AWESOME GOD

Songs of His Power

Volume 1

Kevin Straub

TEACH Services, Inc.
PUBLISHING
www.TEACHServices.com • (800) 367-1844

World rights reserved. This book or any portion thereof may not be copied or reproduced in any form or manner whatever, except as provided by law, without the written permission of the publisher, except by a reviewer who may quote brief passages in a review.

The author assumes full responsibility for the accuracy of all facts and quotations as cited in this book. The opinions expressed in this book are the author's personal views and interpretations, and do not necessarily reflect those of the publisher.

This book is provided with the understanding that the publisher is not engaged in giving spiritual, legal, medical, or other professional advice. If authoritative advice is needed, the reader should seek the counsel of a competent professional.

Copyright © 2022 Kevin Straub for 4th Angel Publications
Copyright © 2022 TEACH Services, Inc.
ISBN-13: 978-1-4796-1303-8 (Paperback)
ISBN-13: 978-1-4796-1304-5 (ePub)
Library of Congress Control Number: 2021915282

Unless otherwise indicated, Scripture references are taken from the King James Version of the Bible.

Scripture taken from the New Revised Standard Version Bible, copyright © 1989 the Division of Christian Education of the National Council of the Churches of Christ in the United States of America. Used by permission. All rights reserved.

Scripture taken from the Revised Standard Version of the Bible, copyright © 1946, 1952, and 1971 the Division of Christian Education of the National Council of the Churches of Christ in the United States of America. Used by permission. All rights reserved.

Scripture taken from the New King James Version®. Copyright © 1982 by Thomas Nelson. Used by permission. All rights reserved.

Scripture texts, prefaces, introductions, footnotes and cross references used in this work are taken from the New American Bible, revised edition © 2010, 1991, 1986, 1970 Confraternity of Christian Doctrine, Inc., Washington, DC All Rights Reserved. No part of this work may be reproduced or transmitted in any form or by any means, electronic or mechanical, including photocopying, recording, or by any information storage and retrieval system, without permission in writing from the copyright owner.

Published by

TEACH Services, Inc.
PUBLISHING
www.TEACHServices.com • (800) 367-1844

Table of Contents

Introduction—The Great Controversy: How God Uses Power 5

Chapter 1—I'm Mad About My Flat; The Language of Wrath and God's "Strange Act" 11

   Inspiration Defines the Wrath of God in Contrast to Carnal Wrath 12

   The Wrath of God and His "Strange Act" 19

Chapter 2—The SDA Church Opines on Divine Wrath and Destruction 26

Chapter 3—Righteous Evil: The Quest for a Hermeneutic for the Standard View 55

Chapter 4—Permissive Will 81

   Part I 81

   Part II 84

   Part III 88

   Part IV 93

   Part V 98

Chapter 5—"Warfare," It Is Called 105

    The Early Days of the Occult 106

    The Council of God; the War Begins 108

    The Luciferian Council 109

    Warfare over the Eternal Deity of Christ. 110

    Contrasting Principles of Warfare. 112

    Divine Compulsion. 113

    Heaven Arraigns the Rebels Before the Divine Tribunal 116

    The Nature of the Expulsion 117

    Maintaining Protection and Freedom 120

Chapter 6—The Role of Angels in Divine Wrath and Punishment 125

Chapter 7—The Ending of the Great Controversy: The Fires 144

    Introduction 146

    The Fire Unquenchable 161

    Fire of Dissolution 190

    The Fire Reservoir 216

Appendix A: The Great Controversy, Chapter 42 233

Appendix B: A Synopsis of the Fires 266

Appendix C: Why so Difficult? 269

Bibliography 272

INTRODUCTION

The Great Controversy: How God Uses Power

*"But I will sing of thy power;
yea, I will sing aloud of thy mercy in the morning:
for thou hast been my defence and refuge in the day of my trouble."*
Ps. 59:16

It dawned on me, in one of those "Aha!" moments, that the great controversy is truly a power struggle, but, not like how earthly entities engage in power struggles. The great conflict is over competing methodological philosophies of governance pertaining to the use of power.

Our cover graphic illustrates a symbol of the Almighty arm of God wielding divine power. The symbol for that power is lightning, which is the discharge of electrical energy. Why is His arm dirty, and why would we choose such an image for the cover of this book?

Have you ever heard of "dirty power"? This refers to the power coming into our homes, which is ideally a pure 60 Hz sine wave, but it gets distorted by transient and harmonic noise generated by interference from various sources, resulting in a fluctuating current with an irregular and altered wave pattern. Nobody would bother about it, except that it can be harmful to sensitive components in electronic equipment, and worse, it generates high-frequency electromagnetic and radio frequency fields that can be harmful to our well-being.

This isn't a science lesson, and you can look up more info online, but I refer to the phenomenon because there is a far more serious problem with "dirty power" in regards to *our concept of God and how He uses power*. All power is His. He is omnipotent. Everything that requires energy (everything that exists requires it) is powered by God because there is no other source.

We know that His power is used to create, sustain, and preserve. The Scriptures have seemingly informed us that He also uses power to destroy: "And the LORD shall cause his glorious voice to be heard, and shall shew the lighting down of his arm, with the indignation of *his* anger, and *with* the flame of a devouring fire, *with* scattering, and tempest, and hailstones" (Isa. 30:30). Isaiah is using images of the physical mayhem in the material world to depict divine wrath in the day of the Lord, which shall be fulfilled in the final conflagration at the second coming and the great-white-throne judgment scene, the two events that serve as bookends to the last millennium before the great controversy is ended and evil is eradicated forever.

There is no doubt that the physical world and its environs will undergo severe chaos. Everything will come apart, and that process begins at the return of Christ as He rescues His church from the earth; it finishes in the events surrounding the final showdown around the Holy City. Fires, storms, and incoming material from the heavens will be unleashed to create a spectacle such as never has been seen by humanity or angels. The flood was global, yet the earth, sun, and moon remained, and life continued, though everything was altered and diminished (see Isaiah 60:20). At the end of the great controversy, prior to the new creation of our planetary home and solar system, the earth and all things touched by sin will not be modified; they will be taken out of existence altogether.

What is in dispute is the belief that when mercy comes to an end and it is time for justice, God turns around and uses power to generate these destructive elements. Yet if we would just pause a moment to consider why He would have to do this, we may see how we have jumped headlong into a false conclusion about how evil gets destroyed because if God is the power source for everything, He would not need to alter His use of power. He would simply have to shut it off. It does not make sense why God would have to generate power to come against His own sustaining power.

The Bible definition of wrath, to which I refer constantly, is when God withdraws His beneficent power. We can read about that in Deuteronomy 31:16–19. We see there that the truth about wrath being *the absence of God as a result of rejecting Him* was to be made into a song. This was for the purpose of ensuring that we might remember how God governs. Every government on earth is based upon power, which is used to bless and destroy; to reward and punish. It employs force to control the will of the people. God's government is based on love and the consent of the governed, wherein power is used to bless and not control the will or destroy. Yet His government does not ignore justice. We do not sacrifice justice for love, not at all, for in the power of choice given to all creatures with moral capacity, they must be able to reject God and His power. In so doing, they will not be able to live anymore for the obvious reason that He sustains our being moment by moment. There is not a breath we take that we do not owe to God.

At that time when the arm of God does His strange work (of withdrawing power), there is a song: "Ye shall have a song, as in the night *when* a holy solemnity is kept; and gladness of heart, as when one goeth with a pipe to come into the mountain of the LORD, to the mighty One of Israel" (Isa. 30:29). This would be a song of deliverance from the ravages of sin, akin to the Song of Moses, which celebrates Israel's deliverance from Egyptian bondage, typifying our deliverance from sin (see Ex. 15).

Even God has joy at this destruction, for it is rooted in the righteousness of His love, which is predicated upon the principles of freedom and non-coercion. He is sad for those who corrupted their ways and sought no remedy, yet He rejoices:

> O Jerusalem, Jerusalem, *thou* that killest the prophets, and stonest them which are sent unto thee, how often would I have gathered thy children together, even as a hen gathereth her chickens under *her* wings, and ye would not! Behold, **your house is left unto you desolate.** (Matthew 23:37, 38, bold emphasis added)

> Say unto them, *As* I live, saith the Lord GOD, **I have no pleasure in the death of the wicked; but that the wicked turn from his way and live:** turn ye, turn ye from your evil ways; for why will ye die, O house of Israel? (Ezekiel 33:11, bold emphasis added)

> And it shall come to pass, *that* as the LORD rejoiced over you to do you good, and to multiply you; so **the LORD will rejoice over you to destroy you,** and to bring you to nought; and ye shall be plucked from off the land whither thou goest to possess it. (Deuteronomy 28:63, bold emphasis added)

God does not rejoice in the destruction itself, but in the redemption from destruction, for the "joy that was set before Him" (Heb. 12:2) includes that work. He rejoices in freedom. His law is established for that purpose. It is the "law of liberty," while sin, the transgression of the law, brings the *wages* of sin, which is death. Death is a prison house of the ultimate bondage from which the relentlessly impenitent will never return. While freedom of choice exercised in the wrong direction will bring that death, God would not have it any other way, because there is no other way than to have a free creation. If there could be no sin, there could be no free moral agents. God would have only a universal hobby farm, populated by wonderful pets that do only what they are programmed to do. In giving moral choice, He had to also allow the results that come of transgression. God rejoices not in the results of transgression, but in the existence of free, moral beings who choose loyalty and willing, joyful service in a friendly and loving relationship with Him.

God has never and will never use power to disrupt, damage, or destroy. Those results reflect the fact that His power is withdrawn, or diminished in its capacity to sustain us, as a result of our request for Him to do so. This is not a verbal request, though that could be part of it, but a request that is made by continuing in sin and selfishness. We often think of biblical destructions as God using power negatively, instead of merely *releasing beneficent restraints* on the existing forces of free moral agents and nature. Notice some inspired words on this concept:

> Pharaoh had his sowing time, and he also had his reaping time. He sowed resistance and obstinacy. He sowed the seed in the soil. *No new power was put into operation by God.* The seed was left to spring up; the man was permitted to act out his true character. When the Lord sees unbelief in the heart against light and evidence, all he has to do is to let the human agent alone; for the seed put into the soil will bring forth seed after its kind…. The character revealed by Pharaoh is similar to that of all the impenitent. *God destroys no man; but after a time the wicked are given up to the destruction they have wrought for themselves.* (White, "Words to the Young," *The Youth's Instructor*, November 30, 1893, emphasis added)

"No new power was put into operation by God." The plagues upon Egypt were not God using power to bring punishment and coerce Pharaoh into doing His will. That kind of "new power" was introduced by Satan, when he "declared that he was prepared to resist the authority of Christ, and to defend his place in Heaven by force of might, strength against strength" (White, *The Spirit of Prophecy*, Vol. 1, p. 22).

The plagues, as in all destructions, were God withdrawing His mighty, saving hand, whereupon other forces may run unchecked, to a degree, bringing chaotic and harmful action. Satan has muddied humanity's perspective of God's arm of power, showing Him to be vested with his own character. Satan will use force to his own ends, which are rooted in self-exaltation. Our work here is to correct the lie.

This collection of studies is provided as a more advanced study, with the assumption that the reader is already familiar with the new teaching on God's character. A good place to cover the groundwork is our previous work, *As He Is: Issues in the 'Character of God' Controversy*. Some of the Bible stories have been covered there, such as the flood and Sodom and Gomorrah, so they will not be covered again in this or the subsequent volume.

CHAPTER 1

I'm Mad About My Flat: The Language of Wrath and God's "Strange Act"

> *"Then my anger shall be kindled against them in that day,*
> *and I will forsake them, and I will hide my face from them,*
> *and they shall be devoured, and many evils and troubles shall befall them;*
> *so that they will say in that day,*
> *Are not these evils come upon us, because our God is not among us?"*
> Deut. 31:17

If somebody were to say to you, "I'm mad about my flat," you might understand the statement in a radically different way if you heard it from a North American than if you heard it from a Brit. As a Canadian, if I were to say this, my fellow citizen would realize that my vehicle is temporarily unusable as it needs repair of a flat tire before I can proceed with my travel plans. The delay would be frustrating to me and could provoke such an expression of anger. However, if I lived in the UK, my use of this expression would likely convey my appreciation of my new apartment dwelling, so pleasing to me that I would be "crazy" in love with it!

In the Scriptures, we are awash in examples of what I call the "language of wrath," which includes the various expressions and descriptions of

God's judgment upon sin and sinners in terms of proactive violence or fiat employment of divine power for punitive/destructive purposes. It occurs to me that when He would be doing that, He would not be acting within the role of "Creator," but quite the opposite, that of "Destroyer."

God's wrath is not anything like human wrath. The wrath of carnal humanity is largely unruly, capricious, and rooted in selfish principles that infected our entire being when humanity, in Adam, changed leaders. Divine wrath functions on an entirely different field than does human wrath. They are not based on feelings or emotions of burning rage, though those kinds of words are used to describe divine anger. In the inspired pages, expressions of God's wrath and the activity that proceeds from it are written, not by a Canadian or Brit in the twenty-first century, but by Hebrews in a time and place far distant from us. This has a tremendous impact on how we should be reading.

Inspiration Defines the Wrath of God in Contrast to Carnal Wrath

This is a study on how to read the Bible and the Spirit of Prophecy. The topic of God's wrath is a subject into which many people are now inquiring. Numerous writers and leading teachers in Adventism have produced their arguments in support of the standard position of divine wrath, which asserts that God exercises wrath by two methods: active and passive. In the former, He uses power proactively for the purpose of punishment and destruction; in the latter, He withdraws protecting power (hides His face).

"God has intervened personally, intentionally, and in some cases violently to put down evil in the past—and that He will do so even more forcefully in the future. The purpose of His active exercise of wrath is either to punish evil people for their sins or to deliver His own people from their grasp, and often both purposes merge into one" (Perspective Digest, https://1ref.us/1hh, [accessed 12/07/2020]).

There is no need for me to take up much space by repeating their arguments. Most of us have grown up in this paradigm in which God's wrath, anger, retribution, judgment, vengeance, jealousy, etc. are read with a carnal understanding and from the perspective of our fallen, fleshly experience of these things. The Bible, upon cursory reading, does seem to make Him the active agent of death and destruction on innumerable occasions.

Apparently, Mel Gibson has nothing on God in the violence department, but let's look at what the Lord thinks of that idea: "Thou thoughtest that I was altogether *such an one* as thyself: *but* I will reprove thee, and set *them* in order before thine eyes" (Ps. 50:21). In the next verse, He admonishes His people to listen up well because cause and effect will surely play out. Using the Hebraic expression of the wrath of Deity, He says, "lest I tear *you* in pieces, and *there be* none to deliver" (v. 22).

The standard view is that God would come at us with lethal power to personally attack our bodies with something undoubtedly very painful. If we were to compare this with human rulers, what would we call that ruler but a despot? What principle is hereby employed but that of fear of punishment? Does God call to repentance with a heart of wooing love, threaten physical violence, or use some combination of the two? In using such a threat, how is He *any* different from human rulers, let alone *altogether* different? James is clearly informing us that we must look at the wrath of God in a completely different way than how we look at the wrath of humanity, for "the wrath of man *worketh not* the righteousness of God" (James 1:20, emphasis added).

The workings of mankind's wrath are not righteous; they are evil. They are not in the same arena in any way. Once we fully grasp this truth, we are ready to make a "sea change" in our understanding of what God's role is in the destruction of the wicked and even all the suffering that comes to *both* the wicked and the righteous.

Isaiah also instructs us to be careful when it comes to making attributions to the character of God: "'For My thoughts *are* not your thoughts, Nor *are* your ways My ways,' says the LORD. 'For *as* the heavens are higher than the earth, So are My ways higher than your ways, And My thoughts than your thoughts'" (Isa. 55: 8, 9, NRSV).

How does God think and what are His ways?

> Earthly kingdoms rule by the ascendancy of physical power; but from Christ's kingdom every carnal weapon, every instrument of coercion, is banished. (White, *The Acts of the Apostles*, p. 12)

> The exercise of force is contrary to the principles of God's government. (White, *The Desire of Ages*, p. 22)

> Compelling power is found *only* under Satan's government. The Lord's principles are not of this order. (White, *The Desire of Ages*, p. 759, emphasis added)

> [Many people] fail of a satisfactory understanding of the great problem of evil, from the fact that *tradition and misinterpretation have obscured the teaching of the Bible concerning the character of God*, the nature of His government, and the principles of His dealing with sin. (White, *The Great Controversy*, p. 492, emphasis added)

Those who are steeped in this vicious view of God can end up with some horrific conclusions:

> So did Christ suffer God's active wrath or His passive wrath on the cross? Certainly He suffered God's passive wrath—God's abandonment of sinners to the results of their sins.... Did God take an active hand in the death of His Son? ... it would certainly be consistent for God to have taken an active role in the death of His Son on the cross.... Christ suffered God's passive wrath on the cross *and very likely His active wrath as well*. (Moore, *Reflections on the Wrath of God*, p. 15, emphasis added).

Is this the kind of "consistency" of character that we want to develop?

Inspired Keys

The Bible contains the keys to understanding the wrath of God. Remember this principle: one text may never be used to destroy or negate another, but the Bible will give us definitions by which we can decode the difficult passages. The mechanism of His wrath, as defined biblically, is when He turns aside, withdraws Himself, and lets the lawbreaker reap the consequence. Those who write against this truth say that it is "a mistake to make the passive model the complete explanation of God's wrath" (Moore 7). Really?

Here is the wrath of God explained as Him hiding His face:

> In a little wrath I hid my face from thee for a moment; but with everlasting kindness will I have mercy on thee. (Isaiah 54:8)
>
> How long, LORD? wilt thou hide thyself for ever? shall thy wrath burn like fire? (Psalm 89:46)
>
> Hide not thy face *far* from me; put not thy servant away in anger … leave me not, neither forsake me. (Psalm 27:9)
>
> Thou didst hide thy face, *and* I was troubled. (Psalm 30:7)
>
> Hide not thy face from me, lest I be like unto them that go down into the pit. (Psalm 143:7)
>
> And the LORD said unto Moses, Behold, thou shalt sleep with thy fathers; and this people will rise up, and go a whoring after the gods of the strangers of the land, whither they go *to be* among them, and will forsake me, and break my covenant which I have made with them. Then my anger shall be kindled against them in that day, and I will forsake them, and I will hide my face from them, and they shall be devoured, and many evils and troubles shall befall them; so that they will say in that day, Are not these evils come upon us, because our God *is* not among us?

> And I will surely hide my face in that day for all the evils which they shall have wrought, in that they are turned unto other gods. (Deuteronomy 31:16–18)

This is an immutable principle that we can apply to God's dealing with His creation at the entrance of sin, throughout the history of fallen humanity, and at the end of the great controversy:

> Jesus Christ the same yesterday, and to day, and for ever. (Hebrews 13:8)

> With [the Father] is no variableness, neither shadow of turning. (James 1:17)

> For I *am* the LORD, I change not. (Malachi 3:6)

> We have only one perfect photograph of God, and this is Jesus Christ. (White, *The SDA Bible Commentary.* Vol. 7, p. 906)

> He who has seen me has seen the Father. (John 14:9, RSV)

God Gives Up, Sin Destroys

Another biblical way of explaining God's wrath is that He "gives over" or "gives up," as depicted in Romans 1:19–24, 26, and 28. When people persist in idolatry and sin, He at last honors them, lets them have their pleasures, and pleads no more. "Ephraim *is* joined to idols: let him alone" (Hosea 4:17). This sense is also employed in 2 Thessalonians 2, speaking of those who cling to the way of lawlessness: "God will send them strong delusion, that they should believe the lie, that they all may be condemned who did not believe the truth but had pleasure in unrighteousness" (vs. 11, 12, NKJV).

When God's wrath is in play, the Bible language will use terms such as "spare not" or "deliver up." This is how Jesus went to His destruction at the cross: "He that spared not his own son, but delivered him up for us all" (Rom. 8:32). It is in this same sense that God "hardened" Pharaoh's heart, sent the flood, rained fire on Sodom and Gomorrah, and sent an evil spirit to Saul, to list a few examples.

> The wages of sin is death. (Romans 6:23)
>
> Then when lust hath conceived, it bringeth forth sin: and sin, when it is finished, bringeth forth death. (James 1:15)
>
> God destroys no man. Everyone who is destroyed will have destroyed himself. (White, *Christ's Object Lesson*, p. 84)
>
> But your iniquities have separated between you and your God, and your sins have hid *his* face from you, that he will not hear. (Isaiah 59:2)

The Fall of Jerusalem

We gain key insights as we look at the "nuts and bolts" of the fall of Jerusalem to Titus' armies in AD 70. God did not raze the city personally, yet it is an action resulting from His wrath. John the Baptist did, in fact, prophesy the coming "wrath of God" against Judea: "Who hath warned you to flee from the wrath to come?" (Matt. 3:7). Connecting John's reference to the "wrath to come" with the destruction of Jerusalem in AD 70, the messenger writes, "The hour of hope and pardon was fast passing; the cup of God's long-deferred wrath was almost full" (White, *The Great Controversy*, p. 20).

Later in the chapter, she enlightens us regarding the function of this wrath, describing events in the invisible world in AD 70: "God withdrew His protection from them and removed His restraining power from Satan and his angels, and the nation was left to the control of the leader she had chosen" (White, *The Great Controversy*, p. 28.1). She reinforces this thought further:

> We cannot know how much we owe to Christ for the peace and protection which we enjoy. It is the restraining power of God that prevents mankind from passing fully under the control of Satan.... God does not stand toward the sinner as an executioner of the sentence against transgression; but He leaves the rejecters of His mercy to themselves, to reap that which they have sown. (White, *The Great Controversy*, p. 36)

The Spirit of Prophecy is clear that the "wrath of God" that destroyed Jerusalem is the same "wrath of God" that will finally destroy our world. In applying inductive reasoning, we will realize that He will not *exercise power* in the destruction of the wicked world, but instead *cease from exercising power* to save and sustain: "In the fate of the chosen city we may behold the doom of a world that has rejected God's mercy and trampled upon His law" (*Ibid.*).

God No Longer Interferes with the Destroyer

> Soon God will show that He is indeed the living God. He will say to the angels, "No longer combat Satan in his efforts to destroy. Let him work out his malignity upon the children of disobedience; for the cup of their iniquity is full.... I will no longer interfere to prevent the destroyer from doing his work." (White, "A Time of Trouble," *The Review and Herald*, September 17, 1901)

> Like Israel of old the wicked destroy themselves; they fall by their iniquity. (White, *The Great Controversy*, p. 37)

We have seen that God does not exhibit a wrath that is anything akin to human wrath. When He is no longer able to fulfill His role of Savior and Protector, the unchecked forces of nature in chaos, evil spiritual forces, and wicked human activity will execute the reward of sin. He has no part in it except to turn aside and allow it, for it is the direct result of sin as a willful separation from God and His righteousness.

The Wrath of God and His "Strange Act"

In the previous section, I presented evidence to show the wrath of God as a thing altogether different from human wrath. We saw the Bible keys that define His wrath point to a God who acts in mercy so far as He can and, at the point of ultimate rebellion, "hides His face" away and permits the sinner to reap the consequence of separating himself/herself from the protective and sustaining power and life of God. Other Bible phrases are employed to mean the same thing (e.g., He "gives them over," "delivers them up," or "spares not").

Those who are coming into the light about the character of God are of the understanding that 1) we must take a different approach to the Bible language in order to be consistent and 2) God does *not* stand as the executioner. Sin itself is what destroys—not because it is a physical power, but because it unleashes harmful, physical power through selfish choices, God is prompted to leave. He ever works only to save, never to destroy. God Himself claims to be eternally consistent. He would not act in violence, contrary to His law, to quell the rebellion at its first stages, and He will not act in violence to end the rebellion in the final scenes either.

> *The Spirit of Prophecy is clear that the "wrath of God" that destroyed Jerusalem is the same "wrath of God" that will finally destroy our world. In applying inductive reasoning, we will realize that He will not exercise power in the destruction of the wicked world, but instead cease from exercising power to save and sustain.*

The Theodicy of Job

"Theodicy" is the term given to an explanation of the existence of evil in a universe ruled by a God of love and mercy. Satan himself, angling to get permission to personally smash Job, said to God, "But put forth thine hand now, and touch all that he hath, and he will curse thee to thy face. And the LORD said unto Satan, Behold, all that he hath *is* in thy power; only upon himself put not forth thine hand" (Job 1:11, 12).

Later, in the same story, the destruction brought upon Job's children by Satan was called the "fire of God" (v. 16). What does this tell us? The Bible writers had a concept of Deity that was akin to the heathen concept, in that all things, good and evil, came from the gods. In the case of the Hebrews, being monotheistic, all things, good and evil, came from YHWH. They did not have a well-developed sense of the devil until the days of Christ. The story of Eve and the serpent was viewed as allegory, and according to orthodox Jews, it is so to this day. They charge Christians with inventing the devil to make excuses for themselves.

Peter Compares the Flood and the Fire

Peter says that the world of old was sustained by the power of God (see 2 Peter 3:5–7). That world was an entirely different ecology. There was a canopy of water over the earth, which was not watered by the same hydrologic cycle that we know today. When God withdrew His sustaining hand, the water came out of suspension, the fountains of the deep also broke up, and water came from hidden places of the earth. In the same way, the final fires of destruction are held in check. God ever acts in mercy while there are yet souls who will repent.

The Wrath of the Powers of God

One writer expresses the concept of divine wrath from another angle:

> God's wrath is not the expression of His personal feelings, for while His wrath is busily destroying man and the world, God is feeling anything but wrathful. He is pained with sorrow and

distress to see His handiwork and His children being committed to so terrible a fate....

See the blasting might of the roaring hurricane, the thunder of a thousand falling buildings and opening crevasses as the earthquake strikes ... *this is wrath*. It is the complete picture of anger and fury and these are the things which the Bible terms "the wrath of God."

From the message God gave through Moses' rod [when the rod was out of Moses' hand, it turned into a snake; when it touched the river, it showed where God would withdraw His sustenance and it turned to blood] He plainly showed that when nature is in this state it has passed out of His control....

It is the wrath of God simply because every power which has gone into the state of wrath through God's directing and controlling power being withdrawn, *is of God*. [e.g., the orbital control of the earth, regulation of the sun, maintenance of the cosmological constants, etc.] They are the powers of God in a wrathful state, therefore it could be called the wrath of the powers of God. Instead, it is simply called, "the wrath of God." (Wright, *Behold Your God*, pp. 389–390)

The Constitution of God's Government

When we maintain that God will at last, by His own action, put down the rebellion by a final act of violence in a global destruction, we are actually saying that He will finally resort to that which He refused to do in beginning of the rebellion, and by that action admit to the claim that the constitution of His government, and by extension, His law and character, are faulty, and an executive judicial extermination is indeed the final solution.

Contrary to this, His constitution has agape love as its foundational motivation, which is self-sacrificing rather than punitive. This means that love, in order to be love, must:

1. give complete freedom of choice
2. never coerce through threat of punishment

The latter needs clarification in that there is, in fact, a threat of punishment for rejecting God, but the threat is not that God will employ power to punish, but instead relinquish His beneficent power and give up those free moral agents to the consequences of their choices within the framework of freedom to choose governing principles under which they shall live out their lives in probationary time. God is not the executioner of the sentence against transgression (see White, *The Great Controversy*, p. 36). Will He personally punish these people for exercising the rights and freedoms He gave them? That would not be love. It would be the actions of an abusive controller.

God's Strange Act

What is God's "strange act"? We often hear this phrase used to depict His final destruction of the impenitent by the unleashing of "fire from God out of heaven." His "strange work" or "strange act" does not apply solely to the final destruction of the wicked. In fact, it applies to *any* time God gives up sinners to destruction. Inspired testimony makes a specific application of the phrase, found once in Scriptures, to the time of the seven last plagues.

It is a mistake to restrict the definition of God's "strange act" or "strange work" to the great-white-throne executive judgment. Curiously, Ellen White never applies the term to the executive judgment. Note the following examples:

- The destruction of the Jewish nation (see *The Desire of Ages*, pp. 582–583)
- The destruction of Jerusalem (note especially how that event is a type of the great time of trouble; see *The Great Controversy*, pp. 17–38)
- The slaughter at Baal-Perazim (see 2 Sam. 5:17–20; Isa. 28:21)

- The slaughter at Gibeon and the capture and slaughter of the five kings (see Josh. 10:12–28; Isa. 28:21)
- God, allowing a state of things to come, gives people up to the deceptions they love; the cry of "Peace, peace" is given by false shepherds, leading to the sudden destruction of the final events (see *Testimonies for the Church*, Vol. 5, p. 77)
- The desolation of the earth after the "national apostasy" (see *Selected Messages*, Book 2, p. 373)
- The pouring out of the plagues (see *The Great Controversy*, pp. 627–628)
- At the "law against the Sabbath of God's creation" ("The Government of God," The Review and Herald, March 9, 1886)

Mount Perazim and Valley of Gibeon

"For the Lord shall rise up as *in* mount Perazim, he shall be wroth as *in* the valley of Gibeon, that he may do His work, his strange work; and bring to pass his act, his strange act" (Isa. 28:21). Focusing on the text from which the term is derived, God's "strange work" is exemplified by two "as in" incidents that occurred on Mount Perazim and in the Valley of Gibeon. We must find how these exhibits stand as similes because God's strange work of destruction will occur in the same way. The Bible records only one significant incident occurring at each of these locations—both confrontations between the forces of God and those of paganism:

1. Mount Perazim: David versus the Philistines (see 2 Sam. 5:17–20)
2. The Valley of Gibeon: Joshua versus Amorites (see Josh. 10:12–19)

In each case, the Lord *delivered up* the Canaanites for destruction because "the Canaanites had filled up the measure of their iniquity, and the Lord would no longer bear with them. *His defense being removed from them*, they would fall an easy prey to the Hebrews" (White, *Testimonies for the Church*, Vol. 4, p. 151, emphasis added). God's strange work is the handing over of the unrepentant to their enemies: "Who knows whether

God will not give you up to the deceptions you love? ... When God shall work His strange work on the earth ... woe will be upon the people" (White, *Testimonies for the Church*, Vol. 5, p. 77).

The Spirit of Prophecy refers repeatedly, as a specific example, to the outpouring of the plagues at close of probation as the time when God will do His strange work:

> Every century of profligacy has treasured up wrath against the day of wrath; and when the time comes, and the iniquity is full, *then God will do His strange work*.... It is *at the time of the national apostasy*, when, acting on the policy of Satan, the rulers of the land will rank themselves on the side of the man of sin—it is then the measure of guilt is full; the national apostasy is the signal for national ruin. (White, *Selected Messages*, book 2, p. 373, emphasis added)

> God's judgments will be visited upon those who are seeking to oppress and destroy His people....
>
> *When Christ ceases His intercession in the sanctuary*, the unmingled wrath threatened against those who worship the beast and his image and receive his mark (Revelation 14:9, 10), will be poured out. The plagues upon Egypt when God was about to deliver Israel were similar in character to those more terrible and extensive judgments which are to fall upon the world just before the final deliverance of God's people. (White, *The Great Controversy*, pp. 627–628, emphasis added)

> Protestantism shall give the hand of fellowship to the Roman power. Then there will be a law against the Sabbath of God's creation, *and then it is that God "will do His strange work in the earth."* ... God keeps a record with the nations: the figures are swelling against them in the books of heaven; and *when it shall have become a law that the transgression of the first day of the week shall be met with punishment, then their cup will be full.*

(White, "The Government of God," *The Review and Herald*, March 9, 1886, emphasis added)

God's "strange act," *properly understood*, is a true definition of His wrath.

When we are speaking about the subject of the wrath of God, invariably His "strange act" will be brought up from the arsenal of misconception. Now we can show that this phrase, while, in principle, will include the final fires of destruction, is not used in inspiration regarding the same, but with several other examples. It is especially important to compare the term with the examples given in the text itself. As we look at the references to Perazim (Baal-Perazim) and Gibeon and go to the Spirit of Prophecy, we find the term applied to *divine recession*, or God *giving over* in the withdrawal of His protecting hand. Mercy comes to an end by the choice of the wicked, leaving them to reap the consequences.

> **When we are speaking about the subject of the wrath of God, invariably His "strange act" will be brought up from the arsenal of misconception.**

CHAPTER 2

The SDA Church Opines on Divine Wrath and Destruction

*"And the brethren immediately sent away
Paul and Silas by night unto Berea:
who coming thither went into the synagogue of the Jews.
These were more noble than those in Thessalonica,
in that they received the word with all readiness of mind,
and searched the scriptures daily, whether those things were so."*
Acts 17:10, 11

The Biblical Research Institute in the Seventh-day Adventist Church is the designated authority on accepted Bible teaching, serving as a gatekeeper for the maintenance of doctrinal purity and the evaluation of teaching. It has been compared to Catholicism's "Congregation for the Doctrine of the Faith," which was founded to defend the church from heresy and promote and defend Catholic doctrine.

The church employs leading theologians to help others answer questions they might have on theological issues. This is a main resource, aside from the official statement of beliefs of the church, which we would access to determine the church position regarding the nature of God's wrath and destructive activity.

We are not disappointed in this, as we find three articles dealing specifically with the subject, beginning with Frank B Holbrook's "Does God Destroy?" (March 20, 1985), at a time when this message was developing and spreading, not *solely* but *primarily* via an Australian independent author, lecturer, and faith leader, F. T. Wright, whose influence spread from Australia to the USA and the Caribbean, where for a short period of time he came into an informal association with Dr. Elliot O. Douglin and other independent elders who were also coming into the new view on God's character and government. Holbrook wrote his rebuttal in answer to the teaching of Dr. Douglin. The posted article on the BRI site is an extract from his critique of Douglin's work. A search on the site will readily yield this and the other two articles that we will discuss in this chapter.

We are not going to make any attempt at providing detailed or thorough responses to any of these BRI studies, as all our objections to the church position are more thoroughly covered in character-of-God (CoG) apologies such as my books *Awesome God: Songs of His Power*, *As He Is: Issues in the 'Character of God' Controversy*, as well as *Light Through the Darkness* by M. M. Campbell, *God's Character: The Best News in the Universe* by Dr. Elliot O. Douglin, and more.

We offer this article as a brief commentary on the main points brought by the church against the teaching of what we call "The Consistent View"

> *In the end, we must own our beliefs for ourselves and not merely submit to those who claim spiritual authority. This is a dangerous approach to deciding what to believe, for the pressure to submit to heresy will come, and we must stand for what we believe as individuals, in defense of our own convictions, not the convictions of other people.*

or "The New View" on God's character, to acknowledge in our answer that we are dealing with a topic that has generated persistent controversy over the years, as well as encourage every Bible student to be as the noble Bereans and study everything for one's own self, that every teaching, including all the official doctrines of the church, may be properly vetted by personal, individual research, under the guidance of those who have gone before and, most importantly, the Holy Spirit who brings us Jesus as our primary revelation of the character of God. In the end, we must own our beliefs for ourselves and not merely submit to those who claim spiritual authority. This is a dangerous approach to deciding what to believe, for the pressure to submit to heresy will come, and we must stand for what we believe as individuals, in defense of our own convictions, not the convictions of other people.

Elder Holbrook states at the outset that he is offering his opinion regarding the problems he sees in the teaching of Dr. Douglin. One of those problems, according to Holbrook, is that Douglin "has discovered *one method* God uses *in probationary time* to discipline and punish sin. This mechanism he applies *to all forms of divine judicial punishment* including the final executive judgment and punishment for sin *after human probation* [the seven last plagues]" (Biblical Research Institute, https://1ref.us/1go [accessed 12/03/2020]). Another of those problems is that Douglin glosses over inspiration on the "concepts of *God's justice* and *human accountability*."

Holbrook proves his point with the scriptures that say that we must give account at the judgment (see Rom. 14:10–12; Acts 24:25), the wicked will be punished (see 2 Cor. 5:10), receiving their recompense according to their deeds (see Rom. 2:6) as an *act of God*, which is to be interpreted as God using personal power in a proactive fashion, to punish and destroy (*Ibid.*). Of course, Holbrook is correct in saying "in my opinion" because the language to which he refers in these Bible passages is subject to interpretation, and if one does not access inspired definitions and keys to interpret the language, relying instead on uninspired sources, this falls squarely into the realm of opinion, not true exegesis of the Scriptures.

We see that the first major issue raised by the church (as represented by Holbrook) is that this new view embraces only "one method God uses ... to discipline and punish sin." The basis of objection here is that the standard view within Adventism is that God has *two* methods of operation with respect to divine wrath: one is the withdrawal of His power and giving up the rebellious to the consequences of their choices, while the other is that He will employ power to do the work personally. In the first, God *moves away* with reluctant sorrow ("how shall I give thee up?" [Hosea 11:8]), while in the second He *moves toward* with aggression ("the LORD will rejoice over you to destroy you" [Deut. 28:63]). The first is called "passive wrath," and the second is called "active wrath."

My problem here is that there is no attempt to prove the standard view, which insists upon dual modalities of wrath. Rather, it is an assumption based on how tradition has interpreted the biblical language of wrath. For the detailed presentation of this issue, we offer the study "Righteous Evil: The Quest for a Hermeneutic for the Standard View," published in this volume. There, we show how the same language of apparently proactive divine wrath and destruction is used in both types of accounts where the mechanism of destruction is revealed (hiding of face, allowing other forces to bear sway) and where it is *not* revealed. The challenge is to show an inspired key that would enable us to classify what type of wrath we are observing, based upon the presence or absence of textual revelation of causation (called technically an "etiological solution"), or some other factor.

A point of contention that Holbrook engages is that while the Bible certainly presents divine recession as a mechanism of wrath and destruction, it *"occurs during probationary time when Satan is active. This mechanism obviously cannot function after the reign of Satan has terminated"* (Biblical Research Institute, https://1ref.us/1go [accessed 12/03/2020]). It is not clear from where this rule comes, other than the invention of opinion. It appears that Holbrook is proffering a common talking point that is heard from detractors, that the consistent view holds that Satan and his devils are always the active agents in destruction.

We do not teach this. We hold that there are *four* areas of restraint in which the Spirit of God, through the angels, keeps a check on destruction. These include, first, the evil spirits, of course, yet not these alone; second, there is the wickedness of the human heart. The individual human posing a threat to itself is under the restraining influence; third, the institutions and nations of humanity are in check; and fourth, nature is held in check. When the Spirit is withdrawn, any or all of these may be given to exert chaotic force. People will commonly point to the flood as an example where Satan did not work directly to bring about the destruction. That is true. Satan feared for his own life in the deluge. God didn't give up the earth to Satan, per se, but to the rampage of the elements passed out of His beneficent control (see *As He Is* for dedicated coverage of the flood and its etiology).

The entire premise of all the apologetics for the standard view is that God has two methods. It is vital to understand that if we solve the problem of single vs. dual modalities of divine wrath, or "passive" only vs. "passive" and "active," then we can move on to explore instances of occurrence and make a determination with regard to sin and how it leads to destruction. Sometimes, we will know certainly because it is given in the narrative. Other times, the narrative does not reveal it. If we do not nail this issue down, we are forever subject to the whims of interpretation and will "pick and choose" for ourselves which destruction is active and which is passive, based upon the presence or absence of revelation. This is not a hermeneutic or key to interpretation. It is mere supposition. We cannot prove a doctrine by a negative. If this were the case, then everything that is *not* stated becomes truth. This is logical fallacy.

In paragraph 12, Holbrook states, "Although God's law forbids killing, it is evident from the biblical data that this is a moral law that forbids murder. It does not apply to judicial executions or ultimate executive justice." This is a common rebuttal that is made, yet the word of the commandment itself, Hebrew *ratsach*, translated "kill," does not make this distinction. It is used both ways. Additionally, we can find other words such as *harag* ("to smite with deadly intent, kill, murder"), used to describe acts of God, such as in Exodus 20:24. We have covered this in our tract series, tract #1CGA, entitled "Do as I Say, Not as I Do: Is God Above His Law?"

Holbrook goes on to say that the commandment does not apply to "judicial executions or ultimate executive justice." This is said to support righteous slaying, whether done by God, angels, or humans. Then he says, "God alone is the fountain of life," a statement derived from *The Desire of Ages*. After quoting Bible passages of God destroying the finally impenitent, Ellen White says of them:

> *This is not an act of arbitrary power on the part of God.* The rejecters of His mercy reap that which they have sown. God is the fountain of life; and *when one chooses the service of sin, he separates from God, and thus cuts himself off from life.* He is "alienated from the life of God." Christ says, "All they that hate Me love death." Ephesians 4:18; Proverbs 8:36. God gives them existence for a time that they may develop their character and reveal their principles. This accomplished, they receive the results of their own choice. By a life of rebellion, Satan and all who unite with him place themselves so out of harmony with God that His very presence is to them a consuming fire. *The glory of Him who is love will destroy them.* (White, *The Desire of Ages*, p. 764, emphasis added)

While the statement is clear that it is not the volitional exercise of physical power on the part of God, His presence will surely slay them. What this means is not worked out in this passage, yet we can get the understanding through research of the writings and bringing together the relevant passages (see "The Ending of the Great Controversy: The Fires," published in this book). Holbrooke says, "God alone is the fountain of life," and while He gives life, He can also "remove it in judicial execution." This is a blurring of the reality, while making it sound like the act of ceasing to issue life is an act that originates with God. It is not that. God is responding to free choice. The passage in *The Desire of Ages* makes it clear that it is the sinner that cuts oneself off from life (God), not the other way around. God acquiesces.

John says that Jesus came to destroy the works of the devil (see 1 John 3:8) through revealing the character of God. Elder Holbrook says, "The actual revelation destroys nothing," but what it does is get us to agree that God should judge sin, which, in the standard view, means He has to use His power to destroy the devil and his followers. Again, all these arguments made by apologists for the standard view are rooted in an a priori assumption that sometimes God executes judgment by exerting destructive power by His own hand. The text does not say that. It says that Christ came to destroy the works of the devil by manifestation and does not go into mechanism. It is not teaching that, by seeing the contrast between Christ and the devil, God gets our permission to torture and at last terminate (kill) the finally impenitent in prolonged physical fire. This is a made-up doctrine that defies substantiation.

The section entitled "Biblical Data on a Direct Action of the Creator (Judicial Execution)" contains several fallacies and assumptions: "true justice demands proper punishment and execution." "Proper" would mean "direct action," or God rolling up His sleeves and getting done the job that apparently sin and the sinner cannot accomplish through voluntary separation from the Source of life, upon which He subsequently gives up sinners to themselves in His presence. Holbrook again appeals to his earlier claim that "after probation," we have a different set of circumstances, and the devil cannot possibly be involved in destructive activity. This is probably true (that the devil is not exerting destruction upon the wicked) in the post-millennial judgment scene, but it is *not true* of the pre-millennial phase of the closure of probation, whereupon the seven last plagues shall be unleashed.

Holbrooke states, "The seven last plagues ... must be by God's direct action. Sin is not a mechanism to produce them; Satan cannot produce them (God and Satan are not copartners). These are judgments that God produces by whatever operation of His laws He chooses." In this statement, he is directly contradicting the Spirit of inspiration:

> When He leaves the sanctuary ... The *restraint which has been upon the wicked is removed, and* <u>Satan</u> *has entire control of the finally impenitent*.... *Unsheltered by divine grace, they have* <u>no protection</u> *from the wicked one.* <u>Satan</u> *will then plunge the inhabitants of the earth into one great, final trouble. As the angels of God* <u>cease to hold in check</u> *the fierce winds of human passion, all the elements of strife* <u>will be let loose</u>. *The whole world will be involved in ruin more terrible than that which came upon Jerusalem of old.* (White, *The Great Controversy*, p. 614, emphasis added)

We do not know why Holbrook contradicts this statement. It would be surprising to find that he has never seen it. He says, "God and Satan are not copartners," yet if God is giving the wicked world over to Satan, who then brings "all the elements of strife" to the planet, while God also is pouring out plagues unrelated to Satan and that strife, we would apparently have them working on the same line.

It is claimed that because punishment is "meted ... according to their works" (White, *Early Writings*, p. 282), it is imposed force from God, for "it could not come simply as a natural result of sin, nor as a simple withdrawal of divine protection" (Holbrook). This all comes from the understanding that the "God does" language is referring to proactive exercise of power and not to the withdrawal of power. Everything hinges on this point, yet it is a point that breaks down in numerous examples, such as 1 Chronicles 10:14, which says God slew Saul. In verse 4, the narrative modifies that language, telling us that Saul committed suicide on his own sword. That is how "God" killed him. He gave Saul over to the results of rejecting Him and His counsel. It ended in Saul exerting power against himself, not God employing power.

Holbrook goes on to highlight the writing of inspiration that speaks of the suffering of the wicked in the fire from God and how there are varied durations of suffering: "Said the angel, 'The worm of life shall not die; their fire shall not be quenched as long as there is the least particle for it to prey upon'" (citing White 1882, *Early Writings*, p. 294). He is failing to connect this statement to the inspired definition of the unquenchable fire:

> We read of *chains of darkness* for the transgressor of God's law. We read of the *worm that dieth not*, and of the *fire that is not quenched*. Thus is *represented* the experience of every one who has permitted himself to be grafted into the stock of Satan, who has cherished sinful attributes. When it is too late, *he will see* that sin is the transgression of God's law. *He will realize* that because of transgression, his soul is cut off from God, and that God's wrath abides on him. *This* is a fire unquenchable, and *by it* every unrepentant sinner will be destroyed. Satan strives constantly to lead men into sin, and he who is willing to be led, who refuses to forsake his sins, and despises forgiveness and grace, will suffer the result of his course. (White, "Christ and the Law," *The Signs of the Times*, April 14, 1898)

This fire is not a proactive, imposed, physical fire of retribution and punishment, but a natural outworking of the mental experience of the sinner, and it destroys the sinner. It is "executive justice," most assuredly, yet the term itself does not necessitate the exercise of divine power. If divine power is the Source of life, all that is necessary in executive justice is the honoring of the freewill choice of the finally impenitent to confirm their rejection of God, which is a rejection of life. God will end the period of grace and mercy granted to sinners because they have chosen to have it ended. This means He gives them over to the results of their decision, and they perish.

That process of realization is the fire, and it is a terrible agony. Some will come to the end of it quickly, and others will not. This is all highly symbolic language. The "particles" to which the angel referred, that the fire "preys upon," are not the physical flesh of the sufferers; they are something else. Holbrook argues that because the impenitent are punished with suffering before they die, under a judicial sentence, it is therefore an imposed physical destruction from God. How it is that we must reach this conclusion is not apparent, other than by bringing a carnal view of wrath and punishment into the picture, attributing mankind's ways to God's ways.

A real problem with the imposed-physical-fire view for varying durations and intensities (see White, *The Great Controversy*, p. 544) is that it appeals to a principle of eye-for-eye justice, which Christ decidedly disavowed (see Matt. 5:38, 39). One must ask the question, Of what necessity or benefit is this kind of justice, and upon what principle(s) is it based? Who benefits and why? We will leave this subject without further comment. Dedicated and detailed treatment of this ultimate destruction scenario is found later, in the chapter "The Ending of the Great Controversy: The Fires."

Holbrook writes another opinion: "In the long view, however, it is really not a specific method that should concern us, but the results." As does the Inspired Word, so do we disagree with such an idea, as it lends itself to some pragmatic notion that the end justifies the means. However, if that is the case, finding that God uses force to effect a victory in any of the battles of the great controversy, the contest then becomes, at least partially, about who is stronger in physical might and ability rather than principles of governance. This lends itself to the "might is right" principle of action, which need not concern itself with things such as morality, loyalty, or the consent of the governed.

> For my thoughts *are* not your thoughts, neither *are* your ways my ways, saith the LORD. For *as* the heavens are higher than the earth, so are my ways higher than your ways, and my thoughts than your thoughts. (Isaiah 55:8, 9)

> Do not err, my beloved brethren. Every good gift and every perfect gift is from above, and cometh down from the Father of lights, with whom is no variableness, neither shadow of turning.... For the wrath of man worketh not the righteousness of God. (James 1:16, 17, 20)

> [Wasted hours] ... should be improved in studying God's plan of government, and gathering lessons from those divine methods.

(White, "Home Duties o the Father," *The Signs of the Times*, December 20, 1877)

The psalmist David in his experience had many changes of mind. At times, as he obtained views of God's will *and ways*, he was highly exalted. Then as he caught sight of the reverse of God's mercy and changeless love, everything seemed to be shrouded in a cloud of darkness....

But *as he wept and prayed, he obtained a clearer view of the character and attributes of God, being educated by heavenly agencies, and he decided that his ideas of God's justice and severity were exaggerated.* He rejected his impressions as being the result of his weakness, ignorance, and physical infirmities, and as dishonoring to God ...

Most earnestly he studied the ways of God, expressed by Christ when enshrouded in the pillar of cloud, and *given to Moses to be faithfully repeated to all Israel* [see Deut. 31:16–19]....

His faith laid hold of God, and he was strengthened and encouraged; *although he recognized God's ways as mysterious, yet he knew they were merciful and good; for this was His character as revealed to Moses*: "The Lord descended in the cloud, and stood with him there, and proclaimed the name of the Lord. And the Lord passed by before him, and proclaimed, The Lord, The Lord God, merciful and gracious, long-suffering, and abundant in goodness and truth." (White, *The SDA Bible Commentary*, Vol. 3, p. 1149, emphasis added)

The Spirit of Prophecy is rife with statements that address God's method of punishment and governance, such as these:

I was shown that the judgments of God would not come directly out from the Lord upon them, but in this way: They place themselves beyond His protection. He warns, corrects, reproves, and points out the only path of safety; then if those who have been the objects of His special care will follow their own course independent of the Spirit of God, after repeated warnings, *if they choose their own way, then He does not commission His angels to prevent Satan's decided attacks upon them.* (White, *Manuscript Releases*, Vol. 14, p. 3, emphasis added)

Again, this is not to say that inspiration only points to Satan as the agent of punishment and destruction. In other places, she outlines the principles of punishment, showing that it can also come from other sources such as aggressor nations or nature:

Earthly kingdoms rule by the ascendancy of physical power; but from Christ's kingdom every carnal weapon, every instrument of coercion, is banished. (White, *The Acts of the Apostles*, p. 12)

The kingdom of God is not concerned with wielding any physical power in a negative manner—controlling, threatening, or punishing; rather, it seeks to encourage the power of our own choice within the framework of the power of love to move us and teach us of a better way, which is ultimately the *only* way to have life and have it more abundantly.

Finally, Holbrook doubles back to "probationary time," during which he seems to concede that passive wrath may be the main method God uses. However, "It would appear from the Scriptures that God has performed some executive acts of justice during probationary time as warnings to the wicked." He cites the flood and Sodom and Gomorrah as such. What warning is that? that God will destroy you if you reject Him?

Regarding the story of the cities of the plains, the critic of the consistent view says, "It is immaterial to speculate what laws God permitted to operate or to fail to operate to produce the fire and brimstone that destroyed these sinful rebels" (*Ibid.*). On this point, we can come to a qualified agreement where we could both say the same words within our own paradigm of understanding, and they would be true, yet we would find that we don't truly agree on principle. It is not necessary that we find substantiation for passive wrath in every instance. It is not given. Sometimes we just don't know with certainty precisely what force or interplay of forces were involved in a specific example of divine wrath.

What *is* given to us for the decoding of the language of wrath is the principle of divine recession, the hiding of God's face, which is the withdrawal of His beneficent power. Remember that God sustains all things by His power. There is no need for Him switch His power use from positive to negative. He simply withdraws power, and the result is negative.

> *The kingdom of God is not concerned with wielding any physical power in a negative manner—controlling, threatening, or punishing; rather, it seeks to encourage the power of our own choice within the framework of the power of love to move us and teach us of a better way, which is ultimately the only way to have life and have it more abundantly.*

Another facet of Holbrook's view is that it doesn't matter whether God's wrath functions actively or passively. It is often said these are simply the two faces of the same coin. The problem with this is that the decision to hide His face and how much of it is not based upon God's determination, but upon the will and choice of the free moral agent. God is bound by the principles of love, which must give freedom of choice. To create a law and design penalties to go with it, which consist, in part, in a discretionary and direct use of force, is an arbitrary system. Freedom of choice is not in it. It now becomes a law that has imposed penalties, which translates, in principle, to deterrence and retributive vengeance (eye for eye). These are fear-based and coercive, not meeting the standard of God's character and government.

According to the consistent view, the flood (which is discussed in *As He Is*) was the relinquishing of nature. Holbrook calls this "speculation," even though there is a good case for it in inspiration. He insists that God caused the flood because "if God had given up control of the forces of this earth, even Noah and his family would have perished." This is not well thought out because it is obvious that there is a continuum on which the more control God relinquishes, the greater potential there is for chaos and ruin. Holbrook seems to take an all-or-nothing approach here, but the fact is that we ourselves are under wrath, yet we survive. All our days are spent in wrath, says the psalmist (see 90:9).

God gave the earth over to corruption. Under the curse it languishes. Death and decay have set in. We battle with weeds, storms, and disease, yet there is still life, beauty, peaceful and prosperous times, good health, etc. that can be enjoyed if we follow His counsel. God still sustains, though the ravages of sin have their effects. We are not yet in the perfection of heaven, nor are we witnessing the total annihilation that is coming at the post-millennial lake of fire.

Holbrook dismisses Douglin's new-view theology by likening it to an executioner of capital punishment, saying, "that the executioner who presses the button doesn't execute the criminal in the chair-the electricity does it!" What the standard view is missing here is that the executioner is not God, the Sustainer of life that the criminal has offended and rejected. The executioner is carrying out arbitrary and imposed penalties for arbitrary and imposed systems of law. God's law is neither. It is the protocol upon which life is built, functioning by the others-centered flow of love and resources in the circuit of beneficence, as opposed to the self-centered retention of these things based on self-protection, fear, and grasping for power and control. The law of God is the transcript of His character. Therefore just as God is life, so it can be said that the law is life. It is the law of life and liberty.

> It will be seen that the glory shining in the face of Jesus is the glory of self-sacrificing love. In the light from Calvary it will be

seen that *the law of self-renouncing love is the law of life for earth and heaven*; that the love which "seeketh not her own" has its source in the heart of God; and that in the meek and lowly One is manifested the character of Him who dwelleth in the light which no man can approach unto....

But turning from all lesser representations, we behold God in Jesus. Looking unto Jesus we see that it is the glory of our God to give. "I do nothing of Myself," said Christ; "the living Father hath sent Me, and I live by the Father." "I seek not Mine own glory," but the glory of Him that sent Me. John 8:28; 6:57; 8:50; 7:18. In these words is set forth *the great principle which is the law of life for the universe*. All things Christ received from God, but He took to give. So in the heavenly courts, in His ministry for all created beings: through the beloved Son, the Father's life flows out to all; through the Son it returns, in praise and joyous service, a tide of love, to the great Source of all. And thus through Christ the *circuit of beneficence* is complete, representing the character of the great Giver, the law of life. (White, *The Desire of Ages*, pp. 19, 21, emphasis added)

Moving forward five years to July 1990, we come to another piece by another professional SDA exegete, Tim Crosby, entitled "Does God Get Angry?", discussing the anger/wrath of God. If we find anything here that was not posed by Holbrook in 1985, we will have a look.

Crosby is framing the argument in a debate of whether God experiences emotion as we experience it, particularly when it comes to anger. His opening argument tracks with Holbrook and the standard view pertaining to the dual modalities of wrath. Apparently, Jesus was so angry with the Jews that He killed a tree to demonstrate what He would do to the rejectors of His grace. We must do better in our reading than this.

In this apologetic for a violent divine wrath, time is spent appealing to the anger *we* feel when we see abuse of the innocent, arousing our personal desire to retaliate against the perpetrators. If we don't see God in this way, then we must have a "love-dovey, namby-pamby, laidback, harmless, and jovial" (Biblical Research Institute, https://1ref.us/1gp [accessed 12/03/2020]) Deity, who is, in the eyes of a man filled with "righteous indignation," a most feckless and weak God. A real man unsheathes the glittering sword of steel, so must a real man's God! This is a popular argument as it holds its appeal in carnal vengeance.

At this point, Crosby moves into a strawman argument, already discussed, in claiming that we tout an "illogical assumption that Satan is always willing to cooperate with God by destroying his own agents who are hindering God's will!" We have discussed that God's wrath is when His mercy is attenuated by the freewill choices of the individual to follow his or her own way. Love dictates that people be given freedom to follow their hearts, but it is meaningless if God does not allow the consequences to follow. This is the Bible definition of divine wrath—note the chiasm of Isaiah 57:17:

> A—For the iniquity of his covetousness
>   B—was I wroth,
>   **C—and smote him:**
>   **C'—I hid me,**
>   B'—and was wroth,
> A'—and he went on frowardly in the way of his heart.

God gives up, and outside forces are given leeway to act in chaotic fashion. These are not *only* the spiritual forces of demons, but also the dark forces of the carnal heart of humanity and the potentially destructive forces in all of nature, from the individual cell to the grandest galaxy of the universe. Should God relinquish anything of His power and control, the imperfection introduced will work in entropic fashion. Having covered this already, there is yet another point to highlight here: When Satan is given leeway to act, he does not always destroy. There are wicked people who have lived out some or all of their lives in luxury, prosperity, and power under satanic blessing.

> The Lord will do just what He has declared that He would—He will withdraw His blessings ... from those who are rebelling ... Satan has control of all whom God does not especially guard. He will favor and prosper some in order to further his own designs, and he will bring trouble upon others and lead men to believe that it is God who is afflicting them. (White, *The Great Controversy*, p. 589)

Crosby follows faithfully along the lines of tradition in the standard view, which strives to understand God's action through the observation of human action. This appeal to human methods as a template for the actions of God is anthropomorphism of the worst kind:

> If great leaders and good men sometimes find it necessary to let the righteous die with the guilty for the achievement of a greater good in the end, then has the Creator Himself no right to discriminatingly (see Genesis 18) destroy evil societies? ...
>
> The doctrine of hell can be understood only as a manifestation of God's retributive justice, in which the sinner is punished until he receives the exact amount of pain he deserves in the light of his crimes.

Under the section "God and Genocide," Crosby showcases the basic philosophy and practice of Constantinian Christianity with its "just war" theory, not showing the slightest awareness of the paradigm of "permissive will," as discussed in our chapter by this name. God gave instructions to Israel in the use of the sword because that is how *they* chose to move forward. It was not His will.

Moses thought God was going to work by military means:

> He, supposing that they were to obtain their freedom by force of arms, expected to lead the Hebrew host against the armies of Egypt ...
>
> Instead of pursuing the direct route to Canaan, which lay through the country of the Philistines, the Lord directed their

course southward, toward the shores of the Red Sea. "For God said, Lest peradventure the people repent when they see war, and they return to Egypt."... The Israelites were poorly prepared for an encounter with that powerful and warlike people. They had little knowledge of God and little faith in Him, and they would have become terrified and disheartened. They were unarmed and unaccustomed to war ... In leading them by the way of the Red Sea, the Lord revealed Himself as a God of compassion as well as of judgment. (White, *Patriarchs and Prophets*, pp. 245, 282)

This does not mean it was initially God's purpose to deliver them by His own methods and later train them in the arts of carnal warfare because He would require them to fight. It was never His purpose for them to fight: "The Lord had never commanded them to "go up and fight." It was not His purpose that they should gain the land by warfare, but by strict obedience to His commands" (White, *Patriarchs and Prophets*, p. 392).

The model of penal justice is one that belongs to this world and the god of this world. Satan is the one who originally preached it: "Every sin must meet its punishment, urged Satan; and if God should remit the punishment of sin, He would not be a God of truth and justice" (White, *The Desire of Ages*, p. 761).

Crosby wants the sinner to receive imposed pain and in the exact amount equal to the crime. This is the God He sees in the Scriptures. Again, I have a one-word question: "Why?" Why is divinely imposed pain necessary in the picture of the great controversy? My follow-up question is two words: "Who benefits?" Or, "What vital function does this carnal style of retribution, which is 'eye-for-eye' justice, play in securing for the universe a closure to the rebellion and prevention from any future rebellion?" These apologists for the standard view have no answer. The *only* appeal that can be made will be grounded in the carnal principles of vengeance/retribution, deterrence, and creature restitution.

None of these apply to God, for none of these effects the result God wants, which is a renewed heart. All of these are fear-based and will not develop loyalty to righteous principles. Crosby goes on to make his defense on this point. He heads straight for the weeds in the section "Reform or Punishment," arguing that somehow the consistent view of wrath would hold forth the finally impenitent as subjects for a program of reform, which apparently could go on forever: "Under the new theory the offender is not punished until the punishment is commensurate with the crime, but is treated until he is cured-which could last forever.... It is clear that God works on the principle of 'an eye for an eye' and that the angels find this praiseworthy."

It is hard to believe this material could make it into the offerings of the prestigious BRI! It sounds as though he would be confusing our view with that of the heresy of universalism. There seems to run in the heart of the standard view a strong desire to mete out the pain that is deserved. However, the pain and suffering for rejecting righteousness and life will come by *consequence*, not by *imposition*.

> **Nobody is saying that the wicked do not get what they deserve. They do! What we are arguing against is the necessity of the imposition of divine power for punitive purposes.**

Allowing the consequences is the action described in inspiration in proactive terms, such as "recompense," "vengeance," and "retribution." Those are "meted" by a natural turning of events, and God ordains it thus, refusing to step in with restraining power because further mercy and restraining action would not change hearts or rehabilitate. The seared conscience would merely continue; the wicked one would simply go on "frowardly in the way of his heart," emboldened by extended mercy beyond hope of any response to the Savior's redemption.

Crosby cites the philosophy of C. S. Lewis: "The humanitarian theory removes from punishment the concept of desert" (*God in the Dock: Essays on Theology and Ethics*. Grand Rapids: Eerdmans, 1970, p. 288). Objection! Nobody is saying that the wicked do not get what they deserve.

They do! What we are arguing against is the necessity of the imposition of divine power for punitive purposes. There is no merit in that. Rather, divine power will be withdrawn according to the choice of the impenitent, and punishment is the result. The argument for imposed punishment goes so far as to say that we rob rebels of their right to be beaten with a stick by God's hand.

A defense of "eye-for-eye" is naturally within the ambit of the traditional view of God's methods. It is claimed that Jesus was not coming against *lex talionis* as a principle of justice, but as something that we would take into our own hands for the sake of vengeance, for that belongs to God, who also grants it to civil authorities. Crosby has thus revealed a major lack of understanding of permissive will, wherein the governments of humanity are given to humans to maintain a semblance of order and safety under the ravages of carnality, selfishness, and wickedness. God gave us these authorities in wrath as He was ejected from the human spirit. "**I gave thee a king in mine anger**, and took *him* away in my wrath" (Hosea 13:11, bold emphasis added).

Not to spend much more time on this, but I just want to say that the vengeance of God is heaping burning coals on the head of those who hate Him. In the end, they do not want any such system of goodness and forbearance and will call for the rocks to fall on them, for the revelation of the Rock will surely crush them as God can do no more good for them.

> But I say unto you, Love your enemies, bless them that curse you, do good to them that hate you, and pray for them which despitefully use you, and persecute you; That ye may be the children of your Father which is in heaven: for he maketh his sun to rise on the evil and on the good, and sendeth rain on the just and on the unjust.... Be ye therefore perfect, even as your Father which is in heaven is perfect. (Matthew 5:44, 45, 48)
>
> Dearly beloved, avenge not yourselves, but *rather* give place unto wrath: for it is written, Vengeance *is* mine; I will repay, saith the Lord. Therefore if thine enemy hunger, feed him; if he

thirst, give him drink: for in so doing thou shalt heap coals of fire on his head. (Romans 12:19, 20)

Wrath is the absence of God. Their minds have permanently rejected God. His goodness is to them as a fire. They don't want it. They invite the vengeance at last so that the life they have already rejected in the spirit of their minds will be made a physical reality (see Deut. 31:16–18).

"One last point. The 'no-wrath' position-robs even the biblical statements about God's love and mercy of all force, for without wrath, there is no mercy.... This caricature of God must be rejected" (Crosby). "Without wrath, there is no mercy"? About what is he talking? Never do we say there is no wrath. We certainly embrace the fact of divine wrath as we seek to define it according to the Inspired Text. What our apologist is essentially saying is, "Without *divinely imposed punishment causing great torture of physical pain*, there is no mercy."

> There is a boundary to the mercy of God, for He does not always strive with men. A record is kept of all the blessings offered and how those blessings are treated; and if we neglect our duty *we shall soon see, as did the Jews*, that *the anger of God* is not withheld but we shall be *given over to the power of Satan* [the power of sin and its result, death]. While it seems astonishing to us that the Jews rejected Christ, we ourselves *will act out the same thing* if we refuse the light for this time. (White, *Manuscript Releases*, Vol. 3, p. 79, emphasis added)

The final-generation wicked will re-enact the same rejection of Christ for a false christ, who is antichrist, and reap the same results. When the anger of God came upon them, they suffered the abomination of desolation, which is defined as being given over to destruction. It came to them in the form of their own vile acts when under siege by the Romans, even to the point of eating of their own children, and then it was finished by wholesale bloodshed as they were slain by the sword of the empire.

Thus, it was that "God" destroyed them—He gave them up to their chosen fate, just as Jesus lamented:

> O Jerusalem, Jerusalem, which killest the prophets, and stonest them that are sent unto thee; how often would I have gathered thy children together, as a hen *doth gather* her brood under *her* wings, and **ye would not!** Behold, **your house is left unto you desolate**: and verily I say unto you, **Ye shall not see me, until** *the time* **come when ye shall say, Blessed** *is* **he that cometh in the name of the Lord**. (Luke 13:34, 35, bold emphasis added)

> And the high priest answered and said unto him, I adjure thee by the living God, that thou tell us whether thou be the Christ, the Son of God. Jesus saith unto him, Thou hast said: nevertheless I say unto you, Hereafter shall ye see the Son of man sitting on the right hand of power, and coming in the clouds of heaven. (Matthew 26:63, 64)

Note the linkage that is made to the second coming, when the truth will be forced from wailing lips. They would see Him again under completely reversed circumstances regarding the balance of power. Jesus, referring to the special resurrection, told those religious persecutors they would see Him coming in the clouds of heaven, on the right hand of power. Their experience will not be theirs alone, but of all who have been special agents of Satan throughout history, and it will also include the wicked living of the final generation who see Him coming:

> The sufferings of every man are the sufferings of God's child, and those who pass by their perishing fellow beings without pity or help, provoke God's grievous anger. His righteous thunders gather. His vivid lightnings flash; it is *the wrath of the Lamb*. Be faithful to your fellowmen, and you will please God. He loves the world; love it too, and you will be accepted by Him. (White, "The Wrath of the Lamb," *The Bible Echo*, May 30, 1898, emphasis added)

The wrath of the Lamb is not reaching out with killing power, but a desolation of those who have chosen sin instead of cleansing. Reading in chapter 40 of *The Great Controversy*, we find that at the second coming, the fear of the wicked is not that He is there to mow them down, or that the elements are in complete chaos, but that they are facing the Holy Christ. What has not been understood about this scenario is that the presence of a Holy God invokes in the human psyche an unprecedented mental terror of guilt and doom. Thus, they prefer the elements, calling for their own destruction. If He were there to kill them, they would welcome it.

However, He is not appearing for that. The Lord is not raising His arm in power to destroy, but in power to raise His own from their graves and gather up His final-generation elect to join them in ascending to Himself, where they will be forever secure. The rest are left to perish. This is how all the wicked are destroyed by the brightness of His coming. It is *truth rejected* that leads to separation from the Source of life and secures the soul in chains of everlasting darkness. The truth about God is the brightness.

Note the typology in the following statement. The manner of destruction called "the brightness of His coming" is a literary device, a symbol, not referring to destruction by energetic radiation but to *the result of rejecting the revelation of Jesus Christ, showing us Who God is*, for *the character of God is His glory* or we can say it this way: *The glory of God is a revelation of His character* (see *The Signs of the Times*, September 3, 1902).

> But *in that day, as in the time of Jerusalem's destruction*, God's people will be delivered, everyone that shall be found written among the living. Isaiah 4:3. Christ has declared that He will come the second time to gather His faithful ones to Himself: "Then shall all the tribes of the earth mourn, and they shall see the Son of man coming in the clouds of heaven with power and great glory. And He shall send His angels with a great sound of a trumpet, and they shall gather together His elect from the four winds, from one end of heaven to the other." Matthew 24:30, 31.

> Then shall they that obey not the gospel be consumed with *the spirit of His mouth* [His Word] and be destroyed with the brightness of His coming [the revealing of His character]. 2 Thessalonians 2:8. *Like Israel of old the wicked destroy themselves*; they fall by their iniquity. By a life of sin, they have placed themselves so out of harmony with God, *their natures have become so debased with evil, that the manifestation of His glory is to them a consuming fire*. (White, *The Great Controversy*, p. 37, emphasis added)

They are destroyed by their own self-knowledge in the face of Jesus Christ, whose presence unveiled causes a psychological meltdown of grief, guilt, and terror. "Now will I rise, saith the LORD; now will I be exalted; now will I lift up myself. **Ye shall conceive chaff, ye shall bring forth stubble: your breath**, *as* **fire, shall devour you**. And the people shall be *as* the burnings of lime: *as* thorns cut up shall they be burned in the fire" (Isa. 33:10–12, bold emphasis added).

Conception takes place in the mind. The word "breath" is *ruwach* (*Strong's Concordance*, H7307), which is "wind, breath, mind, spirit," also denoting the spirit as the seat of emotion, sorrow, trouble, mental acts, and moral character (this is just a hint of what we develop in the study on the fires of destruction).

We thank Tim Crosby for adding his understanding to this exposition of the standard/traditional view, which might be contrasted with the consistent/new view, which is poorly understood by most detractors. He has taken a step to explain why God must impose punishment: they simply deserve it. This is a hollow answer. Yes, they deserve what they will get and get what they deserve. God will bring matters to a close by a sort of imposition: He will rise up and reveal His glory, and this will force the fire of their minds to come out.

The punishment, however, is not by His hand; it is by reality. They choose to remain in their sins—in rejection of Christ and His righteousness—and this is a cognizant choice to die. They will be devoured because God is gone from them (see Deut. 31:17). "And death shall be chosen rather than life by all the residue of them that remain of this evil family, which remain in all the places whither I have driven them, saith the LORD of hosts" (Jer. 8:3).

Fourteen years pass, and on August 12, 2004, Elder Rodriguez adds his very short commentary in an article entitled "What is the wrath of God?", to which we only need to make a short response. He offers five points to consider. The first point is that there is a difference between human wrath and divine wrath, whereas God's wrath is untainted by sin, "primarily intended for healing, procuring the restoration of order within His creation" (Biblical Research Institute, https://1ref.us/1gq [accessed 12/03/2020]).

In point 2, he states, "God's wrath does not appear to be a permanent attribute of God, that is to say something that by nature constantly characterizes Him and His actions." He says it is temporary because it will end, whereas His love is forever. There is an element of truth here, yet it is not accurate on its face because wrath is rooted in love, and God is love. I first heard from an evangelist the bedrock truth: "Love, in order to be love, must be free." That love, which extends absolute freedom, is His eternal character, and how that love responds to rebellion will never change, even though it should never again be tested throughout the ceaseless ages to come. Love does not threaten or coerce in any way. It grants absolute freedom to choose, forever, yet we must remember that it tells the truth.

The free moral agent can rebel through choosing to act outside the law of life, the transcript of God's character. There is a consequence to this, however, with which God will not interfere: that the wage of sin is death. God has let the demonstration of this truth play out and promised us it will never have to be demonstrated again. Therefore, wrath is an eternal feature of God's character because bound up in it is the freedom of choice, which is a constituent attribute of divine agape love.

Rodriguez displays the standard view more prominently in point 3, stating, "This is not self-destruction or impersonal forces acting over sinners and Satan." We have belabored the definition of divine wrath and shown that it is most certainly "self-destruction." This is not contested in Scripture or the Spirit of Prophecy:

> The character revealed by Pharaoh is similar to that of *all the impenitent. God destroys no man;* but after a time *the wicked are given up to the destruction they have wrought for themselves.* (White, "Words to the Young," *The Youth's Instructor*, November 30, 1893, emphasis added)

> For the wages of sin *is* death; but the gift of God *is* eternal life through Jesus Christ our Lord. (Romans 6:23)

> Then when lust hath conceived, it bringeth forth sin: and sin, when it is finished, bringeth forth death. (James 1:15)

> Forasmuch then as the children are partakers of flesh and blood, he also himself likewise took part of the same; that through death he might destroy **him that had the power of death, that is, the devil**. (Hebrews 2:14, emphasis added)

Point 4 brings in the standard view of dual modalities of wrath. Sometimes, according to Rodriguez, God must "directly" intervene and punish the unrepentant in order to curtail the progress of sin as He works to redeem. It seems, in this paradigm of thought, that sin will not check itself. When God withdraws in response to sinful choices, honoring free will, we see the manifestation of all manner of destruction. It is not clear what the "switches" are that trigger the divine hand to go on the offensive, rather than simply let the events play out in revelation of the effects of sin. It appears that sin is not strong enough to tell the story and it needs some extra help from God.

Additionally, we find it is extremely difficult to accept that the great controversy would have been won without interventions, except that God had reached into the entire affair and manipulated it with the application of force. The flood is a primary example of this. If God uses force in this way, then He would have seen that He was losing, as almost the entire world had given over to total corruption, becoming irredeemable. Worried that they might win His last handful of loyal souls, He decided to kill the rest and start over, reducing the scoreboard to "God: 8; Satan: 0."

> **Deterrence doesn't work. People will break laws even though great penalties are assigned. Most citizens can be deterred through the mechanism of avoidance of punishment, but this does nothing to effect change in the heart and can in fact harden it. It does not create loyalty; it creates compliance. God is not after a sullen service. That will ripen into rebellion again.**

No! God saw that humanity was bringing about its own annihilation and devised a means to save His faithful—as well as *any* who would choose to get on board—by having them build a boat to float on the water. God's power guided that boat. His power was to save and only to save. The ones who would not be saved were left to perish in nature, given over to chaotic action as a result of God's hand being rejected. He hid His face in the flood. His action was to forsake, withdrawing His hand from creation (Job 22:15–17; Isa. 54:7–9; 30:26).

Point 5 is not entirely clear, but it seems to be saying that displays of divine destruction in history are a part of God demonstrating His love in that He is interacting with us to show us things in order to save us. Rodriguez is arguing that deterrence against sin, for the remaining observers, is the loving action, which, if it were put into words, in my view, could be accurately described as a divine injunction: "Obey Me because I am God and I am right (because I say so), or I will punish or execute you." Deterrence doesn't work. People will break laws even though great penalties are assigned. Most citizens can be deterred through the mechanism of avoidance of punishment, but this does nothing to effect change in the heart and can in fact harden it. It does not create loyalty; it creates compliance. God is not after a sullen service. That will ripen into rebellion again.

The validity of point 6 is dependent on our definition of divine wrath. It is true that God has saved all humanity from the wrath to come, and whether or not we escape is our own choice. Understanding it as God using power to destroy us would make this point an error. It would be as God saving us from what He will do to us if we refuse to be saved. God wills to save us from sin, not from Himself.

In conclusion, we would re-emphasize the following points:

1. Our first order of business in the study of God's character and government in relation to how He deals with sin and sinners is to obtain the biblical definition of wrath, understanding that God uses power only for beneficent purposes, and when He is pushed out, He takes His power with Him. Not only is the resulting calamity fair and deserved, it is the *only* thing that love can do, for love does not rape. Good, earthly governments attempt to establish themselves as functioning by the consent of the people. God will remain over us only by consent.
2. Once we understand the principle behind divine wrath and how vastly it contrasts with human wrath, we need to get firmly fixed in our minds the Hebrew manner of speech and thought, that *to not exercise power to save is to destroy*. Our second order of business is to apply the definition to our reading of the Bible in context.
3. As soon as we know how divine wrath functions and how to read the Bible, we must be clear that God does not vary in His methods of executing wrath. There is one modality of wrath, and it is passive, not active. It is always the "hiding of His face" (withdrawal of restraints on chaotic forces) in response to free will, never the issuance of punishments by the proactive use of power. There are no inspired statements or any biblical hermeneutic to account for dual modalities of divine wrath.

4. Finally, a thorough understanding of "permissive will" must be developed, seeing that in salvation history, God has made concessions or accommodations to humanity. He has given regulations and instructions in the use of force because He works with errant, carnal humans who do not easily rest in Him, in complete surrender trusting Him in all things. The final generation will be that for which God is looking, and they will not be under any concessions to ignorance that require Him to wink. Permissive will is not grounded in God's principles or reflective of His methods; it is an interim measure and, at the same time, *wrath* (giving over to our errant choices) and *forbearance* (as He is working to bring us to a higher standard).

CHAPTER 3

Righteous Evil: The Quest for a Hermeneutic for the Standard View

"Evil shall slay the wicked."

Ps. 34:21

Does God exercise wrath in two distinct modes of operation? In the standard view of divine wrath, it is claimed that the Creator operates in two distinct modalities of wrath: "active" and "passive." These function by the employment of opposing methodologies. One allows the destructive consequences of evil to bear sway; the other creates those consequences by fiat and deployment of divine power.

In the pursuit of discussion with the mainstream Adventist mind on this subject of the wrath of God and Bible language, this paper was originally produced for open distribution and comment. This author has tried, on many occasions, to arouse an engaged response, thoughtful response, or even *any* response that would attempt to give a rational, biblical, Spirit-of-Prophecy supported answer to the request for an inspired hermeneutical principle that would finally equip us to differentiate between two kinds of wrath that God is alleged to possess and upon which He acts.

The making of this request for a hermeneutical principle asks the correspondent to refrain from simply pointing to instances of biblical language that portrays God in an apparent role of employing power directly to bring destruction, harm, and death. The most popular response, until this time of writing, has been to ignore the request, even after engaging in preliminary correspondence on the broad subject of how God destroys. In a very small number of cases, the recipient has agreed to examine this study and respond in writing, then proceed to either ignore the matter from that point forward or have the courtesy to make a response stating that there is no time available to pursue this any further.

This has caused me to realize that our correspondents likely recognize that there is an interpretive problem and no way to answer the quest for a hermeneutical principle regarding dual modalities of divine wrath. At least, there is no way to answer it from inspired sources without setting up insurmountable contradictions, both from the standpoint of the text itself and the fundamental principles set forth in the law and character of God, the nature of sin, and the issues that are at stake in the great controversy.

The Bible says that God does not change (see Mal. 3:6). It says in another place that there is no variability or "shadow of turning" (James 1:17). James also says in the same passage that every perfect gift comes from the Father of lights—the Father of all manifestations of life. John says that the message of Christ is that in God is all light and no darkness; he also defines that light as the life of mankind (see 1 John 1:5; John 1:4, 9).

While the consistent view of divine wrath holds that God always defaults to "passive wrath," i.e., He withdraws His active power to protect and sustain, the claim that He also has an active mode of wrath means that instead of "giving up" the subject to the consequences of free choice, He comes in with the proactive exercise of power and force to punish the free moral agent for making the wrong choices.

However, God, being perfect, does not need to have two ways to destroy, as if when one way would not work to serve righteousness, then He would have to employ another way. This would go contrary to the declaration of an unchanging, unvarying God and introduce a "shadow of turning," that when one method was not sufficient, He would have to turn to another method. God is consistent, and we want to teach everyone about the consistent view of God, which is, to many, a "new view." It is a new thought that we may read the Bible according to one principle of wrath: "passive wrath." Almost all the Christian world believes in dual modalities of wrath, but very few have examined whether it is actually biblical. Thus, we issue the challenge to each one to prove from the Bible and the Spirit of Prophecy that it is so.

In discussion of the advancing light on the character of God, students of the traditional view may remind us of how the Bible reads, referring to the passage, "I kill, and I make alive" (Deut. 32:39). They may also straighten up in their chairs and say, in a challenging tone, "And just *who* do you think sent the flood?" Or, "Who destroyed Jericho?" That list can go on with many references to biblical accounts of what are apparently divinely instigated destructions.

While the one defending the standard view of divine wrath enjoys sharing many passages such as we just read in Deuteronomy 32:39, we might remind them that students of the advancing light quote them also. We might help them out by bringing some others to the table: "I form the light, and create darkness: I make peace, and **create evil**: I the LORD do all these *things*" (Isa. 45:7, bold emphasis added).

Then we may bring in another that will show God, in this case speaking to David, promoting some evil: "Now therefore the sword shall never depart from thine house; because thou hast despised me, and hast taken the wife of Uriah the Hittite to be thy wife. Thus saith the LORD, Behold, *I will raise up evil* against thee out of thine own house, and *I will take thy wives before thine eyes, and give* them *unto thy neighbour*, and he shall lie with thy wives in the sight of this sun" (2 Sam. 12:10, 11, emphasis added).

Are we to think that David's wives, after being taken by other men and treated as sex objects, under a theological system that attributed such treatment to the direct action of God, are going to say, "Praise the Lord, He is good, His righteousness and mercy endures forever"? How could they possibly think this was a *good* God? To them, He would be a misogynistic tyrant, no more righteous than the culture to which they found themselves subject.

We must be very careful of what we say about God on this matter. Here we are given a scripture verse from Deuteronomy showing God as saying, "I kill" to imply that He is a killer. The traditional view refers to it to support the idea that God wields destructive power in a *proactive* sense, i.e., initiated from within Himself, and He does this at such a point in time and place as determined by Himself, which has been referred to as the "full cup" principle. The view holds that God knows where the full mark is, and when it is reached, the time has come for Him to do the thing that is sung in that extremely popular and terrible song that upholds the "motivate-by-fear" paradigm. "Awesome God" by Rick Mullins is a decided focus on His destructive power.

> **Are we to think that David's wives, after being taken by other men and treated as sex objects, under a theological system that attributed such treatment to the direct action of God, are going to say, "Praise the Lord, He is good, His righteousness and mercy endures forever"? How could they possibly think this was a good God? To them, He would be a misogynistic tyrant, no more righteous than the culture to which they found themselves subject.**

Leaving out the chorus and the one verse that provides a passing acknowledgment of His creative power, we wish to examine this horrible litany of the destructive power of God, which appears to have been written to terrify us through an obvious emphasis of the supposed "active wrath" mode. Noting this author's comments in square brackets, here is how it goes:

When He **rolls up His sleeves** [*to get busy in destructive work*]
He ain't just putting on the ritz [*He isn't fooling around*]
Our God is an awesome God [*His destructive power is the focus of the "awesome" in this song*]
There's **thunder in His footsteps** [*be afraid, be very afraid, lest He be coming for you*]
And **lightning in His fists** [*with which He will personally smite the rebellious*]
Our God is an awesome God [*lightning and thunder in 3-D and surround sound*]
And the Lord wasn't joking
When **He kicked 'em out of Eden** [*With a lightsaber sword, threatening the loss of their heads by the hand of the angel*]
It wasn't for no reason
That He shed His blood [*because God's wrath was avenged on Jesus; the Father needed to be appeased through bloodshed, even a human sacrifice*]
His return is very close
And so **you better be believing** [*or else*] that
Our God is an awesome God …
Judgment and wrath [*by fiat order of fire from the sky, creative power turned to destruction, the wielding of weapons of mass destruction, as in carnal war*]
He poured out on Sodom … [*just like that … God did it*]
Our God is an awesome God [*He reigns "from heaven above," i.e., rains liquid sulfur on the heads of the wicked … awesome!*]
Mercy and grace
He gave us at the cross [*here is the contrasting picture of two Gods—one in the Old Testament, one in the New Testament—pitting judgment and mercy against each other*]
I hope that you have not
Too quickly forgotten that [*keep this as a song ever at the fore-front of your experience with God and live under the threat*]
Our God is an awesome God!

It is with interest that we might observe how God, when instructing Moses on the way His anger works (see Deut. 31:16–18)—by the "hiding of His face," or the *withdrawal principle*—He goes on to instruct him to make the teaching into *a song*, that it might be a witness *for Him* (see v. 19) and not be forgotten through the generations (see v. 21). Songs are powerful; they shape our thinking and become part of our own thoughts when we approvingly listen to and sing them. It is not insignificant that we have two songs, and two opposing ideas of the character of God.

The traditionalist is in opposition to the **new view that has been prophesied to come to God's people**:

> My prayer to God was, that the power of the enemy might be broken, and that the people who had been in darkness might open their hearts and minds to *the message that God should send them*, that they might see *the truth, new to many minds, as old truth in new frame-work. The understanding of the people of God has been blinded; for Satan has misrepresented the character of God*. Our good and gracious *Lord has been presented before the people clothed in the attributes of Satan*, and men and women who have been seeking for truth, have so long *regarded God in a false light* that it is difficult to dispel the *cloud that obscures his glory* [character] *from their view*. (White, "Camp-Meeting at Ottawa, Kansas," *The Review and Herald*, July 23, 1889, emphasis added)

> At no period of time has man learned all that can be learned of the word of God. *There are yet new views of truth to be seen, and much to be understood of the character and attributes of God,*— His benevolence, His mercy, His long forbearance, His example of perfect obedience. "And the Word was made flesh, and dwelt among us, (and we beheld *His glory*, the glory as of the only-begotten of the Father,) full of grace and truth." This is a most *valuable study, taxing the intellect*, and *giving strength to the mental ability*. After diligently searching the word, *hidden treasures are*

> *discovered,* and *the lover of truth breaks out in triumph.* (White, ***Fundamentals of Christian Education***, p. 444, emphasis added)

Those with this new view are shown to be amazed and filled with admiration as they marvel at the singular effectiveness of love alone, without any use of physical weaponry causing destruction and death. What about you, my traditionalist friend? Are you "breaking out in triumph," as God's people are shown to be doing? If you are fighting against this message, *what is it that you now possess* as an advance in light, a "new view," that would invoke jubilation and rapture within your soul? This is not rhetorical. We really would be interested in what could be the new view, if it is not this.

There is no breakthrough in maintaining the status quo on this subject, such as has been done all through the history of Adventism. There must be something in the modern teaching, if it were to fulfill this writing, that would reflect a sent message regarding the character of God. It would be a message that stretches the mind into new territory. Where is this message that would be considered "new views of truth" regarding the "character and attributes of God," causing the heart to soar in fresh revelations, with wonder singing forth the praises of His "awesomeness"?

There are, in fact, many today who *are* rejoicing. Those who hold this "new view" message "break out in triumph" in that they see how God wins a tremendous, universal war of ideology without ever firing a shot, by pure demonstration of the principles of *agape* love, a love that dies for its enemies rather than harms them—*ever*.

Further, this message must be one that comes on to the scene of the closing struggle with an increased clarity and vigor, which will be vehemently opposed by Satan:

> Just before us is the *closing struggle of the great controversy* when, with "all power and signs and lying wonders, and with all deceivableness of unrighteousness," *Satan is to work to misrepresent the character of God,* that he may "seduce, if it were possible,

even the elect." If there was ever *a people in need of constantly increasing light from heaven*, it is the people that, in this time of peril, God has called to be the depositaries of His holy law and to *vindicate His character before the world*. (White, *Testimonies for the Church*, Vol. 5, p. 746, emphasis added)

This message comes at the midnight hour of earth's history, as the "coming of the bridegroom," when there are delusions, heresies, and errors innumerable, in both the world and the churches. God's people will be in sore trial and persecution for their faith, but this will be the time when they will shine the brightest:

> He causes "the light to shine out of darkness." 2 Corinthians 4:6. When "the earth was without form, and void, and darkness was upon the face of the deep," "the Spirit of God moved upon the face of the waters. And God said, Let there be light; and there was light." Genesis 1:2, 3. So in the night of spiritual darkness, God's word goes forth, "Let there be light." To His people He says, "Arise, shine; for thy light is come, and the glory of the Lord is risen upon thee." Isaiah 60:1.
>
> "Behold," says the Scripture, "the darkness shall cover the earth, and gross darkness the people; but the Lord shall arise upon thee, and His glory shall be seen upon thee." Isaiah 60:2.
>
> It is the darkness of misapprehension of God that is enshrouding the world. *Men are losing their knowledge of His character. It has been misunderstood and misinterpreted. At this time a message from God is to be proclaimed, a message illuminating in its influence and saving in its power. His character is to be made known. Into the darkness of the world is to be shed the light of His glory, the light of His goodness, mercy, and truth.*
>
> *This is the work outlined by the prophet Isaiah* in the words, "O Jerusalem, that bringest good tidings, lift up thy voice with strength [loud cry]; lift it up, be not afraid; say unto the cities of

Judah, *Behold your God!* Behold, the Lord God will come with strong hand, and His arm shall rule for Him; behold, His reward is with Him, and His work before Him." Isaiah 40:9,10.

Those who wait for the Bridegroom's coming are to say to the people, "Behold your God." The last rays of merciful light, the last message of mercy to be given to the world, is a revelation of His character of love. The children of God are to manifest His glory. In their own life and character they are to reveal what the grace of God has done for them. (White, *Christ's Object Lessons*, pp. 415, 416, emphasis added)

What she is speaking about in these passages is the very subject that is coming to the forefront and maturing into a full message in the times in which we are now living. The "new views of truth" that are to be understood are specifically concerned with the "character and attributes of God." The timing is clear. As the midnight of apostasy is approaching, this message will be in formation and swelling to a loud cry. Every Seventh-day Adventist needs to be engrossed in this topic, laying aside every other study. It is a message that is to be proclaimed at earth's darkest hour, so we need to know it. Getting the character of God right will open the understanding in all other subjects. It is a "most valuable study" that builds intellectual muscle, as we have seen by the Word of God.

Under the heading **"Many Adventists Brace Themselves Against the Light,"** the prophetess writes, again with regard to a message to come:

> There *is to be* in the [Seventh-day Adventist] churches a wonderful manifestation of the power of God, but it will not move upon those who have not humbled themselves before the Lord, and opened the door of the heart by confession and repentance. In the *manifestation of that power which lightens the earth with the glory of God* [which is His character], they will see only something which in their blindness they think dangerous, something which will arouse their fears, and they will brace themselves to resist it. Because the Lord does not work according to their ideas and expectations, they will oppose the work. "Why," they say, "should we not know the Spirit of God, when we have been in the work so many years?" (White, "Be Zealous and Repent," *The Review and Herald*, December 23, 1890, emphasis added)
>
> The third angel's[1] message will not be comprehended, *the light which will lighten the earth with its glory will be called a false light*, by those who refuse to walk in its *advancing glory*. (White, *Last Day Events*, p. 210, emphasis added)

In this confrontation of the traditional belief system with the advancing light on God's character, the traditionalist is presented with options. Such a one can:

---

[1] When the "third angel's message" is spoken of in the context of the message that "lightens the earth with the glory of God" in power, it is a reference to the fourth-angel work of Revelation 18, which is a repeat of the three angels' messages, under the latter-rain outpouring, which is to perform the task of closing up the work in the earth, ending the great controversy. The term "third angel's message" refers to the package of truths contained in all the messages of the three angels.

They are built on the platform of the righteousness of God, as brought to the Advent people in 1888 and rejected. This historical study is important for believers to undertake today, and I recommend a reading of Ron Duffield's *The Return of the Latter Rain* to get the true history. Most of what is promoted today is revisionist history. The fourth-angel work and message not only gives added impetus and power to the established truths, but also includes "the additional mention of the corruptions which have been entering the churches since 1844" (White, *Early Writings*, p. 277). Most importantly, it sets forth the advancing light on God's character and glory.

1. INVESTIGATE—"go the distance" with our view—that is, determine by investigation if traditional thought can bring peace and satisfaction, while maintaining biblical integrity in its answers to the questions that are posed; or
2. REJECT—"out of hand" and ridicule; avoid the work and trouble, dismiss the discussion with a wave of the hand and label it as heresy, deeming it ridiculous, clinging even more tightly to the traditional paradigm; or
3. AVOID—throw one's arms up in the air in confusion and give up on any hope of understanding the Scriptures or God, avoid the discussion, or go out into the world.

God has promised light to those who seek Him with all their hearts, so He will not give up the *honest* seeker to the third option. The souls that take the second option are automatically disqualified from the discussion by choice, and as earth's history draws to a close, they will find themselves increasingly sidelined in the work of giving the last message of mercy to the world. There is only one correct choice that qualifies as valid inquiry, and to take this nobler approach, which is the God-ordained approach, there must be an honest and probing appeal to the Scriptures and the Spirit of Prophecy, employing a hermeneutical principle derived primarily from the life, teachings, death, and resurrection of Christ.

It is time to come back to developing the theme from the introduction, reminding ourselves once again of Deuteronomy 32:39, depicting a God who says, "I kill." When the traditional mind places this passage on the table, it is often to promote the understanding that God kills proactively because it is in His character to do just that. What I am bringing under the microscope here in these few thoughts is the *traditional* Adventist theology, as published in official church papers such as *Signs of the Times*; as found in books such as Steve Wohlberg's *The Character of God Controversy*; as held forth by top theologians such as Frank Holbrook of the Biblical Research Institute; and as preached by leading media ministry evangelists such as Doug Batchelor of Amazing Facts.

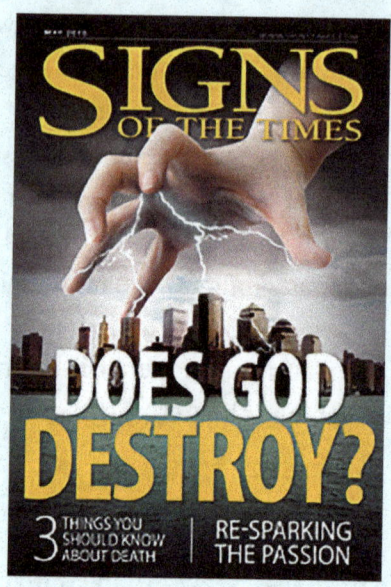

In the traditional view, it is to be understood that God kills only when He can do so *righteously*, when the circumstances call for it, according to divine judgment. In the traditional view, God's statement, **"I kill,"** as mentioned before, is presented in the sense that He does so *proactively*, by direct executive action.

This begs some questions. If this is true, then:

- Why would we not read Isaiah 45:7—**"I create evil"**—in the same way?
- Is there anything in the contexts of these two passages that would indicate diverse principles of operation?
- Can the traditional theology clearly point us to them or provide us any biblical keys that would show us how to make an accurate, situation-specific application of dichotomous principles?

At the same time, while looking at Deuteronomy 32:39, maintaining that God can only kill when He can do so righteously, we would be obligated to apply the principle to Isaiah 45:7 also, which would bring us to articulate that He can only create evil when He can do so righteously. Phrased another way, as the traditional view must admit that God kills in righteousness, so also must He create evil in righteousness. Can we say this? By what principle may we match both statements so they function the same way? For if we make the first one proactive, then we must also read the second one as proactive. We must be able to say that God kills in righteousness and creates evil in righteousness, in a way that is consistent, contradicts no Scripture, and makes sense.

How? Simply by applying the word of the Lord, as given to Moses in Deuteronomy 31:16–18, knowing that evil comes when God withdraws His hand of sustenance and protection—"passive wrath." They must both be passive—by the "hiding of His face." I know that for those to whom these thoughts are new, yet who are on their toes and following closely, this may seem to be really getting into a thorn patch, but I'm not done yet. It's about to get even more prickly!

Walk with me as we bring in the third text: Now that we have a principle established, we can apply it to our reading of the passage that says He gave up innocent women to be sexually abused (see 2 Sam. 12:11). This must be an example of the righteous evil raised up and performed by God, who says through Isaiah that He "*creates* evil," and in 2 Samuel 12:11, the prophet records that He "*raised up* evil." These both must function in the same way. They must be done in righteousness.

Believers in God trust that the Scriptures—*all* Scriptures—are given so that we may understand Him better and grow to love, trust, and serve Him with gladness of heart. I would presume He would have also intended for those wives to know and understand Him by the same things—that He kills and creates evil—because He loves them just as much as He loves us. If it were possible, He would have wanted them to understand how it was that He was "raising up" the evil that was perpetrated on them.

Is there something that is troubling or unsettling in all this? Why? Can you not apply the same principle in one ("I kill") as in the other ("I create evil")? Why not? In other words, where is the evidence that He may *kill* proactively, but when the language changes to "creating evil," it is no longer by executive action, but by giving over to external forces? Is there not some arbitrary, external, interpretive principle coming into play here?

The defender of the standard view is obliged to answer these questions, for he/she must also believe that the truth can afford to be examined closely and not only stand up to the litmus test of logic and reason, but also appeal to and agree with the Bible and Spirit of Prophecy. Most of all, it must harmonize with Christ's life, teachings, death, and resurrection. I have heard it said by church leaders, "Well, we must teach what the church teaches." How can this avoidance of the questions be acceptable? For this author, it is not acceptable in the slightest degree.

The problem here is that 1) according to the standard exegesis of Deuteronomy 32:39, He kills *proactively*, and 2) we have no way of establishing in the biblical text that He "creates evil" by another principle than that by which He kills. **This principle of interpretation, therefore, would be a human imposition and private interpretation.**

The traditionalist must deal with the elephant in the room on this. I do not believe that in the traditional paradigm, there is any sensible, logical way to sort these things out except by producing arguments not found in the Scriptures, nor are they found in any appeal to the life, teachings, and cross of Christ. Rather, a valid exegetical approach will utilize scriptural principles as given *in clear statements* in inspiration and *in Christ*. Without a key or keys to apply the theory of dual principles operating in the destructive acts of God, we would be obliged to take the existing, clearly delineated principles, such as I will show shortly, and apply them *across the board*, to *the entirety* of Scripture. Then it will be found that there is "*evil* evil" in contrast to "*righteous* evil," and we will see some of the precise Biblical keys whereby we may differentiate between the two, according to the inspired principles. This is precisely what the true character-of-God message does.

(I trust the reader understands by now that the phrase "righteous evil" is a play on the paradigm of biblical language—the language of wrath, wherein God is portrayed as *doing that which He allows* or "gives over" to by the mechanism of divine recession—the hiding of His face).

In the traditional paradigm, *if* there is the case on one hand where God's justice is handed down in that **He proactively destroys and kills,** and *if* there is the contrasting case on the other hand where justice is done in that He **gives the wicked over** to evil, the results of their choices, by "hiding His face" (Deut. 31:17, 18), *then* the teacher of the standard theology should be able to graphically set up two columns, according to principles clearly delineated from Scripture. He would place every destructive act of God under either one or the other heading. The teacher of the traditional view would be able to make these placements by clearly showing the biblical principle whereby the student would be able to follow along and clearly identify every scenario as it is being read in the Scriptures, according to contextual clues. Everyone would be able make proper classification, according to one or the other principle.

For example, we would hear the adherent to the standard view readily admit, "Where the Bible says, 'God slew Saul' (1 Chron. 10:14; cf. Hosea 13:11) and we find that he actually committed suicide (see 1 Chron. 10:4), we have the 'giving over' principle in use (passive wrath); then, where we find the walls of Jericho falling (see Josh. 6:5, 16; Heb. 11:30), we have the 'proactive destruction' principle (active wrath)." In these, we could then point to the identifying characteristics in each case that would place them in one or the other category, according to the scriptural keys of interpretation provided by the teacher of the standard view (I would be able to examine these keys if I knew what they were. Therefore, I write this study as a formal invitation to said Bible teacher to come back to me with them so I can throw away this chapter and publish something else).

I am asking for valid and true exegesis. Anything less than an exegetical approach, or an application of a valid scriptural principle (one which is, obviously, a principle shown through evidence provided by the Scriptures themselves) would be an appeal to whatever we think makes the best sense. Historically, this has been done by appealing to how humans do things—by creating God in our own image. Of course, this is nothing less than reading into the text, according to the externally imposed principles of human logic, emotion, and the use of external keys to interpretation such as the dictionary of human language and experience in law, justice, crime, and punishment. The honest Bible student will agree that anything less than true exegesis is inadmissible. It is private interpretation—eisegesis. It simply adds up to worthless human opinion and neither side wants that, right?

As mentioned above, there is also the approach that opts out of the discussion and sidelines oneself by saying, "We can't understand it; it's just one of those things that we'll have to find out in the kingdom." However, the kingdom is within us. Jesus is teaching us. To say, "We can't understand" the character of God, specifically how it relates to how He punishes and destroys, is to deny Christ, the Scriptures, and the Holy Spirit. It is God's purpose in and through Christ that we know Him aright—who He is and as He is—even in all the destructive acts that language portrays Him as doing.

Here again is the crux: The problem with all of this is *not* that there is a "righteous killing" and "righteous evil," but that it is said that He kills **proactively**, at His own discretion and determination, by direct manipulation of the elements or by fiat. Unless the traditionalist can show otherwise, this would necessitate that, by the same token, He creates evil **proactively**. This makes God an evildoer, which is unrighteousness, obviously, so we have to go back to where we took a wrong turn and get on the right path, which takes us to the right conclusion.

Please be patient and do not weary; walk with me yet a little longer. We are going to go back to that fork in the road and set this aright. We will find that there *is* a sense in which God *does* kill and create evil. The Scriptures say these things, as we have read. In order that we do not make God out to be an evildoer, we must have an honest look at *how* He can both kill and create evil *righteously*. This is where we find that God's ways and thoughts are not anything like mankind's ways and thoughts (see Isa. 55:8, 9); that His wrath is not anything like mankind's wrath (see James 1:20).

Therefore, we would have to reexamine the premise upon which the two columns were created, as discussed above. It is found that one of these columns is not valid, as it would be *evil* evil (true evil) and therefore not attributable to God. We are talking about the *"proactively* destroying God" column. Stated plainly, the modality of active wrath is satanic and carnal; it is true evil. We find that God's acts of killing and destruction *all* come under "the hiding of His face" from the sinner, the "giving up," "giving over," "delivering up" the sinner to or "sparing not" the sinner from the consequences of free choice.

This column can be called *"righteous* evil," in keeping with the biblical parlance, as it would harmonize with the God who said, "I kill" and "I create evil" and did many things as expressed in this language, such as raising up evil in David's house (see 2 Sam. 12:11), hardening Pharaoh's heart (see Ex. 4:21), sending the flood (see Gen. 6:17), choosing delusions for the wicked (see Isa. 66:4), sending strong delusions on those who do not love truth (see 2 Thess. 2:10, 11), sending evil spirits or angels (see Judges 9:23; Ps. 78:49), taking off Egypt's chariot wheels (see Ex. 14:25), and hundreds more similar examples.

The Bible language that portrays God as **doing** that which He **allows to play out** to destructive ends is one and the same as what we would call "the language of wrath" and which I am here making a point, in a distinctive and startling fashion, by calling it "righteous evil." In other words, "biblical language," "righteous evil," and "the language of wrath" would all be synonymous terms, referring to the same principle that defines God's wrath, which is nothing like humanity's wrath.

Mankind cannot do *righteous* evil, only *evil* evil. This is because none of us is the Creator God or Sustainer of life. For one **man** will **not** destroy him, unless that other man is vengeful and would kill him. This is how we have viewed God, as if He were a man. For a man to reject God **will** destroy him, but not in the same way. It is not God that will kill the man; it is the nature of the rejection, in that life itself is being rejected. God says, in so many words, "Come to Me, for why will you die?" (see Ezek. 18:31, 32; 33:11; Matt. 23:37, 38). This principle keeps us in harmony with the testimony of Jesus, who said, "[I did] not come to destroy men's lives, but to save *them*" (Luke 9:56), and of John, who tells us that God is light, and in Him is **no darkness at all** (see John 1:5).

A consistent view of the character of God as Giver of life alone removes all the contradictions that come from a surface reading or private interpretation of the Scriptures and/or Spirit of Prophecy. It lets us behold our God, who is unchanging in all His dealings with people; who operates always and absolutely upon pure and righteous principles—principles that depict Him in His true glory as a Being who is of one principle, in whom is no variableness or shadow of turning; as a Being who is nothing other than a Giver and Sustainer of life; a Protector; and a Giver of Himself, the Light/Life of humanity.

Only by having a working principle in place that harmonizes every instance of biblical divine destruction, the "language of wrath" with the "no darkness" principle, can we know Him aright.

> *God does not stand toward the sinner as an executioner of the sentence against transgression*; but He leaves the rejectors of His mercy to themselves, to reap that which they have sown.... *The destruction of Jerusalem is a fearful and solemn warning* to all who are trifling with the offers of divine grace and resisting the pleadings of divine mercy. Never was there given a more decisive testimony to God's hatred of sin and *to the certain punishment that will fall upon the guilty*. (White, *The Great Controversy*, p. 36, emphasis added)

Note the destruction of Jerusalem goes under the "hiding of His face" column in that He gave up Jerusalem to the destruction that befell them under the Roman sword. This is the only mechanism that describes the "certain punishment that will fall upon the guilty." There is no "lightning in His fists," as goes the "Awesome God" song.

To put this together properly, let us reason together by looking at three things God says in the Scriptures regarding Himself and the death of the wicked:

1. "I kill" (Deut. 32:39)
2. "I create evil" (Isa. 45:7)
3. "Evil kills the wicked" (Ps. 34:21)

Do you see where this goes? If we are to harmonize these statements, we must understand that God kills in the very same way He creates evil. God kills and creates evil when He hands sinners over to the consequences of their own choices. It is the evil that destroys through the mechanism of cause-and-effect, even though the Bible language portrays God as the One to bring the effect. The reality or undergirding principle is that God does not stand in the way of the natural effects that come from the bad choices of free moral agents.

No matter how much pain and suffering it brings to God's heart to see His children suffer, He cannot force His sustaining and protecting power into their situation when they are clearly giving themselves over to choices that reject Him. Satan stands by to say, "Give them over, they are mine." God must comply. These are the terms of the great controversy, according to the character and government of God in contrast to the character and government of Satan.

It is no secret that the Bible is written mostly in the modality of active wrath—"God did it" language. This is in accordance with the normal mode of thought and speech in the Hebrew culture and idiom. Ellen White understood it, stating, "It was a maxim among the Jews that a failure to do good, when one had opportunity, was to do evil; to neglect to save life was to kill" (White, *The Desire of Ages*, p. 286). This is how the Bible was largely written and what we call the "major voice" of Scripture, erroneously interpreted as "active wrath." Then we have the lesser-heard voice of passive wrath, which is the "minor voice" of the Bible language, wherein the types of phrases depicting divine recession are used (e.g., 2 Chron. 30:7; Isa. 54:8; Rom. 1:28).

In institutional Adventist theology, the model upheld gives assent to the minor voice, but it is not used as an underpinning or key to interpret the major voice (e.g., Ezek. 25:7; cf. Acts 23:3). It is simply believed that the major voice, *when standing alone* or lacking any modifying narrative, such as in the case of Saul's suicide, must stand as it reads in our own modern mindset and usage of language, without consideration of the Hebrew mindset and manner of speaking. However, there is a problem with this principle of interpretation or hermeneutic. We will break this down as we continue.

We find that the "language of wrath," where God apparently proactively employs destructive power, is used freely in cases where the minor voice is both present and not present. Here is an example of where we have a *direct minor voice* revealed in Scripture relative to a particular biblical narrative of divine destruction:

MAJOR VOICE (ACTIVE WRATH)

"And, behold, I, even I, do bring a flood of waters upon the earth, to destroy all flesh, wherein *is* the breath of life, from under heaven; *and* every thing that *is* in the earth shall die" (Gen. 6:17).

DIRECT MINOR VOICE (PASSIVE WRATH)

For a small moment **have I forsaken thee**; but with great mercies will I gather thee. In a little wrath **I hid my face from thee** for a moment; but with everlasting kindness will I have mercy on thee, saith the LORD thy Redeemer. For this *is as* the waters of Noah unto me" (Isa. 54:7–9, bold emphasis added).

Then there are examples where the major voice is used without the inclusion of a minor voice cue or key, but the curtain is drawn back to clearly show causation (etiology), which is an *indirect minor voice* as a background narrative. Here is an example: The case of Saul states God did it:

MAJOR VOICE (ACTIVE WRATH)

"And [Saul] enquired not of the LORD: therefore [God] *slew him*, and turned the kingdom unto David the son of Jesse" (1 Chron. 10:14, emphasis added).

INDIRECT MINOR VOICE (PASSIVE WRATH)

"And the battle went sore against Saul, and the archers hit him, and he was wounded of the archers. Then said Saul to his armourbearer, Draw thy sword, and thrust me through therewith; lest these uncircumcised come and abuse me. But his armourbearer would not; for he was sore afraid. So *Saul took a sword, and fell upon it*" (1 Chron. 10:3, 4, emphasis added).

The two examples are thus conclusive. The minor voice in them, whether by direct use of biblical phrases depicting divine recession or by the indirect method of providing a narrative-revealing causation, absolutely dictates that it was passive wrath that was being "exercised," in that God gave over to *outside powers*. In the case of the flood, He gave over to the free course of the powers of the elements. In the case of Saul, He gave him over to the archers and the course of his own action, in accordance with the free will that is divinely granted to all moral beings. Free will is therefore rightly classified as an "outside power." God does not interfere with it by exercise of the overruling power that He is certainly capable of employing, if it were in Him to do so.

Then, in the third class of biblical narrative, we lack any indication of the minor voice, either direct or indirect. All we have is the major-voice/active-wrath language as the apparent stand-alone agency of destruction. In other words, it is now perceived that God positively employs the power He possesses to effect destruction by physical manipulation or exertion. In such a narrative, we have no indication that God gave over to anything and cannot prove causation. It simply appears, based on our own interpretation of the language, without reference to the Hebrew idiomatic manner of expression, that God used personal power or the power of holy angels to punish and destroy.

MAJOR VOICE (ACTIVE WRATH)

> "And **the LORD sent fiery serpents** among the people, and they bit the people; and much people of Israel died" (Num. 21:6, emphasis added).

In such a case (although Ellen White makes it clear that it was through the removal of God's restraints on nature), we have nowhere in the Bible either a direct or indirect minor voice brought into the narrative. Here the teacher of the standard view will attempt to apply a hermeneutic from outside the Scriptures, specifically human philosophy, to say God sometimes uses direct power to destroy. Herein, the standard view takes an unwarranted and unauthorized liberty to remove the major voice of apparent "active" wrath from its cultural setting of the biblical/Hebrew idiomatic manner of thought and expression and impose upon it a carnal understanding of judgment, justice, and punishment, after the manner of the world. All of this serves to bring God down to the level of fallen humanity.

We could well assume that the teacher of the traditional view would not like to hear of their model expressed in such radical terms. That teacher, while objecting, would be putting upon oneself the burden of proving how it is not so. This brings us full circle to the quest for a biblical hermeneutic. It is clear that the interpretive principle employed until this time has been that when a story has a clear minor voice element, especially in the indirect sense, telling the story of what really happened (e.g., Saul fell on his own sword, Pharaoh hardened his own heart, etc.), then we may safely interpret the language as passive wrath. However, when we lack an obvious etiological solution or backstory, then we must revert to the idea that God used personal power to effect destruction, according to modern literal or extra-cultural reading of the Hebraic idiomatic manner of expression. The Hebrews would have found our modern, traditional interpretation of the language foreign to its intent.

Now, as we come to the final stretch, as a specific example of how to work with this "language of wrath," let us conduct an exercise. Using our textbook, the Bible, so we may start to practice reading through new eyes, let us take the following case:

> Speak, Thus saith the LORD, Even **the carcases of men shall fall** as dung upon the open field, and as the handful after the harvestman, and none shall gather *them*. Thus saith the LORD, Let not the wise *man* glory in his wisdom, neither let the mighty *man* glory in his might, let not the rich *man* glory in

his riches: But **let him that glorieth glory in this, that he understandeth and knoweth me, that I** *am* **the LORD which <u>exercise lovingkindness,</u> <u>judgment</u>, <u>and righteousness, in the earth: for <u>in these</u>** *things* **<u>I delight</u>**, saith the LORD. Behold, the days come, saith the LORD, that **I will <u>punish</u> all** *them which are* circumcised with the uncircumcised. (Jeremiah 9:22–25, bold and underlined emphasis added)

Cross-reference the above passage with this:

Say unto them, *As* I live, saith the Lord GOD, **I have no pleasure in the death of the wicked**; but that the wicked turn from his way and live: turn ye, turn ye from your evil ways; for **why will ye die**, O house of Israel? (Ezekiel 33:11, bold emphasis added).

What do you see in these texts? Here's what I see: Notice in Jeremiah 9, we have death, judgment, and punishment in juxtaposition with lovingkindness and righteousness, along with the invitation to understand and know God. Further, in stating His delight in these things, it would also mean that He wants us to know *how* it is that He delights in all these things. How does He delight in the carcasses of people fallen in judgment, while in Ezekiel 33:11, we are instructed that He takes no pleasure in the death of the wicked? It is an apparent contradiction.

Here's how we harmonize the two: The judgment that results in the punishment of death is in keeping with principles of righteousness and lovingkindness. It is a judgment in which the Lord delights. Yet in Ezekiel 33:11, we have the clear statement that God has no pleasure or delight in the death of the wicked. Their will to die is all their own (if God willed that they should die, it would come from Him, "at His pleasure," wherein we would take literally what the Bible says in Proverbs 1:26—that He would laugh and mock at the demise of the wicked—or Deuteronomy 28:63, where God will rejoice over the destruction of those who would not obey Him).

His punishment and judgment upon them and their resultant death are found only in the principle of His letting them go to the results of their choices to follow other gods, which are no gods, and the inclinations of their own hearts. This is that in which He delights. This seems to be a strange thought. How is it so? We must continue to unpack this.

God delights in righteousness because there is freedom and life in it. It is righteous that His government is founded and stands ever grounded upon principles of freedom of choice and non-coercion, and by working out the great controversy in accordance with righteous principles, He will at last have a universe entirely rid of rebellion, populated by sons and daughters who serve Him and each other freely, willingly, with unspeakable joy and gladness. However, we all know that along with freedom comes responsibility. Freedom includes the consequences of choosing to reject the Source of life. Of course, He does not delight in the fact that some do not choose life, and despite all that He did in giving up His Son, He will lose some in the end. Yet, in righteousness and according to the principles of freedom, He must give them over to their choices.

> *Only those who are telling the truth about God can have a part in the final message of mercy and bringing an end to the great controversy.*

The ultimate result of God's governing principles will be terrible loss to those who reject Him. It will be a terrible loss to God also, yet it will be victory and eternal security to all those of both heaven and earth who have clung to Him, trusting in His goodness. For the joy that was set before Him, He endured the cross (see Heb. 12:2). He will see the travail of His soul and be satisfied. By Jesus' knowledge and revelation of God's character, many will understand His wrath. It pleased God to "serve justice" on His Son, who "had done no violence," counting Him among sinners, bruising Him through the hiding of His face from Him and giving Him over to the penalty of sin (see Isa. 53:9–12; Matt. 27:46; 2 Cor. 5:21).

Let us fix this principle in our minds regarding the wrath of God. There is a biblical key that we can and should consistently apply in all instances of disease, destruction, or death that are seemingly attributed in any way to God as His own acts:

> Then my **anger shall be kindled** against them in that day, and I will **forsake them**, and I will **hide my face from them**, and **they shall be devoured**, and many **evils and troubles shall befall them**; so that they will say in that day, Are not these evils come upon us, **because our God** is **not among us**? And I will surely **hide my face** in that day for all the evils which they shall have wrought, **in that they are turned unto other gods**. (Deuteronomy 31:17, 18, emphasis added)

This key can be seen again, via the chiastic mechanism of Hebrew poetry. Notice how God "smites" in Isaiah 57:17:

> A—For the iniquity of his covetousness
> B—was I wroth
>   C—and **smote him**
>   C'—**I hid me**
> B'—and was wroth
> A'—and he went on frowardly in the way of his heart.

In conclusion, I pray that this study has served to demonstrate that there is an urgent need for revisiting the standard paradigm in Adventism, with regard to the character of God and how He uses power to advance the truth and establish the universe on correct principles of love and liberty. This demand for a clarification of the hermeneutical principle behind the standard view is a call not only for institutional but also individual self-examination. As my late friend, Dr. Herbert E. Douglass, said to me, "Nothing in the world is more important or more necessary than to get the character of God right." Only those who are telling the truth about God can have a part in the final message of mercy and bringing an end to the great controversy. It is as simple as that.

Another friend wrote to me, saying:

> A church endangers itself when it refuses to operate at more than one level of thinking/maturity. It's natural for someone at a lower level not to be able to understand concepts of someone at any level above them. That is, cognitive dissonance is experienced when you are exposed to or confronted with concepts at a higher level than where you are now. You are then faced with a choice to either be open-minded and figure out why your current understanding or doctrine is insufficient to answer the questions being asked by the "new doctrines" OR to deny, obstruct, obfuscate, twist, or attack the higher-level concepts as heresy (Dean A. Scott, MFA, private comment to K. Straub).

There are many who refuse to engage in this study honestly, for a number of reasons into which I won't go, but I am looking for those who are truly willing to investigate in a spirit that will lift up Christ and cling to Him as our primary hermeneutical principle; as our perfect photograph of God; as One who would rather die for His enemies than destroy them for refusing Him. The truth will bear a candid investigation. Amen!

CHAPTER 4

Permissive Will

> *"Ye have heard that it hath been said,*
> *An eye for an eye, and a tooth for a tooth:*
> *But I say unto you, That ye resist not evil: but whosoever*
> *shall smite thee on thy right cheek, turn to him the other also."*
> Matt. 5:38, 39

Part I

Those holding the traditional view regarding divine wrath and punishment have good, serious questions. They might sound like this:

Q. We have heard several teachers of God's character teaching wonderful things about the non-violent ways of Jesus and how He is the perfect image of the Father. They even show us how God is *not* one who tortures the finally impenitent in the process of the fires of second death, but that there is a natural progression of cause and effect. Our problem is that we do not hear these teachers saying much about some significant issues in violence, which we read about in the Bible. We are interested in knowing more about how to reconcile what we understand to be the non-violent character of God with:

- all His apparent involvement in the Biblical killing
- Him setting up the violent kingdoms of this earth with their various arbitrary laws
- His commands to His people regarding the use of violence, as we see:
  a) in the Mosaic civil code
  b) in dealing with internal dissensions
  c) concerning going to war with their enemies

Some CoG teachers stay silent on many of these issues, but when asked outright, they will tell us that God did in fact play a killing and destroying role by proactively using the "sleep death" to "time them out," and part of this would have been Him killing by proxy, or "by word," in His instructions to His people in the Old Testament theocracy. This seems unsatisfactory to us, still portraying God as one with a mixed character, having not only life, but also death, in Himself. What do we say to all this?

A. Yes, it all tends to perpetuate the notion that somehow being immediately under God's direction as a people means that He will give them instructions in violence. Many of us have heard the question, "Why doesn't God act this way now?" and the quick answer we often hear is "Because we are not under a theocracy."[2] They may give a more complex answer, but it is generally found that they don't have an answer that is much more satisfying than this, and sometimes they get way out in the weeds in their attempt to work with the problem, such as mistaking God for Satan, saying that those commands came from Satan.

I believe that it is problematic for a CoG teacher to present God as one who kills in any way, even though it is said that it is only the "sleep death"

---

[2] This is unfortunate because that is not what is meant by a theocracy. God intends that His church *should* be a theocracy. It is only with mankind out of the way that the third angel's message can go forward with great power and "finish the work." The hierocracy that is the present-day General Conference structure cannot accomplish the work that the Lord will do when He alone is Head over His church…. but that is another subject.

(first death), because it is glaringly obvious that its proactive violence does not harmonize with the peace teachings and their active demonstration in life and death of Jesus, who never put the sleep death on anyone. To the contrary, He only woke them up from that slumber (see John 11:11).

Furthermore, we must consider the scenario of the last-generation, theocratic movement of God. As they, the 144,000, enter the time of final crisis and find themselves surrounded by the enemies of God, we would have to ask the question, "Why would He not also command this final generation of the 'remnant elect' in the use of violent means, as He did in the first theocracy?" Why would they not advance toward the antitypical Promised Land by military conquest? Does this not say that in Jesus, God has changed His methods? He used violence (apparently) with the first Israel, but not with the second. We have three options here:

1. Take up the sword to quell the enemy
2. Declare that God changes His methods
3. Find out how we are misunderstanding God's role in the Old Testament so we can harmonize all Scripture

If we have a changeable God, then what are we saying about His character or the integrity of Jesus' words—"I and my Father are One"—knowing that God declares His unchanging nature (see Mal. 3:6), as does the writer of Hebrews: "Jesus Christ the same yesterday, and to day, and for ever" (13:8)? It must be that in all this, the message of a God who is one, eternal, and perfect, and functions according to the immutable law, which is a transcript of His character, *would be undermined*.

In the examination of God's character and government of love, questions concerning His consistency are raised when we look at His involvement with violence. God's commands to kill are particular points of inquiry that must be addressed, and I believe the subject needs to be covered very early in our explorations of the truths of His character and attributes. Those who start to learn these truths can get very excited at the new views of God opening up to their understanding, but as soon as they start to share with their brethren the non-violence of God, they get stumped with these questions regarding the wars of Israel, civil laws, Him setting up kingdoms of people who rule by force, etc.

We who present the advancing light on God's character to others will generally make our initial launch into the studies with the basic appeal to the life, teachings, and cross of Christ as our fundamental hermeneutic on His attributes, for obvious reasons, as Jesus said plainly: "He that hath seen me hath seen the Father; and how sayest thou *then*, Shew us the Father?" "I have glorified thee on the earth: I have finished the work which thou gavest me to do.... I have manifested thy name [character] unto the men which thou gavest me out of the world: thine they were, and thou gavest them me; and they have kept thy word" (John 14:9; 17:4, 6).

John went on to say that the basic message Jesus came to teach those who walked with Him, which they were then to convey to all of us through their testimony, is "that God is light, and in him is no darkness at all" (1 John 1:5). When we look at what he said earlier in John 1:4, we understand that the "light" of humanity is *life*—Jesus' life. Therefore, darkness is death and not in God. If it is not in God, then He does not give it.... at all! Ever! It comes from somewhere else. Where He is, there is light and life. Any place where He is *not*, there is nothing, which is darkness and death. How is it that we can we be so absolute and "black and white" in our thinking? Jesus, help us!

Part II

Some think that the Achille's heel of the CoG theology has to do with God's directives to ancient Israel in the use of "the sword" (physical coercion and violence). An improper understanding of the function of God's will in the permissive paradigm has caused some modern Christians to come to the conclusion that "there is no room to deny

God's preference for violence as a solution to wickedness," because "God commands violence, it is righteous, because God is perfect," and in light of the advance of the Christian religion in the western world, we should "rejoice that He has given us this incredible gift with which to vanquish our enemies!" I am not making these statements up. They were made to me personally by a Seventh-day Adventist in a discussion on an online SDA forum.

I appreciate this person's ability to cut right to the bottom line in making these statements because they expose the harsh reality of what the standard paradigm of the "destroying God" is saying about His character and how it is carried through in His governance of the universe. Even among most of those who hold to the standard paradigm, these bald statements about God must seem repugnant! The reality is there is no other conclusion that can be made when God is viewed and presented as one who deals with rebellion by the use of proactive violence, i.e.:

1. using weapons of physical force *by His own hand* in the realm of nature
2. in other instances, apparently commandeering demonic forces to work His will
3. in some cases, raising up military forces of the enemies of His apostate people in order to punish them
4. or in the case under study here, when He commands His people in the use of violence

The first three are the more straightforward arenas in which to exercise standard exegesis, wherein we may readily demonstrate that God is *not* actually the destroyer, although often represented as such in Bible language. We aren't delving into those areas here, as they are covered elsewhere. The fourth arena is that which we have called "permissive will" or "permissive command," set forth in contrast to His *"perfect* will."

Another way of defining the permissive paradigm is that, in light of humanity's ignorance, God makes "accommodations" to their erroneous ways. He is the One who meets the darkened mind where it is. We could use the term "accommodative will" interchangeably with "permissive will." What is it, exactly?

This paradigm of thought in the CoG study is the key that unlocks the mysteries of how God could be consistently—unchangingly—the same yesterday, today, and forever—non-violent in all His dealings, *even* in the cases where He commands the use of violent means. Our friend, who has given over to the idea that God gave us violence as a gift with which to vanquish our enemies, believes that those who believe and promote the CoG message must be "double-talkers who play mind games, make excuses, and set up loopholes to contradict the evidence against our claims." We shall see if it is the case as we study it through. We don't want to bring our own interpretations but see what the Scriptures say.

> *On every hand, we get into biblical and logical quagmires, defeating the very heart of SDA "great controversy" theology if we represent God as relying in any way upon—or at any time requiring the use of—violence to move the controversy forward to its righteous conclusion. Such would make force a constituent in His governing principles and violence a component of His character.*

On every hand, we get into biblical and logical quagmires, defeating the very heart of SDA "great controversy" theology if we represent God as relying in any way upon—or at any time requiring the use of—violence to move the controversy forward to its righteous conclusion. Such would make force a constituent in His governing principles and violence a component of His character. To make these things part of what we would call the "attributes of God" sets up irreconcilable contradictions. It produces honest atheists, firm in their convictions, who render for us a horrendous litany of contradictions in their dark evangelism.

Christians in the standard paradigm cannot help the Bible-reading atheist to appreciate and love God. In their feeble attempts to do so, they only inflame his/her natural repugnance and subsequent ferocity.

Let us look at the case of David, for instance. He could not build the house of God because he was declared to be a man of violence: "But God said unto me, Thou shalt not build an house for my name, because thou *hast been* a man of war, and hast shed blood" (1 Chron. 28:3). However, the Scriptures declare that God *Himself* is a man of war: "The LORD *is* a man of war: the LORD *is* his name" (Ex. 15:3).

It gets worse. The Scriptures tell us that God was directly the impetus for David being a man of war: "Therefore David enquired of the LORD, saying, Shall I go and smite these Philistines? And the LORD said unto David, Go, and smite the Philistines, and save Keilah.... So David and his men went to Keilah, and fought with the Philistines, and brought away their cattle, and smote them with a great slaughter" (1 Sam. 23:2, 5).

When we look at this for what it is, through the lenses of reason and logic, we find that if the Lord is a man of war and instructed David to slaughter the Philistine enemy, yet said "no" to David's desire to build His house because he was a man of war, we are left more than puzzled, right?

God elsewhere states His disdain for killing: "Thus saith the Lord GOD; Ye ... shed blood: and shall ye possess the land? Ye stand upon your sword ... and shall ye possess the land?" (Ezek. 33:25, 26). Here are more troublesome examples:

- Isaiah teaches that those who walk in the presence of God do not put violence into their minds. They do not hear of blood or let their eyes look upon evil (see 33:15), yet just a little continued reading brings us to chapter 34, wherein God will destroy all nations with fury (see v. 2) and bathe His sword to the full with blood (see vs. 5, 6) and so on. You can read it all there in that chapter; it is the day of the Lord's vengeance, the time of unquenchable fire.
- The flood came because the earth was filled with violence, but doesn't it seem incongruent that God is then represented as sending that flood

from His own hand, whereby He "drowned the vast world" (White, *Manuscript Releases*, Vol. 12, p. 209; ref. Gen. 6:11, 13)? Is not this filling the earth with violence?
- God hates violence (see Ps. 11:5), yet He will rain fire and brimstone upon the wicked (see v. 6).

These are the things with which we are obliged to contend as we comb through the Scriptures. This is why the atheists have a heyday, spewing acidic sarcasm against the Bible and its supposedly good and loving God, and this is why the agnostics who would like to believe in a benevolent God say they can't see Him as such—not only because of the violence that is *in the world*, but also because they cannot see Him *in the Scriptures* as He is purported to be: good, loving, peaceful, pure, the Source of life, and Giver of the law, which is a transcript of His character. They end up considering both the Scriptures and the God portrayed therein as inconsistent, unreliable, and downright frightening. This is because nobody has shown them how to read the Bible.

We must show them! If we can't, it is imperative that we learn how if we are to properly fulfill the gospel commission and especially the final loud-cry message of mercy to the world, which is about His character of love (see White, *Christ's Object Lessons*, p. 415). This is not optional if we are to be His witnesses and end the great controversy at last.

Part III

We know now, since the peace teachings of Jesus, who is the Way, the Truth, and the Life, God does not instruct us in the ways of violence; He saves us from them (see 2 Sam. 22:3; Rom. 12:17–21). Jesus was prophesied as the tender plant of the Lord who "had done no violence" (Isa. 53:9). "**Yet**," as it is said, "it pleased the LORD to bruise him; he hath put *him* to grief" (v. 10, bold emphasis added). Again, we have a seeming dichotomy, no? How to reconcile all these statements is the study of how God destroys.

It cannot be through proactive violence, as people think. Jesus Himself told Peter to put away his sword because violence begets violence (see Matt. 26:52).

In the same way that the Old Testament "LORD is a man of war" (Ex. 15:3), so also is the New Testament Christ a man of war. He said He did not come to bring peace but a sword (see Matt. 10:34). In Revelation 19:11–14, we see Jesus, as the Word of God, having blood-soaked garments, leading the heavenly armies in war. At last, "the Lord Jesus shall be revealed from heaven with his mighty angels, in flaming fire taking vengeance on them that know not God" (2 Thess. 1:7, 8), destroying the wicked by "the brightness of his coming" (2:8).

I do not want to get off track here and launch into a discussion of how the Father and Son make war in righteousness. Many of the passages I have raised could in themselves become the launching texts for entire articles. What I have attempted to verify to this point is that there is definite language in the inspired account that depicts God and His Christ as waging war on the enemies of righteousness, either directly, indirectly, or in "permissive will"—by *proxy*—and when we juxtapose all of these with God's abhorrence of bloodshed and violence, we see there is a legitimate call for a satisfactory harmonization of the Scriptures and the establishment of a singular principle that undergirds all these apparent modalities of wrath.

God doesn't have a hybrid character with some light (life) and some darkness (death), depending on the situation, nor does He ever act "out of character" (see 1 John 1:5; John 1:4). We have thought that His "strange act" is to go out of character in the exercise of *proactive violence*, but it is rather in *giving over* to the forces of evil and chaos. Included in these forces are the consequences of people's own choices to bring about righteousness by violent means. Even in His instructions to ancient Israel in the use of violence, it had to do with their own choice to pick up the sword. He gave them no such instructions. It did not arise from His own character and style of government.

As we now move into a discussion of the basis of permissive will, we begin with some thoughts on the kingdoms of this world. To live without any application of the force of arms, according to the complete picture of the true character of God, at a general, societal, governmental level, in a world of sinners, governed by sinners, is not possible. It is not according to the Scriptures to promote pacifism as any sort of ideal in the milieu of worldly structures, which were built under the cloud of the great controversy rebellion against God. This would be absolutely out of the question.

I know this may seem like a crazy statement after all I have said. When I talk about replicating the pacifist character and ways of the Lord, it applies to the *believer* who has entered an abiding and personal relationship with the Godhead. The worldly structures are under the god of this world and exist under—in fact *ordained* (Bible language) under—the permissive paradigm or accommodative will of God. Therefore, while we need police and military, it is not our place to service that system, as our time needs to be directed to promoting the kingdom to which we are most fundamentally allied: the spiritual kingdom of God.

As followers of Christ, we should be seeing our way clearly to a total commitment to nonviolence and non-coercion. This is not just talking about physical force but all forms of manipulation. Anything that is not of love—which does not exemplify the spirit of *agape*, which is all-for-the-other, none-for-self, self-sacrificing love—is violence. The principle of sin is separating from the Creator in self-exaltation, and that principle operates by seeking a place for oneself at the top without concern for using or hurting others to get there.

Sin is in contrast to *agape* in that it is an all-for-self, nothing-for-others, others-sacrificing self-interest, and if there is built into the formula anything at all for others, it has a mercenary motive behind it and will drop the others cold if they are no longer beneficial to self-interest. If it doesn't appear now to act entirely as described here, it is because the Spirit of God is having a wooing influence in the direction of light and love. In the final crisis leading to the close of probation for humanity, it will all manifest clearly as to who knows God and who does not, as there will be a waning and ultimately *no* influence for righteousness left in the world.

Stay with me; I am going somewhere with this.

All the systems of mankind work on the principles of the world, which operate by arbitrary rewards for compliance and arbitrary punishments for non-compliance. By nature, having their backing by the force of arms, these systems are inherently violent. They are all manipulative and arbitrary. Their regulations, recompenses, and retributions are subject to continual change and established by the means and to the ends that best suit those with the most power. The pragmatic approach is the highest standard, with the best governments focused on achieving peace and safety with the least number of casualties, while the worst care solely about power and nothing about casualties.

I know this is a cynical and pessimistic worldview, but how else could the world be when it is governed by Leviathan, the king of pride? The terrestrial systems vary in their structuring of power distribution and, therefore, equitability to all people. Invariably, no matter how well they may start out, if they are not based solely on the Word of God, they become decadent and murderous. (In the history of the world, peaceable assumptions of power are rare. America is an exception, and even here we have enough bloody history to realize that nations, like the swords that establish them, are never actually forged without the employment of fire and steel. America can only be understood to arise as a peaceable "lamb" in *relative* terms)

Continuing, the governing powers of mankind end up existing solely for themselves at the expense of the rest. Human governance (whether in the world or in that which calls itself the church of Christ [ref. Isa. 4:1]) ultimately exists to perpetuate the authority and office of its leaders and continually consolidate or centralize power until "all for self and none for others" has come to the full. Therefore, it is an absolutely untenable system of governance and ultimately comes to nothing. Self-exaltation destroys its opponents and when all live by this principle it is every person against the other.

Satan is manipulating all governments and all institutions in this world to the point where he has all power. Worldlings do not yet know that it will cost them everything. Right now, they think they will gain their piece of the pie, but ultimately comes the drying up of the Euphrates, and the dark awakening commences. They will burn the whore with whom they have gotten in bed and proceed to turn on and annihilate her leaders and each other. It is the "Day of the Lord" and the "great conflagration." Revelation 18 and Ezekiel 9 tell the story.

We are talking about civil governance and authority in the institutions of humanity, even though these institutions are said to be "ordained of God." Here, we are looking at sinful structures doomed to second death because they are entirely of the beast. Notice John depicts this in one sentence: "And *in her* [the beast system, Babylon, whose principles are kingly rule, man-over-man, wherein God is removed] was found the blood of prophets, and of saints, and *of all that were slain upon the earth*" (Rev. 18:24, emphasis added).

Note that not only God's people are killed, but all the deaths of every person who ever died a violent death is attributable to the world's systems of rule, which are according to satanic principles of self-exaltation at the expense of others. According to John, there are no souls left of which we can say God killed. *All* violent death comes about by systems of human authority and exercise of arbitrary force, whether authorized or not. Even non-violent or accidental death occurs because of Satan's principles being given to operate in the earth. Nobody escapes it except the final generation. The entire world is given over to a "general wrath," and the "punishment" for sin comes upon all things living and non-living alike, which come to their end, whether violent or non-violent (see Rom. 1:18; 3:10; 5:12; 8:22).

So it is that the wrath of God comes upon this world through the devil, styled the "god of this world" (2 Cor. 4:4), himself having great wrath (see Rev. 12:12), operating in and through the governments of this world—governments that humanity chose for itself in the first Adam. God simply steps aside and says, "Ok, that is what you want and that is what you shall have." The worldly rulers exercise authority over their fellowmen, but it is not to be so in Christ's church (see Luke 22:25, 26). Christ's kingdom is not of this world (see John 18:36), yet God has ordained those

Gentile kings; they are "ministers of God" unto which we are to be subject (see Rom. 13:1–7).

Part IV

How are we to understand all this about God setting up kingdoms and authorities in the world, even ordaining that we should obey them (see Dan. 2:21; Ex. 9:16; 1 Tim. 2:1, 2; Titus 3:1)? It is this way because of the hardness of people's hearts. Bible language is such that God "ordains" many things that are not according to His perfect will. He does not cast people off entirely when He is rejected, but seeks to accommodate them within their darkened thinking. God is in the business of keeping us alive insofar as He may intervene without violating freedom of conscience and choice.

One does not have to think too deeply to realize that it is not God's will that His children should have ever needed earthly governments. They are a present reality due to the fall, in place to mitigate the intensity and frequency of the many ways in which humans violate other humans. Although depicted as "ordained of God," they are deeply flawed from the outset as they have self-interest at their center. Additionally, they function by the inconsistent and ever-changing rules of human law. These systems are arbitrary constructs that prescribe rewards and punishments to ensure compliance. The basis of their appeal is that of self-exaltation/gratification and fear of pain or loss. In other words, they function within a paradigm of promotion and protection of the flesh.

This paradigm cannot comprehend God's ways. It cannot see that when His Spirit directs every individual, perfect love reigns, and love works no ill towards its neighbor. God's perfect will is reflected in His perfect law, perfectly kept, wherein we would look out for the best interest of all others, while the others would be looking out for ours. It is the perfect "all for one and one for all"! It is socialist in nature, yet socialism under carnal principles fails miserably to deliver any sort of classless egalitarianism. The masses are demoted to the realm of servants, horribly abused by the ruling elites and their lackeys with guns.

If people *were* to return to God's perfect will, the kingdoms of this world would fall. If every man and woman in an earthly national government, within its law enforcement, judiciary, military, and financial sectors were to subscribe to Jesus' peace teachings, there would be no more force of arms, and that government would fall. If the armies of the aggressor nation that took over were to do the same thing, they also would topple. It would be a "domino effect."

If righteousness were to fill all the earth, there would be no nations, but since the fall of the kingdom of God in mankind, self-exaltation has replaced God. Without the restraints imposed by human laws, with their arbitrary punishments (fines, imprisonment, physical punishment, death), we know that the ensuing chaos would catapult mankind to a speedy extinction. With the increasing wickedness in the world, we see how it can be so. Truly, we shall see how it will be so on an unprecedented scale. Freedom is the rope that God has given to humanity by which it shall hang on the gallows it built for itself, like Haman in the book of Esther. Therefore, although it is not God's will that people should rule over each other, He gives over to this arrangement in the paradigm of permissive will.

What gets accomplished in this is *probationary time*. Permissive will is none other than forbearance and grace. It puts a check on runaway evil so that the knowledge of God can be preserved in the earth and future generations can at last come out of the darkness, be renewed in His image, and prepared at last for entrance into eternity, where His perfect will reigns. Therefore, when God "ordains" rulers, it is according to the biblical language. It is not that He does it proactively, but He gives mankind over to the various modalities of human governance, ranging from relatively benign and free to tyrannical and murderous. All are ordained of God, even those that run away into absolute depravity. This is because what people do with free choice is out of His hands. No human government is perfect; all operate by satanic principles, but many of them go too far and incur further wrath (giving over) to the point where they fall altogether as God must withdraw further from them.

A nation is strong in proportion to the fidelity with which it fulfills God's purpose for it; its success depends upon its use of the power entrusted to it; its compliance with the divine principles is always the measure of its prosperity; and its destiny is determined by the choices its leaders and people make with respect to these principles (see White, *Education*, pp. 174–178; *Patriarchs and Prophets*, p. 536). God imparts wisdom and power that will keep strong the nations to the degree that they adopt righteous principles but gives up those who ascribe their glory to human achievement and act independently of Him (see p. 501).

People "who refuse to submit to the government of God are wholly unfitted to govern themselves" (White, *The Great Controversy*, p. 584). When, instead of being a protector of its citizens, a nation becomes a proud and cruel oppressor, its fall is inevitable (see White, *Education*, p. 176). As the nations, one after another, have rejected God's principles, their glory has faded, their power departed, and their place been occupied by others (see p. 177). "All are by their own choice deciding their destiny," and in rejecting God's principles, accomplishing their own ruin (p. 178). "The complicated play of human events is under divine control." This is how it is said that "amidst the strife and tumult of nations, He that sitteth above the cherubim still guides the affairs of earth" and overrules "all for the accomplishment of His purposes" (*Ibid*).

We must be very careful how we think about this. If we see God's role in the great controversy as one who guides affairs and overrules by any kind of arbitrary means, moving pieces about on the gameboard out of turn or breaking any of the rules because He is bigger and stronger,

Satan will immediately cry "foul" on Him. We must not subscribe to "sovereignty of God" types of arguments to justify divine violence, for He is not out to win the great controversy by pulling rank. Power of might proves nothing regarding worthiness of character. Love and freedom must win the argument.

It is a very complicated system that only God can order in righteousness, maintaining freedom of choice yet working His influence upon humanity to the maximum limit, never stepping over the line and resorting to force. He gives people over to their choices but hopes to stay in the picture as much as possible, in an advisory capacity, hoping and ever striving to lead them back to a better way until mankind's ways are repudiated and God's ways are once again established.

Hosea relates God's way of overruling (ruling over) the affairs of earth for the accomplishment of His purposes: "I gave thee a king in mine anger, and took *him* away in my wrath" (13:11). Here we see that, in reality, divine permissive will is divine wrath. (Note that the final-generation elect will not function under it. That which is called the church—which we call the "visible church," in the various legal structures of nations—is today organized under permissive will/wrath, but the latter-rain, loud-cry messengers will be organized as a *theocracy*, not a *hierocracy*.)

When Israel clamored for a king to be like the nations (the world), they were asking to be after the *common order*, which is a rejection of God. In keeping with His character of love, it was not God's will to be rejected because it would not be good for *them*. He told them all the bad things that would happen under a king, but then He selected a king for them. This is permissive will in action. He gave them over to their errant desires.

We'll come back and finish commenting on this text from Hosea in a moment, but first we need to look at the establishment of human governance in the camp of the Israelites under Moses as less than God's perfect will and yet another example of permissive will. Turn to Exodus 18 and notice how Moses' father-in-law, Jethro, came to him with a suggestion for human hierarchical organization, and it is all written as though it were ordained of God (see v. 19, 23). However, what is the actual basis for this advice? First, Moses stated that the people would come to him to inquire of God (see v. 15—they needed to be taught to go to God, apparently, as we also must learn today, instead of "making flesh our arm"). Second, Jethro came with advice of his own, and Moses ran with it because it seemed like the easier way (vv. 18, 24). Ellen White concurs:

> The Lord *permitted* Moses to choose *for himself* [not for God because this was not God's choice] the most faithful and efficient men to share the responsibility with him. Their influence would assist in *holding in check the violence of the people, and quelling insurrection*; yet *serious evils would eventually result from their promotion*. They *would never have been chosen had Moses manifested faith* corresponding to the evidences he had witnessed of God's power and goodness. But he had magnified his own burdens and services, almost losing sight of the fact that he was only the instrument by which God had wrought. He was not excusable in indulging, in the slightest degree, the spirit of murmuring that was the curse of Israel. *Had he relied fully upon God, the Lord would have guided him continually and would have given him strength* for every emergency. (White, *Patriarchs and Prophets*, p. 380, emphasis added)

Returning to our text in Hosea to continue our view of how God accomplishes His purposes, notice also that even the taking away of that king was the anger of God, which is a principle of His government in action (i.e., "giving over," "hiding His face," or "sparing not"), wherein God exercises His judgment in that He must allow consequences to fall to such degree that corresponds with the extent to which the free moral agent has rejected Him and His ways. Therefore, in taking away Saul in wrath, the Bible declares that God slew him (see 1 Chron. 10:14), but we know the physical reality is that Saul committed suicide with his own sword (see v. 4). He rejected God, and God withdrew from him. He will not force His way into a situation where He is not wanted, but He strives to stay in the picture to as large a degree as possible, so long as the hardness of heart has not arrived at an unreachable fullness.

Part V

Before moving into the primary discussion in this study, it will be helpful to emphasize that REGULATING, i.e., giving commands, instructions, suggestions, or counsel, regarding the carrying out of an activity in which we are fundamentally opposed on principle, is not the same as agreeing to or condoning that activity in any way. Any argument that might think to implicate God as one who approves of the use of the sword as a method by referring to His commands and counsels regarding the same needs to also deal with and differentiate between this and His commands and counsels on other issues, as though there would be variables that modify the principle of action:

REGULATION OF POLYGAMY [in permissive will]—

If a man have two wives, one beloved, and another hated, and they have born him children, *both* the beloved and the hated; and *if* the firstborn son be hers that was hated: Then it shall be, when he maketh his sons to inherit that which he hath, that he may not make the son of the beloved firstborn before the son of the hated, which is indeed the firstborn. (Deuteronomy 21:15, 16)

If he take him another *wife*; her food, her raiment, and her duty of marriage, shall he not diminish. (Exodus 21:10)

GOD'S WILL REGARDING POLYGAMY—

Thou shalt not commit adultery…. thou shalt not covet thy neighbour's wife [singular]. (Exodus 20:14, 17)

A bishop then must be blameless, the husband of one wife. (1 Timothy 3:2)

REGULATION OF DIVORCE—

When a man hath taken a wife, and married her, and it come to pass that she find no favour in his eyes, because he hath found some uncleanness in her: then let him write her a bill of divorcement, and give *it* in her hand, and send her out of his house. (Deuteronomy 24:1)

GOD'S WILL REGARDING DIVORCE—

It hath been said, Whosoever shall put away his wife, let him give her a writing of divorcement: But I say unto you, That whosoever shall put away his wife, saving for the cause of fornication, causeth her to commit adultery: and whosoever shall marry her that is divorced committeth adultery. (Matthew 5:31, 32)

REGULATION OF SERVITUDE/SLAVERY—

See Exodus 21:2–9; Leviticus 25; Deuteronomy 15:1–18; 23:14, 15

Servants, be obedient to them that are *your* masters according to the flesh, with fear and trembling, in singleness of your heart, as unto Christ; Not with eyeservice, as menpleasers; but as the servants of Christ, doing the will of God from the heart; With good will doing service, as to the Lord, and not to men. (Ephesians 6:5–7)

GOD'S WILL REGARDING SERVITUDE/SLAVERY—

And they that have believing masters, let them not despise *them*, because they are brethren; but rather do *them* service, because they are faithful and beloved, partakers of the benefit. These things teach and exhort. (1 Timothy 6:2)

For ye are all the children of God by faith in Christ Jesus. For as many of you as have been baptized into Christ have put on Christ. There is neither Jew nor Greek, there is neither bond nor free, there is neither male nor female: for ye are all one in Christ Jesus. (Galatians 3:26–29)

But Jesus called them *to him*, and saith unto them, Ye know that they which are accounted to rule over the Gentiles exercise lordship over them; and their great ones exercise authority upon them. But so shall it not be among you: but whosoever will be great among you, shall be your minister: And whosoever of you will be the chiefest, shall be servant of all. (Mark 10:42–44)

REGULATION OF PUNISHMENT AND RETRIBUTIVE JUSTICE—

Eye for eye, tooth for tooth, hand for hand, foot for foot, Burning for burning, wound for wound, stripe for stripe. (Exodus 21:24, 25)

GOD'S WILL REGARDING PUNISHMENT AND RETRIBUTIVE JUSTICE—

Ye have heard that it hath been said, An eye for an eye, and a tooth for a tooth: But I say unto you, That ye resist not evil: but whosoever shall smite thee on thy right cheek, turn to him the other also. (Matthew 5:38, 39)

Then said Jesus unto him, Put up again thy sword into his place: for all they that take the sword shall perish with the sword.

> Thinkest thou that I cannot now pray to my Father, and he shall presently give me more than twelve legions of angels? (Matthew 26:52, 53)

> Jesus answered, My kingdom is not of this world: if my kingdom were of this world, then would my servants fight, that I should not be delivered to the Jews: but now is my kingdom not from hence. (John 18:36)

Finally, coming to God's commands to Israel in the use of the sword, we find that it was not His will that He should have led His people to the conquest of Canaan by violence. His deliverance would have taken the "purer" form, if I may use that term, of "giving over" instead of permissive will (in reality, however, the permissive paradigm is also "giving over" in that God, winking at ignorance, meets people where they are in their thinking, even giving instruction within an errant mode of governance; even in His instructions to them to destroy their enemies with the use of carnal weapons).

Moses thought God was going to work by military means: "He, supposing that they were to obtain their freedom by force of arms, expected to lead the Hebrew host against the armies of Egypt" (White, *Patriarchs and Prophets*, p. 245). Moses later understood this was not God's way and became the meekest man who ever lived (see Num. 12:3). However, it was not so with the general body. Therefore, God, in giving over to their paradigm, did not forsake them when He saw them pick up weaponry from the bodies of the Egyptian soldiers washed up on the shore. "As morning broke it revealed to the multitudes of Israel all that remained of their mighty foes—the mail-clad bodies cast upon the shore" (pp. 288, 289). They came out of Egypt "unarmed and unaccustomed to war" (p. 282), and there was no other way for them to have obtained weapons.

There are no direct records confirming they rushed down and took the armor from the Egyptians, but all the evidence points strongly in that direction. Here are the facts: They approached, crossed, and emerged from the Red Sea without implements of war. Shortly after leaving the Red Sea, they engaged in warfare against the Amalekites, in which they did not use sticks and stones. As there were no swordsmiths between the Red Sea and the location of this battle, the only way they could have become equipped was by salvaging the weaponry washed ashore (see Straub, *As He Is*, p. 242).

This taking up of the sword reveals that they intended to fight their enemies their way. God never intended for it: "The Lord had never commanded them to 'go up and fight.' It was not His purpose that they should gain the land by warfare, but by strict obedience to His commands" (White, *Patriarchs and Prophets*, p. 392).

> I will send my fear before thee, and will destroy all the people to whom thou shalt come, and I will make all thine enemies turn their backs unto thee. And I will send hornets before thee, which shall drive out the Hivite, the Canaanite, and the Hittite, from before thee. I will not drive them out from before thee in one year; lest the land become desolate, and the beast of the field multiply against thee. By little and little I will drive them out from before thee, until thou be increased, and inherit the land. And I will set thy bounds from the Red sea even unto the sea of the Philistines, and from the desert unto the river: for I will deliver the inhabitants of the land into your hand; and thou shalt drive them out before thee. (Exodus 23:27–31)

God intended they would drive out the inhabitants of the land merely by advancing at His direction. They would take over the land by multiplying on the borders of the heathen habitations and moving in as their enemies moved out. It would certainly not be done through military conquest, bathing their swords in their blood, or taking by force what did not belong to them. The heathen would have been forced to retreat under perilous circumstances—by things of a pestilential or disastrous nature; or they could have been reduced by war among themselves or with other nations.

Any or all these things would descend upon their heads because God was not with them, protecting and sustaining them.

However, Israel wanted to do the work of driving them out by the sword. Therefore, God worked with them in their own modality, for as long as they still had not entirely cast Him off, He was able to stay in their picture to a greater degree than He could for the heathen nations. The hands of Deity were tied, so to speak. It was God working with their own choice. He instructed them in the terrible work they must therefore do if they were to stay alive and have a place. Conquest by war and bloodshed is not ever God's way. Not only is war the way of force, but also deception, as the waging of war is done utilizing methods of intrigue, theft, intrusion, and lies (i.e., by feigning, espionage, and propaganda). Satan is the father of lies.

Although God wills to work in the modality of human hardheartedness, the permissive paradigm is not the place to remain. In the end, the results are still death; it just takes longer to get there. God intends to bring His people up and out of permissive will to the point where He no longer has to make accommodations for their weaknesses, trying to get them through it with a minimum of casualties, but rather leading them from strength to strength by the power of His name—His character of love. He would have taken them under His wing, but they would not.

That is why they rejected Christ. They wanted a military deliverer who would thrust through the Roman oppressor with the sword of conquest. This is why Jesus told Peter to put up his sword, for the way of the sword ends in escalating, retributive violence. Thus, the Jews were desolated. God "destroyed" them by giving them over to their choice. "His blood *be* on us, and our children"; "we have no king but Caesar" (Matt. 27:25; John 19:15).

In conclusion, it is quite easy to believe in a non-violent God when we just look to Christ, but when coming to terms with the Bible language, with God setting up human kingdoms and commanding ancient Israel, we have to study many hours, carefully comparing line upon line in the Scriptures. We must read history with the understanding of principles, that we may settle into the new paradigm without throwing away the Bible. Even so, we receive the accusations of rewriting the Scriptures, creating loopholes, and such things. As we amass the evidences for the "new views ... of the character and attributes of God," we are richly rewarded as "hidden treasures are discovered" (White, *Fundamentals of Christian Education*, p. 444).

I believe we must truly *want* to believe in a consistently gentle and non-violent God, as depicted in Christ, in order to see Him in this way at last—to see Him *as He is*. We must pray without ceasing to overcome our hardheartedness and desire for revenge and eye-for-eye justice. It is true that as a man thinks in his heart, so he is. If we want to retain the idea that God gave humanity violence as a way of dealing with enemies, we will not see otherwise, no matter how many careful studies are produced to the contrary. "Blessed *are* the peacemakers: for they shall be called the children of God" (Matt. 5:9).

CHAPTER 5

"Warfare," It Is Called

The artist's conception of the war in heaven as a physical contest, as promoted by SDA ministry Amazing Facts

In great mercy, according to His divine character, God bore long with Lucifer (Patriarch and Prophets, p 39).

Again and again he was offered pardon on condition of repentance and submission.... Lucifer was convinced that he was in the wrong,

> *that the divine claims were just,*
> *and that he ought to acknowledge them as such before all heaven*
> (The Great Controversy, p. 496).

> Then there was the council in heaven—warfare, it is called (Ms34-1906).

> [The angels who followed Lucifer] had learned the lesson of genuine rebellion against the unchangeable law of God, and this is incurable (The Story of Redemption, p. 17).

It is the concept of many that when rebellion came to full fruition in heaven, there was a great martial conflict of some type, where angels pitted strength of might against one another in the physical realm. Through all our study about how God operates His government, we have clearly seen that He *never* employs physical force to establish or maintain righteousness. This is a principle that must ever stand, for moral "right" can never be established or upheld by physical "might."

> *God is a pacific social scientist and leadership genius, not a political manipulator or propagandizing warlord.*

All that is proven in a contest of physical strength is who is *physically* stronger. Any other issues must be proven by other means—by the implementation of principles of righteousness—not pragmatism—that a verdict may be rendered through empirical observation of the outcomes of the application of love and freedom, not fear and coercion. God is a pacific social scientist and leadership genius, not a political manipulator or propagandizing warlord.

The Early Days of the Occult

When Lucifer first got strange ideas into his head about his own greatness, he started to move about among the angels with suggestions. Little by little, he came to indulge thoughts of self and turn the allegiance of his peers from God to himself (see White, *The Great Controversy*, p. 494).

> Leaving his place in the immediate presence of God, Lucifer went forth to diffuse the spirit of discontent among the angels. *Working with mysterious secrecy,* and for a time *concealing his real purpose* under an appearance of reverence for God, he endeavored to excite dissatisfaction concerning the laws that governed heavenly beings, intimating that they imposed an unnecessary restraint. Since their natures were holy, he urged that the angels should obey the dictates of their own will. He sought to create sympathy for himself by representing that God had dealt unjustly with him in bestowing supreme honor upon Christ. He claimed that in aspiring to greater power and honor he was not aiming at self-exaltation, but was seeking to secure liberty for all the inhabitants of heaven, that by this means they might attain to a higher state of existence. (White, *The Great Controversy*, p. 495, emphasis added)

A long time passed by while Lucifer continued to spread his propaganda. At first, by insinuation and misrepresentation, he planted discontent in heaven, which later ripened into outright falsehood and open rebellion. Even while he was plying his trade, he came under conviction that "he was in the wrong, that the divine claims were just, and that he ought to acknowledge them as such before all heaven.... He had not at this time fully cast off his allegiance to God" though "he had forsaken his position as covering cherub" *(Ibid.,* p. 495). God tried to help him.

> [Lucifer] did not see whither he was drifting. But such efforts as infinite love and wisdom only could devise, were made to convince him of his error. His disaffection was proved to be without cause, and he was made to see what would be the result of persisting in revolt. Lucifer was convinced that he was in the wrong.... *He had not at that time fully cast off his allegiance to God. Though he had left his position as covering cherub, yet if he*

had been willing to return to God, acknowledging the Creator's wisdom, and satisfied to fill the place appointed him in God's great plan, *he would have been reinstated in his office. The time had come for a final decision; he must fully yield to the divine sovereignty or place himself in open rebellion.* He nearly reached the decision to return, but pride forbade him. It was too great a sacrifice for one who had been so highly honored to confess that he had been in error, that his imaginings were false, and to yield to the authority which he had been working to prove unjust. (White, *Patriarchs and Prophets*, p. 39, emphasis added)

The Council of God; the War Begins

As he went on stubbornly, the channel of conviction was blocked and Lucifer's light all but went out.

God called an assembly of the angels.

Then there was <u>the council</u> in heaven—<u>warfare</u>, it is called (*Manuscript* 34, March 23, 1906, "A Message to A.T. Jones and Others in Battle Creek," emphasis added).

This council that God had arranged was a call to choose leaders. That is why we have the term "warfare" being applied. The council drew the line in the sand. Before this, it was not open rebellion. Prior to the great assembly, Lucifer had been moving about with subtle sophistry, planting seeds of dissatisfaction and insinuating doubts. After the council, it ripened into a revolt. This council called for "a final decision; he must fully yield to the divine sovereignty or place himself in open rebellion" (White, *Patriarchs and Prophets*, p. 39).

Amazingly, during this assembly, which was not only called to bring the rebellion to a head, but also to confer open honor and affirm the status of Christ as having in Himself eternal divine nature and authority, we find Lucifer's heart thrilled with heavenly love, as he was naturally caught up in the scene of worship and praise: "As songs of praise ascended in melodious strains, swelled by thousands of glad voices, the spirit of evil seemed vanquished; unutterable love thrilled his entire being; his soul went out, in harmony with the sinless worshippers, in love to the Father and the Son" (p. 36). Yet, he determined to resist: "But again he was filled with pride in his own glory. His desire for supremacy returned, and envy of Christ was once more indulged."

Satan, at this time, sealed his own decision, while the grace period for the angels lingered on. As he went out from there to work his deception, he admitted he had stepped over the line.

The Luciferian Council

The warfare commenced in earnest as Lucifer called his own council, which was tantamount to a bid for creature worship in keeping with the principles of self-exaltation he had been cultivating:

> He left the immediate presence of the Father [*not as covering cherub*, as that was already done, but *the presence of the Father in the heavenly council*], dissatisfied, and filled with envy against Jesus Christ. Concealing his real purposes, *he assembled the angelic host*. He introduced his subject, which was *himself*. As one aggrieved, he related the preference God had given Jesus to the neglect of himself.... He stated to them that he had called them together to assure them that he no longer would submit to this invasion of his rights and theirs; that never would he again bow down to Christ; that *he would take the honor upon himself* which should have been conferred upon him, and *would be the commander of all who would submit to follow him and obey his voice. There was contention among the angels.* (White, *The Spirit of Prophecy*, Vol. 1, pp. 18, 19, emphasis added)

> He told them that himself and they also had now gone too far to go back, and he would brave the consequences; for to bow in servile worship to the Son of God he never would; that God would not forgive, and now they must assert their liberty and *gain by force* the

position and authority which was not willingly accorded to them. (White, *The Spirit of Prophecy*, Vol. 1, p. 20, emphasis added)

He declares *he cannot submit to be under Christ's command, that God's commands alone will he obey*. Good angels weep to hear the words of Satan, and to see how he despises to follow the direction of Christ, their exalted and loving commander. (White, *Spiritual Gifts*, Vol. 3, p. 38, emphasis added)

Warfare over the Eternal Deity of Christ

It is most interesting to note that Lucifer, now Satan, seemed to set up in his mind that Christ was somehow a lesser being than the Father was, for he indicates that he will obey the Father but not Christ. The nature of the contention confirms this. After the Luciferian council, at which point the polemic nature of this struggle is seen to intensify, the loyal angels pled with him and reasoned thus: "They clearly set forth that Jesus was *the Son of God, existing with him before the angels were created; and that he had ever stood at the right hand of God*" (White, *The Spirit of Prophecy*, Vol. 1, p. 19, emphasis added).

We must not miss an important point here. A major element of this warfare was contention over the eternal deity of Christ. In this, I tremble for those among the professed people of God who are involved in the so-called "non-trinitarian" or "antitrinitarian" movement, for the warfare they have decided to wage is in this aspect a rerun of the rebellion. Here we are today, right along with the loyal angels, trying to convince these folks that they are tearing away at the foundation of the eternal pre-existence of Christ, the Son of God, who has "ever stood at the right hand" of the Father.

The Spirit of Prophecy is clear on this matter that the status of Christ as the Only Begotten Son of God is an eternal status. In other words, He was *always* there with the Father. The contention by a modern, fanatic element of independent Adventism is that the Only Begotten Son is a Being who was not previously in existence before He was "begotten."

Angels were expelled from heaven because they would not work in harmony with God. They fell from their high estate because they wanted to be exalted. They had come to exalt themselves, and they forgot that their beauty of person and of character came from the Lord Jesus. This fact the [fallen] angels would obscure, *that Christ was the only begotten Son of God*, and they came to consider that they were not to consult Christ.

One angel {LUCIFER} began the controversy and carried it on until there was rebellion in the heavenly courts among the angels. (White, *This Day with God*, p. 128, emphasis added)

The rebellion was, at its core, about the status of Christ as the Almighty, Eternal, Only Begotten Son of God.

Again, the popular concept held by many of the denominational organization of the General Conference of SDAs is that angels pitted forces of physical strength against one another, and by this means, the rebels were finally ejected from heaven. In this depiction, martial-arts style of combat is used, including the use of a "Star Wars" type lightsaber emanating from a handheld dagger.

Contrasting Principles of Warfare

Now, we turn to a little further thought on the idea of the loyal and rebel forces engaging in a battle of hand-to-hand combat, finding it not only to be against the nature of God's character and governing principles, but logically untenable:

1. This is not a controversy over physical might. God created all things, and the laws of physics belong to Him. There would be no need to commit His creatures to crude, physical struggle over any issues of ideology, theology, or governance. "He could have handled Satan and all his sympathizers as easily as one can pick up a pebble and cast it to the earth" (White, *Manuscript Releases*, Vol. 18, p. 361). This not only would have frustrated God's purposes to establish the security of the universe on the sole basis of loyalty to goodness and truth, "but by this he would have given a precedent for the violence of man which is so abundantly shown in our world in the compelling principles" (*Ibid.*).
2. Truth is never established by force. "Earthly kingdoms rule by the ascendancy of physical power; but from Christ's kingdom every carnal weapon, every instrument of coercion, is banished" (White, *The Acts of the Apostles*, p. 12). Truth and righteousness are established through the work of demonstration over the course of time and the often painful process of letting principles show the results of their own implementation.
3. If we believe God arbitrarily forced Satan out of heaven by application of physical force, that is one thing. Another thing that would cause us to question the nature of God's character and government would be that it seems He would have passed off the problem of the rebellion in heaven and handed it down to the new creation of humanity, where they would hardly be ready or able to defend against such a foe. It seems like a setup for failure! What would this tell us about God?

Divine Compulsion

While it is true that there was, at the end, an expulsion from heaven, which by its nature was compulsive, it came after the rebels had fully exhausted their bid for supremacy, which included a stated determination to take heaven by force after ideology had failed. (Note that the nature of this compulsion would be with regard to *occupation of space*, not *choice of beliefs or allegiance*. This distinction is important.) The contest could not yet be considered finished, however, because the demonstration of Satan's claims needed more time to manifest, especially for the onlooking worlds, the new human race, and even those loyalists who remained in heaven. Therefore, while the testing of Satan's claims must go forward, it had to do so in a theater of living beings. He was given a chance to gain further adherents in the universe, and all were free to take part in the trial on either side—God's or Lucifer's. The trial of the universe was to be especially easy, and Satan's power to be heavily curtailed. More on this will be discussed later.

> **Though God never intended for Satan to win any more rebels to his side, the unfallen universe could not be so sheltered that there would be no opportunity for any others to take up his cause. This would go against the principles of freedom.**

Though God never intended for Satan to win any more rebels to his side, the unfallen universe could not be so sheltered that there would be no opportunity for any others to take up his cause. This would go against the principles of freedom. We can only speculate how the controversy would have ended had every inhabited world successfully passed their period of probation, but we will refrain from such an exercise.

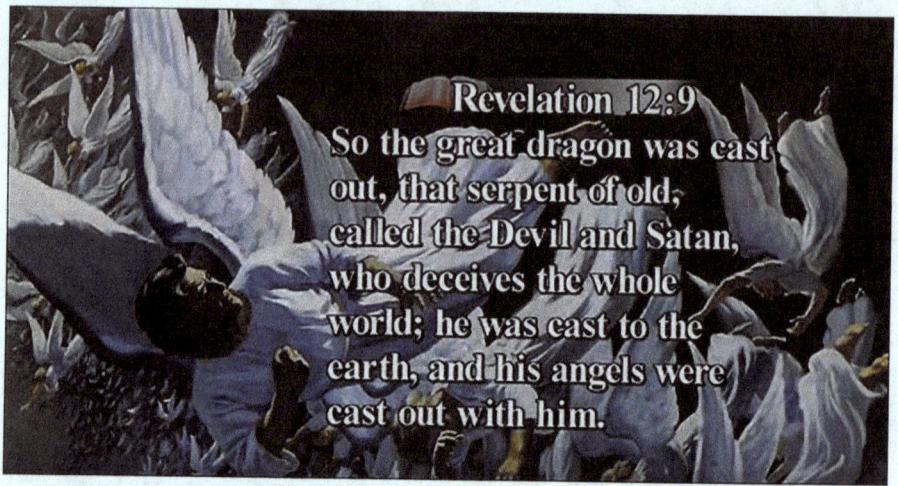

Kenneth Cox Ministries publishes this picture, again, depicting a violent overthrow, as though cast over the edge of a precipice, flailing headlong to the earth.

The expulsion of Satan from heaven was more decidedly a *rejection* than an *ejection*. He was given free rein to move about and develop his thesis, even using artifice to promulgate it. Once every mind was fully decided as to what each individual position would be, there was nothing left to do but leave that place because there would be no more reception for the arch rebel. His work there would be finished. Would God have to force him out? Revelation 12:9 certainly depicts a "casting out," but must we read physical combat into this, or can it be that he was "cast out" by finding that there were none left to hear his arguments anymore? that the philosophical lines were drawn, and he would be winning no more to his side in rebellion? Now, owning nothing in heaven, he would need to seek for a new place to establish his kingdom.

It is interesting to read and makes one ponder deeply as to the nature of the conflict. We read first that "the great God could at once have hurled this archdeceiver from heaven; but this was not His purpose. He would give the rebellious *an equal chance to measure strength and might* with His own Son and His loyal angels. In this battle every angel would choose his own side and be manifested to all" (White, *The Story of Redemption*, p. 17, emphasis added).

We have learned already that this "strength and might" is the pitting of truth against error. It is ideological. If it were to be a physical struggle, it would not make sense to say "an equal chance to measure strength and might" because God possesses omnipotence. All the powers in the universe are made by Him and sustained by Him. Creatures would know this. Yet the very next sentence states, "It would not have been safe *to suffer any who united with Satan in his rebellion to continue to occupy heaven*" (emphasis added).

This seems to indicate to us that God was prepared to use force, but is it so? We immediately find a disclaimer to this idea in that God knows that if He were to exercise power in this way, the "disaffected angels would not have been manifested." Lucifer had to be allowed to mature his plans to the full in order that the angels would all come to an open statement of their position and intent. "If God had *exercised His power to punish* this chief rebel, *disaffected angels would not have been manifested*; hence, God took another course, for He would manifest *distinctly* to all the heavenly host His justice and His judgment" (emphasis added).

Having thus given up their posts of duty, determining, along with their rebel leader, that they would no longer submit to God, they would have therefore found themselves unemployed in heaven. Would we think they would seek to keep the real estate while evicting the Owner, especially with a minority vote? Perhaps they would expect this, but God did not allow for it, expelling them instead.

How was it to be done? Would God be enlisting His angels to engage in some sort of physical fighting? Satan did say he himself would use force. What could he have been thinking? He would surely know he could never win in this way. Would he be attempting to bait God into physical combat? This way, he could play the victim, claiming God was playing the part of a bully, using His inherent omnipotence against the underdog. Whatever Satan was thinking, it didn't work. Praise God!

Heaven Arraigns the Rebels Before the Divine Tribunal

After the initial council of God, the Luciferian council, and the ensuing ideological warfare that took place among the angels, God "summoned" all the inhabitants of heaven before Him once again. Satan proudly trumpeted his determined resistance, pointing to the great numbers that had joined his side and declaring his intent to wage physical warfare, "to defend his place in heaven *by force of might*, strength against strength" (p. 18, emphasis added).

Even so, we read in Jude that they "kept not their first estate, but left their own habitation" (v. 6). We are not compelled to read into the heavenly expulsion of the rebels any kind of physical combat, whether by lightsaber, kickboxing, or any other method that angels might devise to conduct physical warfare.

"God declared that the rebellious should remain in heaven no longer.... Then there was war in heaven" (White, *The Story of Redemption*, pp. 18, 19). We are not explicitly informed of the exact nature of the warfare at this point. While it is safe to say that heretofore there would have been no kind of physical push against one another, it seems inconclusive as to what exactly and specifically ensued after Satan's declaration to use physical force. The words at this point seem to indicate some sort of physical struggle while coming short of actually saying it.

> The Father decides the case of Satan, and declares that he must *be turned out of Heaven* for his daring rebellion, and that all those who united with him in his rebellion, should *be turned out with him*. Then there was war in Heaven. Christ and his angels fought against Satan and his angels, for they were determined to remain in Heaven with all their rebellion. But they prevailed not. Christ and loyal angels triumphed, and *drove Satan and his rebel sympathizers from Heaven*. (White, *Spiritual Gifts*, Vol. 3, p. 38, emphasis added)

The Son of God, the Prince of heaven, and His loyal angels engaged in conflict with the archrebel and those who united with him. The Son of God and true, loyal angels prevailed; and Satan and his sympathizers were expelled from heaven. (White, *The Story of Redemption*, p. 19, emphasis added)

The Nature of the Expulsion

Here is where we must not judge the text by what it appears to say, but rather by the principles we have seen in operation thus far, in consideration of the fact that God never changes in how He operates. First, we saw earlier He determined not to use force, even though He would be fully capable of doing so. "God took another course, for *He would manifest distinctly* to all the heavenly host His justice and His judgment" (White, *The Story of Redemption*, p 17, emphasis added). He would reveal His justice and judgment in a *distinct* fashion. This means He would manifest a course that would be different from what we might expect—use of physical violence.

Second, we recall also that to use force would have set a precedent "for the violence of human beings that is so abundantly shown in our world in the compelling principles" (White, *Manuscript Releases*, Vol. 18, p. 361). From these strong indicators of principle, we may safely conclude that while God compelled the rebels to leave, He did not use physical compulsion, as in force of hand-to-hand or even armed combat. What then, did He use?

"(For the weapons of our warfare *are* not carnal, but mighty through God to the pulling down of strong holds;) Casting down imaginations, and every high thing that exalteth itself against the knowledge of God" (2 Cor. 10:4, 5). The centurion with the sick servant called upon Christ, understanding that He needed to "speak the word only" and that it would be done (Matt. 8:8). God would merely need to speak the command to leave, and evil would be compelled to leave, the same as when Christ asserted authority by the unveiling of His divinity, speaking a command, clearing the earthly temple of those trafficking in unrighteousness, saying, "Take these things hence" (John 2:16).

We can also take our cue from other events where Christ commanded spirits to depart. Notice how the devils grovel before Him: "What have we to do with thee, Jesus, thou Son of God? art thou come hither to torment us before the time?" (Matt. 8:29). Jesus needed only to say, "Depart," and they must obey, for they cannot stand in the presence of unveiled glory and the authority of righteousness. When divinity manifests, it has automatic, irresistible power and authority. In the wilderness of temptation, Jesus commanded, "Get thee hence, Satan" and the evil one had no power to stay (see 4:10). "Christ's divinity flashed through suffering humanity. Satan had no power to resist the command to depart. Humiliated and enraged, he was forced to withdraw from the presence of the world's Redeemer" (White, *Sermons and Talks*, Vol. 2, p. 219).

Therefore, we may correctly understand that during all the earlier stages of the heavenly conflict, God remained relatively silent, in the background, but when the time came such as Lucifer and his host were prepared to go so far as to think foolishly that they might exert physical pressure against the loyal host and even Christ Himself, all that would need to happen is Christ would stand up in unveiled glory and His heretofore veiled divinity would flash through, causing the wicked to flee. This same authority would also be given the loyal angels to wield.

> So *we* may resist temptation and *force* Satan to depart from us.... We cannot save ourselves from the tempter's power; he has conquered humanity, and when we try to stand in our own strength, we shall become a prey to his devices; but "the name of the Lord is a strong tower: the righteous runneth into it, and is safe" *Satan trembles and flees before the weakest soul who finds refuge in that mighty name.* (White, *Christ Triumphant*, p. 219, emphasis added)

There would be no contest. The rebel forces would be compelled to "tuck tail and run." There is nothing that can resist the full presence of the Lord when He manifests His glory, even when we, in pure hearts of faith, invoke His all-powerful name, for it is nothing less than a consuming fire. "Understand therefore this day, that the LORD thy God *is* he which goeth over before thee; ***as* a consuming fire he shall destroy them, and he shall bring them down before thy face: so shalt thou drive them out**, and destroy them quickly, as the LORD hath said unto thee" (Deut. 9:3, bold emphasis added).

It is the righteousness of the Lord and the Lord alone, in the face of wickedness, that drives out and destroys the wicked. The unveiling of His glory, which is His character, is the only way our Lord exercises compelling power in the face of intransigent rebellion. Stated yet another way, executive judgment is always by "giving over" to the results of evil and, when the ultimate is required, by revelation of Himself after free choice is fixed.

"Speak not thou in thine heart, after that the LORD thy God hath cast them out from before thee, saying, For my righteousness the LORD hath brought me in to possess this land: **but for the wickedness of these nations the LORD doth drive them out** from before thee" (v. 4, bold emphasis added).

> *Another way we can look at this is that the very harmonious and loyal atmosphere of heaven would become torturous to those developing characters of evil and rebellion.*

This is such an important principle that God saw fit to say it twice, back to back: "Not for thy righteousness, or for the uprightness of thine heart, dost thou go to possess their land: **but for the wickedness of these nations the LORD thy God doth drive them out** from before thee" (v. 5, bold emphasis added). So it is that "evil shall slay the wicked: and they that hate the righteous shall be desolate" (Ps. 34:21).

Another way we can look at this is that the very harmonious and loyal atmosphere of heaven would become torturous to those developing characters of evil and rebellion. Speaking of those who have hardened themselves in sin, it is written that heaven "would be torture to them; the glory of God would be a consuming fire. They would long to flee from that holy place. They would welcome destruction, that they might be hidden from the face" of Christ (White, *The Great Controversy*, p. 543).

Maintaining Protection and Freedom

Of course, seeing that Satan and his followers would not give up trying to badger and browbeat the angels, the rebel host would have been prevented from having further access to the loyal forces. Minds being made up, God protected the rights of His own to free enjoyment of their estate in heaven without continual harassment. Yet:

> God knew that such determined rebellion would not remain inactive. Satan would invent means to annoy the heavenly angels, and show contempt for his authority. As he could not gain admittance within the gates of Heaven, he would wait just at the entrance, to taunt the angels and seek contention with them as they should pass in and out. He would seek to destroy the happiness of Adam and Eve. He would endeavor to incite them to rebellion, knowing that this would cause grief in Heaven. ("The Great Controversy. Between Christ And His Angels and Satan And His Angels." *The Signs of the Times*, January 16, 1879)

When Satan, with his ideas, was no longer welcome, he would yet push his philosophy on unreceptive ears. This is a form of force. There is physical force and there is a force that comes by verbal mechanism or that of ideological or psychological pressuring, the coercive "hounding" of an individual or society through the methodology of hijacking the means of communication for purposes of propaganda. God would give the gatekeepers His authority to simply repel the rebels by the Word of God. This is how it is done.

Note how the disciples marveled at the power they had over the devils, saying, "Lord, even the devils are subject unto us through thy name" (Luke 10:17). Jesus knew exactly what that power was, reminding them, "I beheld Satan as lightning fall from heaven" (v. 18). He knew He needed to only speak, and the departure of the wicked would be as rapid as a bolt of lightning. No *Star Wars* lightsabers would be needed; no protracted dance of thrust and parry. He told them, "Behold, I give unto you power to tread on serpents and scorpions [demons], and over all the power of the enemy: and nothing shall by any means hurt you" (v. 19).

God's people need to keep this principle ever in mind, as it is also a call to continual digging into His Word, that we may be knowledgeable and so settled in the truth that no heresy will disturb our peace. We must realize that many will come in, seeking contention through persistent pushing of an idea upon unreceptive minds—not unreceptive because they are not willing to examine an unfamiliar thought, but because they know the Word of God does not agree with that thought. We can know that this is unrighteous harassment, often witnessed in individuals who seek to gain acceptance of doctrines espoused by their fanatic and cultic movements.

God's people are safeguarded by commitment to the practice of the truth—a practice cultivated by knowledge gained through the study of the Scriptures and the Spirit of Prophecy. Those seeking to gain admittance for their error will be repelled by a people strong in these things, and there will be no need to call upon any human authority—not the temple guards nor the Roman soldiers. The Word of God alone is mighty. The opposers of God's people will find that there "is no place found for them" with their ideas.

Satan did not win a majority in heaven, so now it was up to him to establish for himself a place to call his own, where he could rule according to his own ideas. Therefore, he turned to the newly created human race to see if he could subvert them to his system of lies. God, in mercy, devised a simple and easy test for Adam and Eve and even the inhabitants of other planets, while warning them about what was taking place.

God says of Adam, "I gave him the noblest qualities and the highest powers, my requirements were light upon him. It was because he did not believe my word, did not choose to stand the simple test I imposed upon him, but believed the word of the enemy, that he fell from his holy estate" ("They That Have Done Good," *The Signs of the Times*, August 29, 1892).

He allowed the rebel to have a soapbox for his ideas, and even while warning His children, He would allow anyone who cared to listen to those ideas to come and hear. Yet, it would be a restricted platform: only at one tree.

> Should he seek to intimidate them because of his power, so recently an angel in high authority, he could accomplish nothing. He decided that cunning and deceit would do what might or force could not.
>
> God assembled the angelic host to take measures to avert the threatened evil. It was decided in Heaven's council for angels to visit Eden and warn Adam that he was in danger from the foe....
>
> They told them that Satan purposed to do them harm, and it was necessary for them to be guarded, for they might come in contact with the fallen foe; but he could not harm them while they yielded obedience to God's command; for, if necessary, every angel from Heaven would come to their help rather than that he should in any way do them harm. But if they disobeyed the command of God, then Satan would have power to ever annoy, perplex, and trouble them....
>
> The angels charged them to follow closely the instructions which God had given them in reference to the tree of knowledge; for in perfect obedience they were safe, and the foe could then have no power to deceive them. God would not permit Satan to follow the holy pair with continual temptations. He could have access to them only at the tree of knowledge of good and evil. ("The Great Controversy. Between Christ And His Angels and Satan And His Angels." *The Signs of the Times*, January 16, 1879)

Satan had tried and failed with other populated planets. God had allowed him freedom to try his philosophies, but he was restricted to one venue on each planet: a tree. It was the same on earth. In keeping with the fairness and consistency of God came the warning to the inhabitants that there was an enemy and to listen to him would be folly.

> The Lord has given me *a view of other worlds*. Wings were given me, and an angel attended me from the city to a place that was bright and glorious.... The inhabitants of the place were of all sizes; they were noble, majestic, and lovely. They bore the express image of Jesus, and their countenances beamed with holy joy, expressive of the freedom and happiness of the place. I asked one of them why they were so much more lovely than those on the earth. The reply was, "We have lived in strict obedience to the commandments of God, and have not fallen by disobedience, like those on the earth." Then *I saw two trees*, one looked much like the tree of life in the city. The fruit of both looked beautiful, but *of one they could not eat. They had power to eat of both, but were forbidden to eat of one*. Then my attending angel said to me, "None in this place have tasted of the forbidden tree; but if they should eat, they would fall." (White, *Early Writings*, pp. 39, 40, emphasis added)

As mankind was tested, so were all the worlds given the same trial of obedience. "Like the inhabitants of all other worlds, he must be subjected to the test of obedience" (White, *Patriarchs and Prophets*, p. 332). Satan did not come down to them to physically wrest from them an allegiance through threat of violence, nor would they have been turned out from those worlds through violent expulsion. He would have come to them at the one place allowed by God, who, never changing, would have done the same for these worlds, warning them of the conflict underway—that the foe would be allowed to speak at the tree and the best course would be to stay away and not eat the fruit of disobedience, lest they also die.

They passed their tests. We did not. Now we live under the knowledge of good and evil—knowledge that God never intended we should have. It is a terrible thing to be a sinner, but praise God, all of heaven was poured out that we need not remain in this condition or sink into oblivion. We have a Savior! The Lord God reasons with us on this point, saying, "In [your] fallen condition did I not send help? I sent my Son, who was equal with myself, that he might live an example upon earth, and die for man's transgressions, that you might make no mistakes or failures in obtaining eternal life" ("They That Have Done Good." *The Signs of the Times*, August 29, 1892).

There He hung, upon His cursed tree between two souls—one choosing the tree of life and the other choosing the tree of death. Let us avail ourselves of every provision in Christ, choosing life. Then, one day soon, all the universe will shout together in victory with us, knowing that the night of trial is over and we are home at last, free forever. And so today, we lift Him up in hope of that day and that shout of victory!

CHAPTER 6

The Role of Angels in Divine Wrath and Punishment

*"For he shall give his angels charge over thee,
to keep thee in all thy ways."*
Ps. 91:11

"Angels are sent from the heavenly courts, *not to destroy*, but to watch over and guard imperiled souls, to save the lost, to bring the straying ones back to the fold. 'I came not to condemn, but to save,' Christ declared" ("The New Life in Christ," *The Review and Herald*, May 10, 1906, emphasis added).

We could stop right there. We have our answer. The Bible and the Spirit of Prophecy tell us that angels are sent to keep us in God's care and save the lost. In addition, it is stated clearly that they are *not* sent to destroy. There is no exception given to the rule. This is in keeping with Jesus' own statement to the disciples, when they wanted to call fire on the heads of the inhospitable Samaritans: "You don't know what spirit is motivating you, because I have not come to destroy anyone, but to save everyone" (Luke 9:55, 56, paraphrased). Yet, the Bible and SoP continually portray angels as being involved in destruction, and the language *appears* to depict them as being involved *proactively*, by direct exertion of the power they are given to wield in God's service.

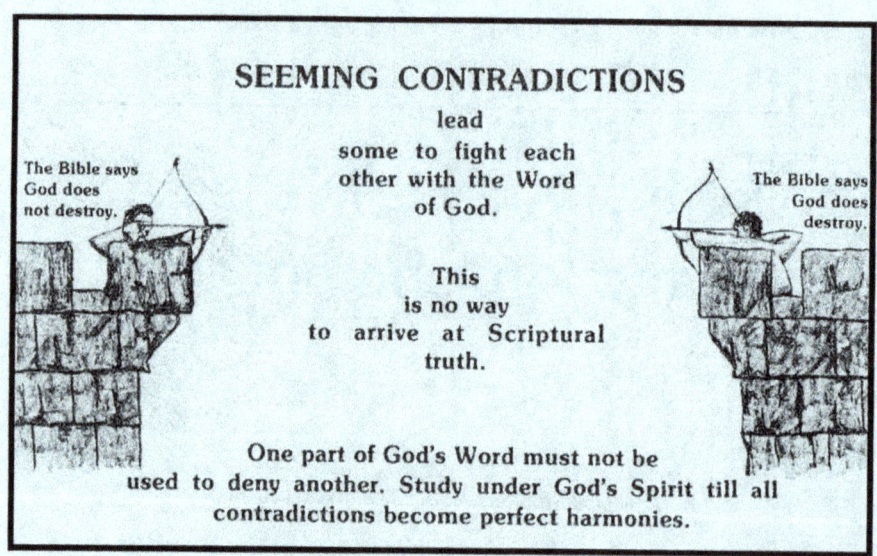

The writings of inspiration must harmonize. One text must not contradict another. Also, "One saying of the Saviour must not be made to destroy another" (White, *The Great Controversy*, p. 370). If we are finding an apparent contradiction, we must study further until the mystery is resolved. With this in mind, we proceed to look at some samples of *apparent* contradictions.

On the one side, we have the bedrock principle, well established by the Word of God through inspiration, that God does *not* destroy:

- "Satan is the destroyer; Christ is the restorer" (White, *Medical Ministry*, p. 240).
- "God does not stand toward the sinner as an executioner of the sentence against transgression" (White, *The Great Controversy*, p. 36).
- "Rebellion was not to be overcome by force. Compelling power is found only under Satan's government. The Lord's principles are not of this order" (White, *The Desire of Ages*, p. 759).
- The destruction of the wicked "is not an act of arbitrary power on the part of God" (White, *The Desire of Ages*, p. 764).

- "I was shown that the judgments of God would not come directly out from the Lord upon them, but in this way: They place themselves beyond His protection. He warns, corrects, reproves, and points out the only path of safety; then if those who have been the objects of His special care will follow their own course independent of the Spirit of God, after repeated warnings, if they choose their own way, then He does not commission His angels to prevent Satan's decided attacks upon them" (White, *Manuscript Releases*, Vol. 14, p. 3).
- "Earthly kingdoms rule by the ascendancy of physical power; but from Christ's kingdom every carnal weapon, every instrument of coercion, is banished" (White, *The Acts of the Apostles*, p. 12).

What about these kinds of statements?

> The angels revealed to Lot the object of their mission: "*We will destroy* this place, because the cry of them is waxen great before the face of the Lord; and *the Lord hath sent us to destroy it*." (White, *Patriarchs and Prophets*, p. 159, emphasis added)

> *The same angel* who had come from the royal courts to rescue Peter, had been the messenger of wrath and judgment to Herod. *The angel smote Peter to arouse him from slumber; it was with a different stroke that he smote the wicked king*, laying low his pride and bringing upon him the punishment of the Almighty. *Herod died in great agony* of mind and body, under the retributive judgment of God. (White, *The Acts of the Apostles*, p. 152, emphasis added)

> At length *the destroying angel was bidden to slay* the first-born of man and beast among the Egyptians. That the Israelites might be spared, they were directed to place upon their doorposts the blood of a slain lamb. Every house was to be marked, that when *the angel came on his mission of death*, he might pass over

> the homes of the Israelites. (White, *The Desire of Ages*, p. 51, emphasis added)
>
> The mark of deliverance has been set upon those "that sigh and that cry for all the abominations that be done." Now *the angel of death* goes forth, represented in Ezekiel's vision by the men with the slaughtering weapons, to whom the command is given: "Slay utterly old and young, both maids, and little children, and women; but come not near any man upon whom is the mark; and begin at my sanctuary." Says the prophet, "They began at the ancient men which were before the house." [Ezekiel 9:1-6.] The *work of destruction* begins among those who have professed to be the spiritual guardians of the people. The false watchmen are the first to fall. There are none to pity or to spare. Men, women, maidens, and little children perish together. (White, *The Great Controversy*, p. 656, emphasis added)

On one hand, we have many key statements regarding God not using His power to bring punishment and death by His hand, and this would also mean He would not use His servants, the angels, to do it by proxy. On the other hand, the language, on its face, says God kills, destroys, exacts vengeance, sends evil, etc. Now, with careful attention and study, we know how to interpret all of this, accessing the principle of divine recession or the hiding of His face (see Deut. 31:16–18).

Inspiration gives the keys to interpret divine wrath and destruction, as we have shown above. In like manner, we must consistently apply this rule to angels. The language, again, on its face, suggests God uses angels to destroy. However, the reality is that He never initiates or carries out the destruction itself; He only honors freedom of choice and removes protections and restraints. Likewise, by initiating instructions through the chain of command of the angel ranks to retreat and stand down, destruction generally ensues.

God works through the angels for the benefit of mankind and when He doesn't, it is wrath. It really is as simple as that. Thereby, it is written that the angels "destroy." The angels do not exercise destructive power in the sense we normally would understand. The power that is exerted is that of destroying forces outside themselves. The guardian angels remove their power to restrain forces of chaos and evil when righteousness is repelled by the free moral agent. They permit the evil or chaotic powers to destroy by "checking out," and thus it is said that they themselves exercise the destructive power. It is hard to get the mind around this because the language says the angels exercise destructive power, but they don't exercise destructive power *personally*; they create the condition whereby the destructive power is unleashed and is exercised by evil angels, evil humans, or nature.

It should be mentioned at the outset that Satan does not always respond the same way to the lifting of restraints. Devils will use power two ways. Satan is a deceiver and manipulator. He, with his angels, will sometimes hold back from destruction and bring apparent good; or they will harass and destroy. Holy angels can only exercise power beneficently or *not* exercise it by the righteous command of God. He will say, "Leave them alone, they are joined to their idols." What can the Almighty do? (see Hosea 4:17; Job 22:17). This is the range of their activity.

On one hand, we have many key statements regarding God not using His power to bring punishment and death by His hand, and this would also mean He would not use His servants, the angels, to do it by proxy. On the other hand, the language, on its face, says God kills, destroys, exacts vengeance, sends evil, etc.

These principles regarding the role and action of evil angels versus holy angels must apply consistently and should guide us in all our studies. "Satan has control of all whom God does not especially guard. He will favor and prosper some in order to further his own designs; and he will bring trouble upon others and lead men to believe that it is God who is afflicting them" (White, *The Great Controversy*, p. 589).

We read in 1 Chronicles 21:1 that "Satan stood up against Israel, and provoked David to number Israel." This was, on the part of David, an act of national pride and trust in human might. It was a rejection of God. "When David offended against God by numbering the people, one angel *caused* that terrible destruction by which his sin was punished" (White 1911, p. 614, emphasis added).

God commanded a holy angel to release the destruction, and the word "caused" is used. How did this angel "cause" the destruction? When God hides His face, the angels retreat. As we call this "divine recession," so we might extend it to the angels, calling it "angelic recession." In the volume *Patriarchs and Prophets*, with regard to the punishment for David's sin, we read, "The "land was smitten with pestilence, which destroyed seventy thousand in Israel" (p. 748). Note the angel did not employ his own power to destroy, but it was the power of the pestilence that destroyed. However, in the inspired language, it is spoken of as the action of "the angel of the Lord destroying" (*Ibid.*), or in another place, "the destroying angel" (*Ibid.*).

Therefore, when holy angels abandon their posts, whatever forces are in that vicinity comprise the arsenal poised for destruction. Allowed to run their course, whether they be the forces of nature gone to chaos, demons left to do their mischief, or human passion under the control of evil angels and carnal impulses, they will naturally bring evil. In the case of this pestilence, it was the forces of nature left to run amok, without the protection of God to keep disease in check. How devils might be involved in this, we are not given to know, except that Satan is "the author of disease" (White, *Spiritual Gifts*, Vol. 4a, p. 15).

Note also, in another place in this story, it says, "the anger of the LORD was kindled against Israel, and *he* moved David against them to say, Go, number Israel and Judah" (2 Sam. 24:1, emphasis added). How easily the

Scriptures move back and forth between the literal language—"Satan ... provoked David to number Israel"—and the idiomatic language—"the LORD ... moved David" to take the census of the fighting men. These are both the same event.

It is all about freedom of choice. David was tempted by Satan and drawn away of his own desire, and God is depicted as doing it because He allowed David to follow his own heart in the matter (see James 1:13, 14, Isa. 57:17). Seeing how this works, it is not difficult to understand that God and angels are said to destroy, when the fact is they allow destruction to take place due to the exercise of freedom to move out of God's protective sphere.

Let us look at the discussion of the coming destructions of the last plagues and how it is that holy angels are involved:

> I saw *an angel with a commission from Jesus*, swiftly flying to *the four angels who had a work to do on the earth*, and waving something up and down in his hand, and crying with a loud voice— **"Hold! Hold! Hold! Hold!** until the servants of God are sealed in their foreheads." I asked my accompanying angel the meaning of what I heard, and what the four angels were about to do. He shewed me that *it was God that restrained the powers, and that he gave his angels charge over things on the earth*, and that *the four angels had power from God to hold the four winds, and that they were about to let the four winds go*, and while they had started on *their mission to let them go*, the merciful eye of Jesus gazed on the remnant that were not all sealed, then he raised his hands to the Father and plead with him that he had spilled his blood for them.—*Then another angel was commissioned to fly swiftly to the four angels, and bid them hold* until the servants of God were sealed with the seal of the living God in their foreheads. (White, "Dear Brethren and Sisters," *The Review and Herald*, August 1, 1849, emphasis added)

This "angel with the commission from Jesus" is the destroying angel. When he should issue the instruction, the four sentinel angels of the earth will leave their posts, with the gates unlatched, and destruction will come. Yet, the actual work of destruction is attributable to Satan, the destroyer:

> *Unsheltered by divine grace, they have no protection from the wicked one. Satan will then plunge the inhabitants of the earth into one great, final trouble. As the angels of God cease to hold in check the fierce winds of human passion, all the elements of strife will be let loose.* The whole world will be involved in ruin more terrible than that which came upon Jerusalem of old. (White, *The Great Controversy*, p. 614, emphasis added)

Let us now examine some inspired text, which reveals the very principle under discussion regarding the role and function of holy angels in relation to the language of inspiration, i.e., the language of wrath. To set the table, we review the physical work that took place in the destruction of the temple at Jerusalem, noting especially who did that work. We know from history how the city was razed. Josephus is very clear. However, we need not rely solely on the historians because inspiration also recounts the story of Titus' soldiers going so out of control that they would not follow orders to save the temple:

> The blind obstinacy of the Jewish leaders, and the detestable crimes perpetrated within the besieged city, excited the horror and indignation of the Romans, and Titus at last decided to take the temple by storm. He determined, however, that if possible it should be saved from destruction. But *his commands were disregarded*. After he had retired to his tent at night, the Jews, sallying from the temple, attacked the soldiers without. In the struggle, *a firebrand was flung by a soldier through an opening in the porch*, and immediately the cedar-lined chambers about the holy house were in a blaze. Titus rushed to the place, followed

by his generals and legionaries, and *commanded the soldiers to quench the flames. His words were unheeded. In their fury the soldiers hurled blazing brands into the chambers adjoining the temple*, and then with their swords they slaughtered in great numbers those who had found shelter there. Blood flowed down the temple steps like water. Thousands upon thousands of Jews perished. Above the sound of battle, voices were heard shouting, "Ichabod!"—the glory is departed.

"*Titus found it impossible to check the rage of the soldiery*; he entered with his officers, and surveyed the interior of the sacred edifice. The splendor filled them with wonder; and as the flames had not yet penetrated to the holy place, *he made a last effort to save it*, and springing forth, *again exhorted the soldiers to stay the progress of the conflagration*. The centurion Liberalis endeavored to force obedience with his staff of office; but *even respect for the emperor gave way to the furious animosity against the Jews, to the fierce excitement of battle, and to the insatiable hope of plunder*." (White, *The Great Controversy*, pp. 33, 34, emphasis added)

Understanding the causation of the destruction of the temple, we now read words that, if not applied according the key principle of divine/angelic recession, would appear to blatantly contradict the historical story:

Men will continue to erect expensive buildings, costing millions of money; special attention will be called to their architectural beauty, and the firmness and solidity with which they are constructed; but the Lord has instructed me that despite the unusual firmness and expensive display, these buildings will share the fate of the temple in Jerusalem. That magnificent structure fell. *Angels of God were sent to do the work of destruction, so that one stone was not left one upon another that was not thrown down.* (White, *The SDA Bible Commentary*, Vol. 5, p. 1098, emphasis added)

Therefore, here is a clear example of how it works. It says, "Angels were sent to do the work of destruction." To any modern reader, the words mean just what they say: the angels exerted their powers to directly apply physical force to the stones so that they toppled. However, that is *not* what it means in the context of inspiration, which is in the Hebrew manner of thought and speech in both the Bible and the Spirit of Prophecy. The etiology of this—what actually happened—was that the enraged and out-of-control Roman soldiery did the work of destruction when the angels of God ceased "to hold in check the fierce winds of human passion," just as they will do when the wrath of nations will be let loose at the close of probation.

We could apply the very same language to all instances of modern destruction. The buildings in New York city fell because of human political violence, yet we can readily say, "Angels of God were sent to do the work of destruction, so that" not one floor was left upon another. In another place in her writings, Ellen White had a vision while in New York City and saw these great buildings going up, as monuments to the pride of the men who built them and who boasted of their indestructibility. They were built upon wealth accumulated through taking advantage of the poor.

> The scene that next passed before me was an alarm of fire. Men looked at the lofty and supposedly fire-proof buildings and said: "They are perfectly safe." But these buildings were consumed as if made of pitch. The fire engines could do nothing to stay the destruction. The firemen were unable to operate the engines.
>
> I am instructed that when the Lord's time comes, should no change have taken place in the hearts of proud, ambitious human beings, men will find that *the hand that had been strong to save will be strong to destroy*. No earthly power can stay *the hand of God*. No material can be used in the erection of buildings that will preserve them from *destruction when God's appointed time comes to send retribution* on men for their disregard of His law and for their selfish ambition. (White, *Testimonies for the Church*, Vol. 9, p. 13, emphasis added)

See how the buildings came down, and it is "the hand of God" that is involved in it. But how? Did God apply force? did He *apply* His hand of power? or did God *remove* His hand of protecting and sustaining power? These are opposite actions. We must get it right if we are to understand correctly the character of God and the nature of His government.

Many would probably like to take up for discussion some of the destroying-angel texts like the ones cited at the beginning of this study. It is interesting and enriching to take up these cases once we are familiar with the mechanism of action. We could go on and examine case after case of the angels' *apparent* use of violence as they go about their normal functions in their dual role of protecting God's people and bringing souls to Christ (but "not to destroy," see White, "The New Life in Christ," cited above).

Many of these cases are discussed in other studies. However, there is a specific statement that we will take time to examine momentarily. This is an especially important passage to consider. In it, we have a representation of both the holy angels and the evil angels regarding the mechanism of destruction. Many have unwittingly played into the hands of the enemy of all that is good by employing this passage, believing that in it they have a "silver bullet" proof text showing holy angels as the executioners of sinners at God's command. Let's look at that single paragraph before we go to the context:

> A single angel destroyed all the first-born of the Egyptians and filled the land with mourning. When David offended against God by numbering the people, one angel caused that terrible destruction by which his sin was punished. The *same destructive power* exercised by *holy angels* when God *commands*, will be exercised by *evil angels* when He *permits*. There are forces now ready, and only waiting the divine permission, to spread desolation everywhere. (*The Great Controversy*, p. 614, emphasis added)

Always remember the saying that "a *proof text* without a *context* is a *pretext*." That is certainly the case with how this passage is used by those who are apologists for the standard view. Look at the last sentence. What forces are "only waiting … to spread desolation"? These are the forces who act *by permission*. They are the evil angels. The permission for them to act comes from holy angels, *per God's command*.

Take special note that inspiration declares of the plagues of Egypt, "Ruin and desolation marked the path of the destroying angel" (White, *Patriarchs and Prophets*, p. 269). They are ever at the ready to cause mayhem, as Peter informs us that they are in service of one who "as a roaring lion, walketh about, seeking whom he may devour" (1 Peter 5:8). However, evil angels cannot always act as they would like because they are restrained. They need a permit. Holy angels are waiting for no such permission. They are "all ministering spirits, sent forth to minister for them who shall be heirs of salvation" (Heb. 1:14).

> *Thus, it is that evil pushes hard, and good must push back to keep protection in place. If good should no longer resist, devils rush into the vacuum.*

There are no angels of God in this passage that are engaged in the physical work of destruction. The four angels and the solitary angel are the highest ranking (levels one and two) angelic entities in charge of *restraining the destruction* (see White, "Dear Brethren and Sister" above). The solitary angel is undoubtedly the one called "the destroying angel," likely named Gabriel. It was Gabriel who, joined by Christ, withstood Satan working through the king of Persia to keep in check his malicious intent against God's people. Thus, it is that evil pushes hard, and good must push back to keep protection in place. If good should no longer resist, devils rush into the vacuum.

> The king of Persia was controlled by the highest of all evil angels. He refused, as did Pharaoh, to obey the word of the Lord. Gabriel declared, He withstood me twenty-one days by his representations against the Jews. But Michael came to his

help, and then he remained with the kings of Persia, holding the powers in check, giving right counsel against evil counsel.

Good and evil angels are taking a part in the planning of God in His earthly kingdom. It is God's purpose to carry forward His work in correct lines, in ways that will advance His glory. But Satan is ever trying to counterwork God's purpose. (White, *Manuscript Releases*, Vol. 11, p. 99)

Our *Great Controversy* passage under study is difficult because it seems to make a holy angel into the destroyer. The holy angel "causes" the destruction because he releases the destroyer. In this way, the destroyer gains permission to destroy. Yet, the commanding angel, as a holy angel, can be represented as a "destroying angel." However, the holy angel is not "the destroyer" in name. Who, then, is "the destroyer"?

> All who failed to heed the Lord's directions would lose their first-born *by the hand of the destroyer*. (White, *Patriarchs and Prophets*, p. 278, emphasis added)

We know the Bible identifies the destroyer as Satan in both the Greek and Hebrew:

> And they had a king over them, *which is* the angel of the bottomless pit, whose name in the Hebrew tongue *is* Abaddon, but in the Greek tongue hath *his* name Apollyon. (Revelation 9:11)

Paul uses the term "destroyer" to refer to Satan:

> Neither murmur ye, as some of them also murmured, and were destroyed of the **destroyer**. (1 Corinthians 10:10, bold emphasis added)

Looking at this word in the Greek, we find an interesting connection to the snake:

ὀλοθρευτής
olothreutēs
ol-oth-ryoo-tace'
From G3645; a ruiner, that is, (specifically) a venomous serpent: —destroyer.

Joining the above statement in *Patriarchs and Prophets* with the one below:

> If man refuses to yoke up with Christ, if he refuses to learn of the great Teacher, he cannot receive God's protection.
>
> If he feels and acts independently of God, walking in the path of disobedience, *Satan will exercise his power, after deceiving, to destroy*. (White, *Letter 22*, Feb. 13, 1900, emphasis added)

In another place:

> Sometimes men do pass the boundary line beyond God's protecting care, and *then Satan exercises his power upon them, and God does not interpose*. (White, *The SDA Bible Commentary*, Vol. 3, p. 1140, emphasis added)

If we conduct a search for the phrase "exercise his power" in the Spirit of Prophecy database, we will find it is always Satan who uses it to deceive, vex, ruin, and destroy; God always uses it to tell the truth, create, heal, protect, and save.

The key to understanding our *Great Controversy* passage is that it is "the same destructive power," which is not God's power but Satan's power. (Yes, all power is *from* God—He is the "Father of lights" [James 1:17]— yet *how* it is exercised is not all *of* God. Power used with true beneficence is of God; destructive power is not of God.) God *commands* His angels to step aside, and by doing so, *permits* evil angels to do Satan's work. These are one and the same in their effect.

POINT OF NOTE: The power, therefore, that is exercised when holy angels step aside by God's command is the power that is exercised by the evil angels by His permission. They are one and the same issue from the throne.

In other words, holy angels do not physically exercise destructive power, but they *allow* evil angels to execute the destructive power. This is consistent with the "hiding of face" principle by which divine wrath functions (see Deut. 31:16–18).

God does not use His holy angels to kill by proxy. Neither does He kill personally. In another place, we read about the destruction of Satan and the wicked, with attending explanation:

> "Because thou hast set thine heart as the heart of God; ... I will destroy thee, O covering cherub, from the midst of the stones of fire.... Thou shalt be a terror, and never shalt thou be any more." Then "the wicked shall not be: yea, thou shalt diligently consider his place, and it shall not be;" "they shall be as though they had not been." Ezekiel 28:6–19; Psalm 37:10; Obadiah 16.
>
> *This is not an act of arbitrary power on the part of God.* The rejecters of His mercy reap that which they have sown. God is the fountain of life; and when one chooses the service of sin, he separates from God, and thus cuts himself off from life.... By a life of rebellion, Satan and all who unite with him place themselves so out of harmony with God that His very presence is to them a consuming fire. The glory of Him who is love will destroy them. (White, *The Desire of Ages*, pp. 763, 764, emphasis added)

Coming back to our "same destructive power" quote, it is now time to have a brief look at the context. First, in the *preceding* paragraph, we note that Ellen White is setting up for our highlight paragraph by discussing what happens at the close of probation, when the world will be subjected to the seven last plagues:

> When He leaves the sanctuary, darkness covers the inhabitants of the earth. In that fearful time the righteous must live in the sight of a holy God without an intercessor. *The restraint which has been upon the wicked is removed, and Satan has entire control* of the finally impenitent.... The wicked have passed the boundary of their probation; the Spirit of God, persistently resisted, has been at last withdrawn. *Unsheltered by divine grace, they have no protection from the wicked one. Satan will then plunge the inhabitants of the earth into one great, final trouble. As the angels of God cease to hold in check the fierce winds of human passion, all the elements of strife will be let loose.* The whole world will be involved in ruin more terrible than that which came upon Jerusalem of old. (White, *The Great Controversy*, p. 614, emphasis added)

It is clearer than noontide light that she is carefully applying the principle we have been discussing: that of destruction as the result when God removes His protection. The final plagues on earth are the results of Satan's activity, which God allows to proceed unchecked.

The paragraph following our "same destructive power" quote continues to develop the theme of the "judgments" that are brought upon the world in the last plagues:

> Those who honor the law of God have been accused of bringing judgments upon the world, and they will be regarded as the cause of the fearful convulsions of nature and the strife and bloodshed among men that are filling the earth with woe. The power attending the last warning has enraged the wicked; their anger is kindled against all who have received the message, and Satan will excite to still greater intensity the spirit of hatred and persecution. (White, *The Great Controversy*, pp. 614, 615)

In the following statement, we find that these judgments are said by the wicked world to be punishments of God upon them because He is angry for the desecration of the "Christian Sabbath"—their Sunday. Satan plays up this idea that God brings angry, direct destructions when He is not obeyed, and this is how he gets the world to come against God's people with murderous intent—with genocide on their mind. The reality of the mechanism of the judgments that come, as already proven, is the withdrawal of divine power, which restrains Satan:

> This time is right upon us. *The Spirit of God is being withdrawn from the earth. When the angel of mercy folds her wings and departs, Satan will do the evil deeds he has long wished to do.* Storm and tempest, war and bloodshed,—in these things he delights, and thus he gathers in his harvest. And so completely will men be deceived by him that *they will declare that these calamities are the result of the desecration of the first day of the week. From the pulpits of the popular churches will be heard the statement that the world is being punished because Sunday is not honored as it should be. And it will require no great stretch of imagination for men to believe this. They are guided by the enemy, and therefore they reach conclusions which are entirely false.* (White, "A Time of Trouble," *The Review and Herald,* September 17, 1901, emphasis added)

Believe what? What false conclusions? THIS: That God's wrath is punitive in the same way as is humanity's wrath and punishment; that He will directly destroy His children if they go against His authority and government.

> As the Sabbath has become the special point of controversy throughout Christendom, and religious and secular authorities have combined to enforce the observance of the Sunday, *the persistent refusal of a small minority to yield to the popular demand will make them objects of universal execration.* It will be

urged that the few who stand in opposition to an institution of the church and a law of the state ought not to be tolerated; that *it is better for them to suffer than for whole nations to be thrown into confusion and lawlessness.* The same argument many centuries ago was brought against Christ by the "rulers of the people." "It is expedient for us," said the wily Caiaphas, "that one man should die for the people, and that the whole nation perish not." John 11:50. This argument will appear conclusive; and a decree will finally be issued against those who hallow the Sabbath of the fourth commandment, *denouncing them as deserving of the severest punishment and giving the people liberty, after a certain time, to put them to death.* Romanism in the Old World and apostate Protestantism in the New will pursue a similar course toward those who honor all the divine precepts. (White, *The Great Controversy,* pp. 615, 616, emphasis added)

In conclusion, when we examine *The Great Controversy,* page 614, paragraph 2 in the revealing light of its context, the whole point Mrs. White is making is that in the last great conflict of earth before the second coming, God stands aside and lets Satan and his angels do the destroying work. In drawing a parallel to that, she cites both the punishment on David for numbering Israel and the slaying of the firstborn in Egypt. The angel that destroys "by permission" in these cases was not a holy angel. It was a "pestilence" administered by an evil angel in both cases, as is clearly spelled out below:

> He cast upon them the fierceness of his anger, wrath, and indignation, and trouble, **by sending evil angels among them.** He made a way to his anger; he spared not their soul from death, but **gave their life over to the pestilence; and smote all the firstborn in Egypt.** (Psalm 78:49–51, emphasis added)

> So Gad came to David, and said unto him, Thus saith the LORD, Choose thee either three years' famine; or three months to be destroyed before thy foes, while that the sword of thine enemies

overtaketh *thee*; or else three days **the sword of the LORD, even the pestilence, in the land, and the angel of the LORD destroying** throughout all the coasts of Israel. Now therefore advise thyself what word I shall bring again to him that sent me. And David said unto Gad, I am in a great strait: let me fall now into the hand of the LORD; for very great *are* his mercies: but let me not fall into the hand of man. **So the LORD sent pestilence upon Israel**: and there fell of Israel seventy thousand men. (1 Chronicles 21:11–14, bold emphasis added)

In summary, it is just as one writer commented to me: "While our Creator issues a command for holy angels to withdraw, the same command permits evil angels to destroy. As one set leaves the other takes its place" (Lorraine L. Henry, social media communication). This is precisely what we are saying. This is a consistent principle. "The same destructive power" is *satanic power* wherein holy angels loosen their restraints on demons. It is a manifestation of the "divine recession" mechanism of punishment/judgment/destruction in the execution of divine wrath, biblically termed the "hiding of God's face."

Notice Jesus said not to despise the little ones. Why? Because "in heaven their angels do always behold the face of my Father" (Matt. 18:10). Do you see something amazing here? I do. The face of God turned toward us is His favor, protection, and sustenance. This two-edged metaphor of face toward/face turned away is a basic, Hebrew, cultural norm, in both physical and verbal expression, denoting favor and "looking upon" or displeasure and looking away.

This is the key to God's wrath as depicted in Deuteronomy 31:16–18. His face is turned toward us through the ministration of angels. It is turned away from us when the angels are told to cease their ministry. Any time judgment comes, it must be through the withdrawal of the ministration of angels, to whatever degree God must withdraw them, according to the choices of the free moral agent. By corollary, to this same degree may evil angels exercise their malice.

May God add rich blessings to this reading of His Word.

CHAPTER 7

The Ending of the Great Controversy: The Fires

> *"I will ascend above the heights of the clouds;*
> *I will be like the Most High."*
> *"Ye shall be as gods."*
> *"Do as thou wilt; this is the whole of the law."*
> *(Lucifer, as cited in Isa.14:14; Gen. 3:5;*
> *and through Aleister Crowley, Satanist)*

The whole wicked world stand arraigned at the bar of God, on the charge of high treason against the government of heaven. They have none to plead their cause; they are without excuse; and the sentence of eternal death is pronounced against them. It is now evident to all that the wages of sin is not noble independence and eternal life, but slavery, ruin, and death.... Satan seems paralyzed as he beholds the glory and majesty of Christ. He who was once a covering cherub remembers whence he has fallen. A shining seraph, "son of the morning;" how changed, how degraded! (White, *The Faith I Live By*, p. 356)

That at the *name of Jesus every knee should bow, of *things* in heaven, and *things* in earth, and *things* under the earth; And *that* every tongue should confess that Jesus Christ *is* Lord, to the glory of God the Father. (Philippians 2:10, 11)

*G3686 ὄνομα

Onoma on'-om-ah

From a presumed derivative of the base of G1097 [*ginosko*] (compare G3685 [*oninemi*]); a "name" (literally or figuratively), (*authority, character*): - called, (+ sur-) name (-d).

> When thus it shall be in the midst of the land among the people,
> *there shall be* as the shaking of an olive tree,
> *and* as the gleaning grapes when the vintage is done.
> They shall lift up their voice, they shall sing for the majesty of the LORD,

they shall cry aloud from the sea.
Wherefore glorify ye the LORD in the fires,
even the name of the LORD God of Israel in the isles of the sea (Isa. 24:13–15).

Introduction

These *things* hast thou done, and I kept silence; thou thoughtest that I was altogether *such an one* as thyself: *but* I will reprove thee, and set *them* in order before thine eyes (Ps. 50:21).

Do Not Be Surface Readers

To know God is to love Him. The only way we can know Him is if we have the right concept of who He is. We must know His character. The only way to know Him is to seek Him with your whole heart and soul. A mere surface reading and understanding of the Scriptures will not reveal to us the deep things of God.

> Seek ye the LORD while he may be found, call ye upon him while he is near: Let the wicked forsake his way, and the unrighteous man his thoughts: and let him return unto the LORD, and he will have mercy upon him; and to our God, for he will abundantly pardon. For my thoughts *are* not your thoughts, neither *are* your ways my ways, saith the LORD. For *as* the heavens are higher than the earth, so are my ways higher than your ways, and my thoughts than your thoughts. (Isaiah 55:6–9)

We should study the Scriptures more earnestly; for their treasures of wisdom and knowledge do not lie upon the surface for the superficial reader. ("The Relation of Christ to the Law Is Not Understood," The Review and Herald, February 4)

The Ending of the Great Controversy

In fact, surface reading will get us in trouble, for oftentimes, what is right on the surface, or the "obvious" reading, is not what is being said at all. Here is an example of this:

> And there came a voice to him, Rise, Peter; kill, and eat. But Peter said, Not so, Lord; for **I have never eaten any thing that is common or unclean.** And the voice *spake* unto him again the second time, **What God hath cleansed,** *that* **call not thou common.** (Acts 10:13–15, bold emphasis added)

The context of this passage makes it clear that food is not the point, yet many have seized upon these and similar passages to claim Jesus declared all that is used by humans for food as admissible and clean.

> Forbidding to marry, *and commanding* to abstain from **meats, which God hath created to be received with thanksgiving** of them which believe and know the truth. For **every creature of God** *is* **good, and nothing to be refused**, if it be received with thanksgiving: For **it is sanctified by the word of God and prayer**. (1 Timothy 4:3–5, bold emphasis added)

The surface meaning would encourage the surface reader to serve up a roast pig for Thanksgiving dinner, so long as the patrons pray over it. As another example, there are texts that would, on the surface, seem to indicate that upon death, we go immediately to glory:

> And I knew such a man, (whether in the body, or out of the body, I cannot tell: God knoweth;) How that **he was caught up into paradise**, and heard unspeakable words. (2 Corinthians 12:3, 4, bold emphasis added)

> But if I live in the flesh, this *is* the fruit of my labour: yet what I shall choose I wot not. For I am in a strait betwixt two, having a desire **to depart, and to be with Christ**; which is far better: Nevertheless to abide in the flesh *is* more needful for you. (Philippians 1:22–24, bold emphasis added)

To know God is to love Him. The only way we can know Him is if we have the right concept of who He is. We must know His character. The only way to know Him is to seek Him with your whole heart and soul.

A mere surface reading and understanding of the Scriptures will not reveal to us the deep things of God.

Surface reading is the reason so many unthinkingly accept the highly unsatisfying standard fare from institutionalized religion on the subject of God's wrath. Human governance is predicated on force. It gets compliance by threat of coercion or punishment. Order is enforced strictly, and weapons of physical force will be employed if need be. This is not a discussion of whether they should function this way. Our discussion throughout this volume is how God functions. They are not the same; there is no comparison (see Mark 4:30). Note how the human paradigm of justice in a carnal world is drawn upon as an exegetical tool, that we might overlay the function of human governmental concepts onto that of divine punishment and wrath. Here is a little reading of an example of church teaching materials:

> Read *2 Thessalonians* 1:7–9. **What is the primary reason for the destruction of the wicked at the time of Jesus' second coming? How are we to understand these verses with the idea of God as being full of love, grace, and forgiveness?**

Many people are uncomfortable with the language of these verses. They feel that "pay back" *(NIV)*, vengeance, punishment, and the infliction of suffering are unworthy of a God of love, grace, and mercy. But just punishment and retribution is a frequent theme of Paul's *(Rom. 2:5, 12:19)*. Paul is unequivocal: God's justice will one day be powerfully made manifest. *And why not? Any good government in today's world must at some point exercise force in order to restrain evil.* Though force is not always violent (as when you are stopped for a traffic violation or audited for your taxes), *in some cases, especially when the criminals are using violence themselves, they must be answered with violence.* Good governments provide a necessary restraint so that we can all live together in peace. Many times outright evil will not give way voluntarily. And *the greater the power and brutality of evil, the greater the force often needed to undo that evil.*

The images in this passage are not pretty, but they assure us that *God will do whatever it takes to end violence and oppression....*

Through His own experience, Jesus understands the cost of suffering. *He can be trusted to exercise divine justice but without overkill. Divine justice will result in suffering, but not one iota more than necessary.* If we can trust God in anything, we can trust that His justice will reveal a wisdom and fairness that we cannot currently comprehend.

The goal of this passage is not to rejoice in vengeance but to encourage the abused and oppressed. The day of justice is coming. We don't need to take justice into our own hands. (*Seventh-day Adventist Quarterly*, Teachers' ed., 3rd quarter, 2012, p. 129, italic emphases added)

This model of divine justice instructs us plainly that it is God who exercises power to inflict suffering. There is no discussion in these types of teachings that would give us any reason why somebody going to eternal death would need to be tortured first. I have never received a straight answer to that question.

We must do better; dig deeper. Many complain of intensive studies that seek to extract more in-depth understandings, saying, "We must take the plain and simple reading of the Bible that even a child can understand, etc." However, spiritual riches are concealed beneath the surface, and we must become miners of truth.

> Let all seek to comprehend, to the full extent of their powers, the meaning of the word of God. A *mere superficial reading of the inspired word will be of little advantage*; for *every statement* made in the sacred pages requires *thoughtful contemplation*. It is true that some passages do not require as earnest concentration as do others; for their meaning is more evident. But the student of the word of God should *seek to understand the bearing of one passage upon another until the chain of truth is revealed* to his vision. As veins of precious ore are hidden beneath the surface of the earth, so *spiritual riches are concealed in the passages* of Holy Writ, and it *requires mental effort and prayerful attention* to discover the *hidden meaning* of the word of God. Let every student who values the heavenly treasure put to the *stretch his mental and spiritual powers*, and sink the shaft deep into the mine of truth, that he may obtain the celestial gold,—that wisdom which will make him wise unto salvation. (White, *Christian Education*, p. 101, emphasis added)

Truth Advances

We may at times be required to lay aside that which we have held.

> There is no excuse for any one in taking the position that there is no more truth to be revealed, and that all our expositions of Scripture are without an error. The fact that certain doctrines have been held as truth for many years by our people, is not a proof that our ideas

are infallible. Age will not make error into truth, and truth can afford to be fair. No true doctrine will lose anything by close investigation. We are living in perilous times, and *it does not become us to accept everything claimed to be truth without examining it thoroughly; neither can we afford to reject anything that bears the fruits of the Spirit of God*; but we should be teachable, meek and lowly of heart. *There are those who oppose everything that is not in accordance with their own ideas, and by so doing they endanger their eternal interest* as verily as did the Jewish nation in their rejection of Christ. *The Lord designs that our opinions shall be put to the test*, that we may see the necessity of closely examining the living oracles to see whether or not we are in the faith. ("Christ Our Hope," *The Review and Herald*, December 20, 1892, emphasis added)

All the peculiarities given us as an inheritance or acquired by indulgence or *through erroneous education* must be thoroughly overcome, decidedly resisted. Love of esteem and *pride of opinion*, all must be brought to the sacrifice. They must be overcome. There is no compromise to be made with the enemy of righteousness. (White, *Daughters of God*, p. 169, emphasis added)

The *sin that is most nearly hopeless and incurable is pride of opinion*, self-conceit. This *stands in the way of all growth.... How can one improve when he thinks his ways* [or beliefs] *perfect*? (White, *Counsels for the Church*, p. 46, emphasis added)

And so, as we present to you that which claims to be an advance in the light of truth in this time of the fourth angel—which sheds abroad the glory of the Lord—we must ask the question:

How do you know but that the Lord is giving fresh evidences of his truth, placing it in a new setting, that the way of the Lord may be prepared? What plans have you been laying that new light may be infused through the ranks of God's people? What evidence have you that God has not sent light to His children? All self-sufficiency, egotism, and *pride of opinion must be put away*. We must *come to the feet of Jesus, and learn of Him* who is meek and lowly of heart. (White, *Selected Messages*, Book 1. p. 414, emphasis added)

The history of the Reformation teaches us that the *church of Christ is never to come to a standstill and cease reforming*. God stands at the head, saying to them as He did to Moses, "Go forward." "Speak unto the children of Israel, that they go forward." God's work is onward; step by step His people advance onward through conflict and trial to final victory. The history of the church teaches us that God's people are not to be stereotyped in their theories of faith, but to *be prepared for new light, for opening truth revealed in His Word*. (White, *Christ Triumphant*, p. 317, emphasis added)

The Character of God and the Nature of Sin

It is a fact that God's ways and thoughts are much higher than ours are. It is also true that God would have us forsake our own ways and thoughts, seeking rather to know His ways and thoughts because therein is life eternal (see Isa. 55:7–9; John 17:3). It is His desire that not one should perish but all would have everlasting life. Satan realizes the way of salvation depends on our understanding God and trust in Him, so his best efforts have been to cast *misunderstanding* and darkness upon God's character.

The earth was *dark through misapprehension of God*. That the gloomy shadows might be lightened, that the world might be brought back to God, Satan's deceptive power was to be broken. This could not be done by force. *The exercise of force is contrary to the principles of God's government*; He desires only the service of love; and love cannot be commanded; it cannot be won by force or authority. Only by love is love awakened. To know God is to love Him; *His character must be manifested in contrast to the character of Satan.* This work only one Being in all the universe could do. Only He who knew the height and depth of the love of God could make it known. Upon the world's dark night the Sun of Righteousness must rise, "with healing in His wings." (White, *The Desire of Ages*, p. 22, emphasis added)

Satan would also have us misunderstand the nature of sin and its results. As long as we are deceived about these two very important things—the character of God and the nature of sin—he remains alive.

> The people of God should awaken to a keen perception of the grievous character of transgression. Sin is disguised, and many are deceived in regard to its nature.... [which] is faithfully portrayed in the inspired pages,—its offensive character before God, its corruption, its shame, and its results. ("A Living Church," *The Review and Herald*, June 3, 1880, emphasis added)

As we delve into the nature of sin as the cause of all death, it becomes immediately imperative that we need to have a better understanding of divine wrath. When we come to a view of God's wrath from a biblical standpoint, we will come to understand just how poignant is the statement that God's ways are nothing like Satan's ways, which are also the ways of carnal humanity.

Satan was a liar and murderer from the beginning. The great controversy is between

Christ and antichrist, whose respective characters and methodologies are diametrically opposed. A study of the conflict reveals how God rules His universe: by selfless love, liberty, and truth; and how Satan rules: by self-exaltation, force, and deception. In order to win this controversy, God must prove that His ways are superior and the true principles of love and liberty, without any resort to the use of force, agreed to by all on a basis of informed loyalty, constitutes the only viable government that will produce eternal life for all living beings in a safe, secure, and joyful society.

> Satan's representations against the government of God, and his defense of those who sided with him, were a constant accusation against God. These murmurings and complaints were groundless. Yet God allowed Satan to work out his theories. He could have handled Satan and all his sympathizers as easily as one can pick up a pebble and cast it to the earth. But by this He would have given a *precedent for the violence* of man which is so abundantly shown in our world in the compelling principles. The Lord's principles are not of this order. All the compelling power is to be found under Satan's government. God would not work in this line. He would not give the slightest encouragement for any human being to set himself up as God over another human being, and *cause him mental or physical suffering. This principle is wholly of Satan's creation.*
>
> In the councils of heaven it was decided that principles must be acted upon which would not at once destroy Satan's power, for it was [God's] purpose to place things upon an eternal basis of security.... God's order must be contrasted with the new order after Satan's devising. The corrupting principles of Satan's rule must be revealed. The principles of righteousness expressed in God's law must be demonstrated as unchangeable, eternal, perfect. (White, *Manuscript Releases*, Vol. 18, p. 361, emphasis added)

We are told that in the time of the end, even the final-generation formation of the 144,000 loud-cry messengers, we shall understand the "wrath" of God perfectly:

> Behold, a **whirlwind of the LORD** is gone forth in *fury*, even a grievous whirlwind: it **shall fall grievously upon the head of the wicked**. The **anger of the LORD** shall not return, until he have executed, and till he have performed **the thoughts of his heart: in the latter days ye shall consider it perfectly**. (Jeremiah 23:19, 20, bold emphasis added)

> Then they that feared the LORD spake often one to another: and the LORD hearkened, and heard *it*, and a **book of remembrance was written** before him **for them** that feared the LORD, and **that thought upon his name** [character]. And they shall be mine, saith the LORD of hosts, **in that day when I make up my jewels**; and I will spare them, as a man spareth his own son that serveth him. Then shall ye return, and **discern between the righteous and the wicked, between him that serveth God and him that serveth him not**. (Malachi 3:16–18, bold emphasis added)

> And after these things I saw another angel come down from heaven, having great power; and the **earth was lightened with his glory**. (Revelation 18:1, bold emphasis added)

> *The glory of God is His character*…. This character was revealed in the life of Christ. That He might by His own example condemn sin in the flesh, He took upon Himself the likeness of sinful flesh. *Constantly He beheld the character of God; constantly He revealed this character to the world. Christ desires His followers to reveal in their lives this same character.* (White, *That I May Know Him*, p. 131, emphasis added)

The glory of God is His character. While Moses was in the mount, earnestly interceding with God, he prayed, "I beseech thee, show me thy glory." In answer God declared, "I will make all my goodness pass before thee, and I will proclaim the name of the Lord before thee; and will be gracious to whom I will be gracious, and will show mercy on whom I will show mercy." *The glory of God— His character—was then revealed*: "The Lord passed by before him, and proclaimed, The Lord, The Lord God, merciful and gracious, longsuffering, and abundant in goodness and truth, keeping mercy for thousands, forgiving iniquity and transgression and sin, and that will by no means clear the guilty." (White, *God's Amazing Grace*, p. 322, emphasis added)

Wrath and Punishment

God would not have us err in understanding from where temptation, sin, and death come or that mankind's wrath is not the same as is God's.

> Let no man say when he is tempted, I am tempted of God: for God cannot be tempted with evil, *neither tempteth he any man*: But every man is tempted, when he is drawn away of his own lust, and enticed. Then when *lust hath conceived, it bringeth forth sin: and sin, when it is finished, bringeth forth death. Do not err, my beloved brethren.* Every good gift and every perfect gift is from above, and cometh down from the Father of lights, with whom is no variableness, neither shadow of turning. Of His own will begat he us with the word of truth, that we should be a kind of firstfruits of His creatures. Wherefore, my beloved brethren, let every man be swift to hear, slow to speak, slow to wrath: *For the wrath of man worketh not the righteousness of God.* (James 1:13–20, emphasis added)

It was generally believed by the Jews that sin is punished in this life. Every affliction was regarded as the penalty of some wrongdoing, either of the sufferer himself or of his parents. It is true that all suffering results from the transgression of God's law, but this truth had become perverted. Satan, the author of sin and all its results, had led men to look upon disease and *death as proceeding from God,—as punishment arbitrarily inflicted* on account of sin. Hence one upon whom some great affliction or calamity had fallen had the additional burden of being regarded as a great sinner. (White, *The Desire of Ages*, 471.1, emphasis added)

Their sufferings are often represented as a punishment visited upon them by the direct decree of God. It is thus that the great deceiver seeks to conceal his own work. By stubborn rejection of divine love and mercy, the Jews had caused the protection of God to be withdrawn from them, and Satan was permitted to rule them according to his will. The horrible cruelties enacted in the destruction of Jerusalem are a demonstration of Satan's vindictive power over those who yield to his control. (White, *The Great Controversy*, pp. 35, 36, emphasis added)

The sinner who refuses salvation will experience the "wrath" of God—the very same wrath Christ suffered when He took our place.

Those who reject the mercy so freely proffered, will yet be made to know the worth of that which they have despised. *They will feel the agony which Christ endured upon the cross* to purchase redemption for all who would receive it. And they will then realize what they have lost,—eternal life and the immortal inheritance. ("Be Zealous and Repent," *The Review and Herald*, September 4, 1883, emphasis added)

We should not try to lessen our guilt by excusing sin. We must accept God's estimate of sin, and that is heavy indeed. Calvary alone can reveal the *terrible enormity of sin*. If we had to *bear our*

> *own guilt, it would crush us*. But the sinless One has taken our place; though undeserving, He has borne our iniquity. (White, *Thoughts from the Mount of Blessing*, p. 116, emphasis added)

> They will call on the rocks and mountains to fall on them and *hide them from the face of Him* that sitteth on the throne and from the wrath of the Lamb. "The wrath of the Lamb,"—One who ever showed himself full of tenderness, patience, and long-suffering, who, having given himself up as the sacrificial offering, was led as a lamb to the slaughter, to save sinners from *the doom now falling upon them because they would not allow Him to take away their guilt*. ("A Message for Today," *The Review and Herald*, June 18, 1901, emphasis added)

How are we to interpret the above "doom" that falls upon the guilty? Does Jesus say, "You did not accept My gift of redemption from sin and eternal life. Therefore, *I* condemn you and *I* must kill you"? or, "You did not accept Me. For this I will burn you alive"? It is not lost on this writer that it is ugly to state it like this, but it is not done for mere rhetoric or shock value. We must understand that truly, in effect, this is what we must say if we believe God takes sinners into His own hands and slays them by His own exercise of lethal power.

No, it is not *God* who kills; it is *sin*. We do not understand it fully, but there is enough light on the subject for us to have a fair concept of how sin destroys. We start to understand it correctly only when we know Him aright. We can start to work into this subject by establishing in our thinking, as a foundation upon which to build, that the *complete* revelation of God's goodness has everything to do with life and death, depending upon what choices we make in relation to that revelation.

> Jacob had been guilty of a great sin in his conduct toward Esau; but he had repented. His transgression had been forgiven, and his sin purged; therefore he could endure the revelation of God's presence. But wherever men came before God while willfully

cherishing evil, they were destroyed. At the second advent of Christ the wicked shall be consumed "with the Spirit of His mouth," and destroyed "with the brightness of His coming." 2 Thessalonians 2:8. *The light of the glory* [character] *of God, which imparts life to the righteous, will slay the wicked.* (White, *The Desire of Ages*, p 108, emphasis added)

To understand the Father, we look to Jesus, who came to glorify Him. To understand the "wrath" of God, we look to the cross, for Christ is the only one who has suffered that ultimate wrath, which is the second death. The cross reveals the truth about the character of God as well as the nature of sin and its consequences.

> The sacrifice of Christ as an atonement for sin is the great truth around which all other truths cluster. In order to be rightly understood and appreciated, *every truth* in the word of God, from Genesis to Revelation, *must be studied in the light that streams from the cross of Calvary.* (White, *Gospel Workers*, p. 315, emphasis added)

> The mystery of the cross explains all other mysteries. In the light that streams from Calvary, the attributes of God which had filled us with fear and awe appear beautiful and attractive. Mercy, tenderness, and parental love are seen to blend with holiness, justice, and power. (White, *The Spirit of Prophecy*, Vol. 4, p. 469, emphasis added)

> If sinners can be led to give one earnest *look at the cross*, if they can obtain a full view of the crucified Saviour, they will *realize the depth of God's compassion and the sinfulness of sin.* (White, *The Acts of the Apostles*, p. 209, emphasis added)

> The death of Christ was to be the convincing, everlasting argument that the law of God is as unchangeable as His throne.

> The agonies of the Garden of Gethsemane, the insult, the mockery, and abuse heaped upon God's dear Son, the horrors and ignominy of the crucifixion, furnish sufficient and thrilling demonstration that *God's justice, when it punishes, does the work thoroughly.* The fact that *His own Son*, the Surety for man, *was not spared*, is an argument that will stand to all eternity before saint and sinner, before the universe of God, to testify that He will not excuse the transgressor of His law. Every offense against God's law, however minute, is set down in the reckoning, and *when the sword of justice is taken in hand, it will do the work for impenitent transgressors that was done to the divine Sufferer. Justice will strike; for God's hatred of sin is intense and overwhelming.* (White, *The SDA Bible Commentary*. Vol. 3, p. 1166, emphasis added)

What was it that killed our Savior? What was the "wrath" that He suffered?

> Upon Christ as our substitute and surety was laid the iniquity of us all. He was counted a transgressor, that He might redeem us from the condemnation of the law. The guilt of every descendant of Adam was pressing upon His heart. The wrath of God against sin, the terrible manifestation of His displeasure because of iniquity, filled the soul of His Son with consternation. All His life Christ had been publishing to a fallen world the good news of the Father's mercy and pardoning love. Salvation for the chief of sinners was His theme. But now with the terrible weight of guilt He bears, He *cannot see the Father's reconciling face.* The *withdrawal of the divine countenance* from the Saviour in this hour of supreme anguish *pierced His heart* with a sorrow that can never be fully understood by man. *So great was this agony that His physical pain was hardly felt.* (White, *The Desire of Ages*, p. 753, emphasis added)

Therefore, physical fire is not what brings the second death. In fact, as we examine the suffering of Christ and His taste of the second death, we see that any kind of physical affliction, while coming into the picture, is not the thing that destroys. He did not die of the physical torture. The physical is incidental. When God gives up the sinner, physical suffering may be involved, but the real suffering is spiritual and mental. While physical suffering is not imposed by God, neither is the spiritual and mental suffering that destroys the sinner an imposed condition. It is a result of the sinner's cumulative choices to live without reference to the Creator and a final reckoning with the implications of those choices.

> Satan with his fierce temptations wrung the heart of Jesus. The Saviour could not see through the portals of the tomb. Hope did not present to Him His coming forth from the grave a conqueror, or tell Him of the Father's acceptance of the sacrifice. He feared that sin was so offensive to God that their separation was to be eternal. Christ felt the anguish which the sinner will feel when mercy shall no longer plead for the guilty race. It was the sense of sin, bringing the Father's wrath upon Him as man's substitute, that made the cup He drank so bitter, and broke the heart of the Son of God. (White, *The Desire of Ages*, p. 753)

Yet **we** did esteem Him stricken, smitten **of God**, and afflicted. (Isaiah 53:4, bold emphasis added)

The Fire Unquenchable

"Unquenchable Fire" Is a Parabolic Term

> And say to the forest of the south, Hear the word of the LORD; Thus saith the Lord GOD; Behold, I will kindle a fire in thee, and it shall devour every green tree in thee, and every dry tree: the

flaming **flame shall not be quenched**, and all faces from the south to the north shall be burned therein. And all flesh shall see that **I the LORD have kindled it: it shall not be quenched**. Then said I, Ah Lord GOD! they say of me, **Doth he not speak parables**? (Ezekiel 20:47–49, bold emphasis added)

I use this text realizing that those who exclaim, "Doth he not speak parables" are mockers. They are saying, "This 'prophet' is telling us fables." However, the truth of the matter is that the unquenchable fire *is* a parable—a metaphor. The wicked of today, especially, who do not understand the Bible language correctly are responding to the idea of God sending literal fire as a fairy tale. That part would be true. That God is a torturer and killer is a misrepresentation, and it actually fosters a rejection and hatred of God.

However, the wicked are ultimately denying God will at last give them up to destruction. They have found a convenient way of rejecting Him so that they need not make any further personal investigation into who He is. They are rejecting a false picture of God and using this as an excuse to embrace sin and godlessness. The fire unquenchable is a final reckoning of their willingness to so readily reject God, and with that comes the realization of the result of the transgressions they have loved. It is bound up with remorse, despair, bitterness, hatred, terror, shame, and burning guilt.

> In His great suffering, Christ felt no pang of bitterness against His Father. He felt no remorse for His own sins, but for the sins of the fallen race. But *those who refuse the gift of Christ will one day feel the sting of remorse.* Entire obedience to the law of God is the condition of salvation. Those who refuse this, *who refuse to accept Christ, will become embittered against God. When punished for transgression, they will feel despair and hatred.* This will be *the experience of all who do not enter into Christ's suffering*; for it is *the sure consequence of sin.*
>
> We read of chains of darkness for the transgressor of God's law. We read of the worm that dieth not, and of *the fire that*

is not quenched. Thus is represented the experience of every one who has permitted himself to be grafted into the stock of Satan, who has cherished sinful attributes. When it is too late, *he will see* that *sin is the transgression of God's law. He will realize* that because of transgression, *his soul is cut off from God*, and that *God's wrath abides on him. This is a fire unquenchable, and by it every unrepentant sinner will be destroyed.* Satan strives constantly to lead men into sin, and he who is willing to be led, who refuses to forsake his sins, and despises forgiveness and grace, *will suffer the result* of his course. ("Christ and the Law," *The Signs of the Times*, April 14, 1898, emphasis added)

Every word they have spoken against the world's Redeemer will be reflected back upon them, and will one day *burn into their guilty souls like molten lead*. They will be overwhelmed with terror and shame as they behold the exalted one coming in the clouds of heaven with power and great glory. Then shall the bold defier, who lifted himself up against the Son of God, see himself in the true blackness of his character. The sight of the inexpressible glory of the Son of God will be intensely painful to those whose characters are stained with sin. *The pure light and glory emanating from Christ will awaken remorse, shame, and terror*. They will send forth wails of anguish to the rocks and mountains, "Fall on us, and hide us from the face of Him that sitteth on the throne, and from the wrath of the Lamb: for the great day of his wrath is come; and who shall be able to stand?" ("The Temptation of Christ," The Review and Herald, April 1, 1875, emphasis added)

The unquenchable fire is the broken law coming back to do what God's law does:

> Against every evildoer God's law utters condemnation. He may disregard that voice, he may seek to drown its warning, but in vain. It follows him. It makes itself heard. It destroys

his peace. If unheeded, it pursues him to the grave. It bears witness against him at the judgment. *A quenchless fire, it consumes at last soul and body.* (White, *Education*, pp. 144, 145, emphasis added)

The destruction of the wicked is not due to blasts of destructive energy or lava from the sky breathed from God's creative power. We must fix in our understanding that the wage of sin is death, that God does not pay it. It is rather the inherent nature of *sin itself* and it does not come from external forces:

> *This is not an act of arbitrary power on the part of God.* The rejecters of His mercy reap that which they have sown. God is the fountain of life; and when one chooses the service of sin, he separates from God, and thus cuts himself off from life. He is "alienated from the life of God." Christ says, "All they that hate Me love death." Ephesians 4:18; Proverbs 8:36. God gives them existence for a time that they may develop their character and reveal their principles. This accomplished, *they receive the results of their own choice*. By a life of rebellion, Satan and all who unite with him place themselves so out of harmony with God that His very presence is to them a consuming fire. The glory of Him who is love will destroy them.
>
> At the beginning of the great controversy, the angels did not understand this. Had Satan and his host then *been left* to reap the full *result of their sin* [note the phrase "been left" denotes the withdrawal of divine power to sustain—*not* the result of God blasting them with some type of physical energy], they would have perished; but it would not have been apparent to heavenly beings that this was the inevitable result of sin. A doubt of God's goodness would have remained in their minds as evil seed, to produce its deadly fruit of sin and woe. (White, *The Desire of Ages*, p. 764, emphasis added)

God does not stand toward the sinner as an executioner of the sentence against transgression; but He leaves the rejectors of His mercy to themselves, to reap that which they have sown. (White, *The Great Controversy*, p. 36)

God's "strange act" will not be inconsistent with who He is, for He is the same yesterday, today, and forever.

God has given to men a declaration of His character and of His method of dealing with sin.... "All the wicked will He destroy."... yet *all the manifestations of retributive justice will be perfectly consistent with the character of God* as a merciful, long-suffering, benevolent being....

And all who have a just conception of these qualities will love Him because they are drawn toward Him in admiration of His attributes. (White, *The Great Controversy*, p. 541, emphasis added)

God's Weapon

The Word of God is His weapon, represented in figures of fire, arrows, hail stones, coals, thunder, sword, and rod. These are all symbols of wrath, which is in reality the result of the rejection and subsequent absence of His Word, which will devour, discomfit, pierce, smite, break, and "dash in pieces" the wicked:

Wherefore thus saith the LORD God of hosts, Because ye speak this word, behold, I will make **my words in thy mouth fire**, and this people wood, **and it shall devour them**. (Jeremiah 5:14, bold emphasis added)

Then the earth shook and trembled; the foundations also of the hills moved and were shaken, because he was wroth. There went up a smoke out of his nostrils, and fire out of his mouth devoured: coals were kindled by it.... At the brightness **that**

was before him his thick clouds passed, hail **stones** and coals of fire. The LORD also thundered in the heavens, and the Highest gave his voice; hail **stones** and coals of fire. Yea, he sent out his arrows, and scattered them; and he shot out lightnings, and discomfited them. (Psalm 18:7, 8, 12–14, bold emphasis added)

He hath said, which heard the words of God, which saw the vision of the Almighty, falling **into a trance**, but having his eyes open... he shall eat up the nations his enemies, and shall break their bones, and pierce **them** through with his arrows. (Numbers 24:4, 8, bold emphasis added)

And take the... the sword of the Spirit, which is the word of God. (Ephesians 6:17)

For the word of God *is* quick, and powerful, and sharper than any twoedged sword, piercing even to the dividing asunder of soul and spirit, and of the joints and marrow, and *is* a discerner of the thoughts and intents of the heart. (Hebrews 4:12)

And out of his mouth goeth a sharp sword, that with it he should smite the nations: and he shall rule them with a rod of iron: and he treadeth the winepress of the fierceness and wrath of Almighty God. (Revelation 19:15)

Psalm 2 is an interesting, poetic depiction of the wicked—who set themselves against the Word of God, which sets forth His Begotten Son as His Anointed King—and how their rejection of Him brings wrath. The declarations of God are likened to a rod. Those who trust in that rod are blessed, but it destroys the wicked. Why? Because God will physically and proactively destroy them? No! Because they have rejected salvation in Christ! This is all the language of wrath, not to be read as a literal rendition according to normal, modern, dictionary understanding of the words.

Why do the heathen rage, and the people imagine a vain thing?
The kings of the earth set themselves, and the rulers take counsel

> together, against the LORD, and against his anointed, *saying*, Let us break their bands asunder, and cast away their cords from us. He that sitteth in the heavens shall laugh: the Lord shall have them in derision. Then shall he speak unto them in his wrath, and vex them in his sore displeasure. Yet have I set my king upon my holy hill of Zion. I will declare the decree: the LORD hath said unto me, Thou *art* my Son; this day have I begotten thee. Ask of me, and I shall give *thee* the heathen *for* thine inheritance, and the uttermost parts of the earth *for* thy possession. Thou shalt break them with a rod of iron; thou shalt dash them in pieces like a potter's vessel. Be wise now therefore, O ye kings: be instructed, ye judges of the earth. Serve the LORD with fear, and rejoice with trembling. Kiss the Son, lest he be angry, and ye perish *from* the way, when his wrath is kindled but a little. Blessed *are* all they that put their trust in him. (Psalm 2)

Perhaps the most powerful statement is made by Isaiah, who shows us that Jesus Himself is the Rod and the word of His mouth is what destroys the wicked. We also know John says Jesus is the Word of God.

> And there shall come forth a rod out of the stem of Jesse, and a Branch shall grow out of his roots: And the spirit of the LORD shall rest upon him, the spirit of wisdom and understanding, the spirit of counsel and might, the spirit of knowledge and of the fear of the LORD; And shall make him of quick understanding in the fear of the LORD: and he shall not judge after the sight of his eyes, neither reprove after the hearing of his ears: But with righteousness shall he judge the poor, and reprove with equity for the meek of the earth: and he shall smite the earth with the rod of his mouth, and with the breath of his lips shall he slay the wicked. (Isaiah 11:1–4)

> In the beginning was the Word, and the Word was with God, and **the Word was God**. (John 1:1, bold emphasis added)

The Word judges, not by sitting on high and handing down a verdict based upon His observations of the wicked; rather, His judgment comes of bringing truth, not only by speaking, but by exemplification, for what He *says* is righteous, He *does*. He is not a "say and do not" as is the Pharisee, whom He rebukes.

The final realization of destruction is not set in motion until the great-white-throne judgment, aka "executive" judgment. The guilt the unrepentant sinners will feel when their life records will be laid open to them is one of the components of bearing wrath.

> The guilt is upon the soul that sinneth. He is accountable for all the evil arising through his influence, conscious or unconscious, that works disaster in the world. By his unfaithfulness he prepares himself for the second death. ("Words to the Young," *The Youth's Instructor*, December 21, 1893)

The consciousness of sin will cause intense suffering. For those with great sin upon them, that suffering will be multiplied.

> As soon as the books of record are opened, and the eye of Jesus looks upon the wicked, **they are conscious of *every sin* which they have ever committed**. They see just where their feet diverged from the path of purity and holiness, just how far pride and rebellion have carried them in the violation of the law of God. (White, *The Great Controversy*, p. 666, emphasis added)

> As the Holy One upon the throne slowly turned the leaves of the ledger, and His eyes rested for a moment upon individuals, His glance seemed to **burn into their very souls**, and at the same moment every word and action of their lives passed before their minds as clearly as though **traced before their vision in letters of fire**. Trembling seized them, and their faces turned pale. Their first appearance when around the throne was that of

careless indifference. But how changed their appearance now! The feeling of security is gone, and in its place is a **nameless terror**. A dread is upon every soul, lest he shall be found among those who are wanting. Every eye is riveted upon the face of the One upon the throne; and as His solemn, searching eye sweeps over that company, there is a quaking of heart; for they are **self-condemned without one word being uttered**. In anguish of soul each declares his own guilt and with terrible vividness *sees* that by sinning he has thrown away the precious boon of eternal life. (White, *Testimonies for the Church*, Vol. 4, p. 385, emphasis added)

When the records of heaven shall be opened, the Judge will not in words declare to man his guilt, but will cast one penetrating, convicting glance, and every deed, every transaction of life, will be vividly impressed upon the memory of the wrongdoer. The person will not, as in Joshua's day, need to be hunted out from tribe to family, but his own lips will confess his shame. The sins hidden from the knowledge of men will then be proclaimed to the whole world. (White, *Patriarchs and Prophets*, p. 498)

God places every action in the scale. What a scene it will be! What impressions will be made regarding the holy character of God and the terrible enormity of sin, when the judgment, based on the law, is carried forward in the presence of all the worlds. Then before the mind of the unrepentant sinner there will be opened all the sins that he has committed, and he will see and understand **the aggregate** of sin and his own guilt. (White, *The Seventh-day Adventist Bible Commentary*, Vol. 7, p. 953, emphasis added)

These preceding passages and others like them are the keys to discerning what is meant by the following depiction, written in the tradition of the biblical metaphor but sadly misinterpreted to teach that God tortures with physical fire while keeping subjects alive:

> Satan rushes into the midst of his followers and tries to stir up the multitude to action. But fire from God out of heaven is rained upon them, and the great men, and mighty men, the noble, the poor and miserable, are all consumed together. I saw that some were quickly destroyed, while others suffered longer. They were punished according to the deeds done in the body. Some were many days consuming, and **just as long as there was a portion of them unconsumed, all the sense of suffering remained**. Said the angel, "The worm of life shall not die; **their fire shall not be quenched as long as there is the least particle for it to prey upon**." (White, *Early Writings*, p. 294, emphasis added)

The "portions" and "particles" that are "consumed" are symbols of the consciousness of every sin. There is no pre-determined amount of suffering imposed upon the wicked except by their own lives of sin. This is all that is implied in the depiction of the millennial work of judgment in which Christ and the saints review the life records of the lost and "mete out to the wicked... that which they must receive at the execution of the judgment" (White, *Early Writings*, pp. 52, 53). This review and "sentencing" during the thousand years will only confirm what is already a reality. (It is in the same vein as the idea of "predestination," in that the Bible language would depict the matter of salvation and damnation as being predetermined by God [see Acts 13:48; Eph. 1:5; Rom. 8:29, 30]. *Foreknowledge* is not *foreordination*. Free choice will always remain intact, unmolested by any interference stemming from divine omniscience.)

The more wicked the being, the more "particles" there are for the "fire" to "prey upon." The fuel for this fire is spiritual: it is their sins. They have therefore an accumulation or "aggregate of sin;" they have stored up wrath for its unleashing at the time of revelation (see Rom. 2:5). This is the fire within that is brought out at execution. Remember Jesus said the one who is forgiven much loves much (see Luke 7:47). By contrast, the one who has sinned much will struggle much against love, seeking for a way to live without God but ultimately finding it impossible. Every wicked being will ultimately come to terms with their fate, but some will take longer than others will.

In an unpublished paper of unknown date by Pr. Roland Rogers, we read the following:

> An evil hard heart develops through the process of rejecting God and committing evil deeds. And the greater the evil deeds, the harder the heart. The wicked's hard heart would not readily accept their guilt. They would stubbornly try to hold on to their self-righteousness. They would persist in trying to justify themselves. They would not readily acknowledge the enormity of their wickedness. Therefore, for them to come to the point of admitting and embracing guilt would take some time.
>
> Mental anguish comes only if the wicked accept or embrace their guilt. If they do not, there would not be the mental anguish and it would not accomplish its destructive work. God does not force the wicked to have mental anguish. It comes through God's revelation of what He is and what they are. For some it just takes longer for both to happen. (*Wrath of God*, p. 35)

Grieving, Desolation, and Fear

> The righteous shall be in everlasting remembrance. He shall not be afraid of evil tidings: his heart is fixed, trusting in the LORD. His heart *is* established, he shall not be afraid, until he see *his desire* upon his enemies. He hath dispersed, he hath given to the poor; his righteousness endureth for ever; his horn shall be

exalted with honour. **The wicked shall see** *it*, **and be grieved; he shall gnash with his teeth, and melt away.** (Psalm 112:6–10, bold emphasis added)

Matthew also alluded to this experience by the symbol of "outer darkness," a place of "weeping and gnashing of teeth" (8:12), a crushing place of spiritual agony where there is no hope. In the setting of the executive judgment, Isaiah said, "Ye shall conceive chaff, ye shall bring forth stubble: **your breath,** *as* **fire, shall devour you** (33:11, bold emphasis added).

> *It can be noted, even in our present reality, that the secular person is often uncomfortable around the devout. This phenomenon will be amplified to excruciating levels of spiritual discomfort.*

breath = "*ruach*," or "spirit," "mind," "character" of a rational being.

"And the people shall be *as* the burnings of lime: *as* thorns cut up shall they be **burned** in the **fire**" (v. 12, bold emphasis added).

burned = "*yatsath*," figuratively, to desolate

fire = "*aysh*" can be taken figuratively or literally

"Hear, ye *that are* far off, what I have done; and, ye *that are* near, acknowledge my might. **The sinners in Zion are afraid; fearfulness hath surprised the hypocrites**" (vs. 13, 14, bold emphasis added).

Note in this next verse, whose fire is it? "LORD, *when* thy hand is lifted up, they will not see: *but* they shall see, and be ashamed for *their* envy at the people; yea, **the fire of thine enemies shall devour them**" (26:11, bold emphasis added).

At the revelation of sin, which they don't want to see, but which God will show them, a fire is kindled within. This is destruction to their souls. As we continue, we will see that the very unveiling of holiness is what kindles the fire—not only of the presence of deity but also the presence of the holy angels and the redeemed. At the presence of righteousness, there is torment. Note how the confrontation between Christ and the demoniacs at the Gadarenes resulted in an anxious response from the demons: "Have you come here to torment us before the appointed time?" (Matt. 8:29, NABRE). It can be noted, even in our present reality, that the secular person is often uncomfortable around the devout. This phenomenon will be amplified to excruciating levels of spiritual discomfort.

> For the day of the LORD *is* near upon all the heathen: as thou hast done, it shall be done unto thee: thy reward shall return upon thine own head. For as ye have drunk upon my holy mountain, *so* shall all the heathen drink continually, yea, they shall drink, and they shall swallow down, and they shall be as though they had not been. But upon mount Zion shall be deliverance, and there shall be holiness; and the house of Jacob shall possess their possessions. **And the house of Jacob shall be a fire, and the house of Joseph a flame**, and the house of Esau for stubble, and they shall kindle in them, and devour them; and there shall not be *any* remaining of the house of Esau; for the LORD hath spoken *it*. (Obadiah 15–18, bold emphasis added)

The wicked are afraid because the presence of God and all of His holy ones brings about their destruction by that which is called the "unquenchable fire" (see Zech. 14:14; Ps. 149:6–9; Ezek. 25:14; Matt. 13:41–43; Dan. 12:3). This fire is simply the "presence of the holy angels" and "the presence of the Lamb" (Rev. 14:10). "As **smoke** is **driven away**, *so* drive *them* **away**: as wax **melteth before the fire**, *so* let the wicked **perish at the presence of God**" (Ps. 68:2, bold emphasis added).

The language of fear and driving away is a reference to this process of standing before the revealing presence of the Lord. To the wicked, His fire is the symbol of all His goodness and penetrating knowledge, in direct confrontation with the full revelation of sin and its results, with no solution or place to run and hide. This brings to them a fear more intense than we can imagine or reference in history, except in a small way: at the cleansing of the temple.

A significant display of this effect will be seen at the second coming, which ends in a first-death experience during the general mayhem among warring men and unprecedented, violent, global upheavals in nature, including great fires of the literal kind. This is a limited demonstration involving only the wicked living at the time of His coming. At the great white throne (GWT) judgment, all the wicked who ever lived are present and *ultimately* destroyed in the second death, by the *ultimate* and specific revelation of their sins brought out from their own minds, in Christ's presence.

> Behold, I will bring **a fear upon thee** [speaking about the backsliding daughters that trusted in her treasures], saith the Lord GOD of hosts, from all those that be about thee; and **ye shall be driven out every man** right forth [the language of the soul's realization of the wrath of God, which is their own abandonment of God]; and **none shall gather up** [the language of desolation; it is too late for salvation] him that wandereth. (Jeremiah 49:5, bold emphasis and comments added)

Living in the Fire

> What is the lie that Satan has foisted upon us? What is the distortion that all too many have bought into? Isn't it just this, the place you don't want to go, the place you don't want to be for eternity is the place of eternal burnings and consuming fire, in other words, the traditional Christian concept of hell? And yet the Bible says that this place is God's very presence, His throne surrounded by a sea of glass mingled with fire (Rev 15:2)! ("The Question of Punishment Part III," Come and Reason Ministries, https://1ref.us/1gr [accessed 12/03/2020])

Of the righteous who stand in this presence, Isaiah said, "Who among us **shall dwell with the devouring fire**? who among us shall **dwell with everlasting burnings**? **He that walketh righteously**" (33:14, 15a, emphasis added). The righteous dwell in the presence of God. "**Thine eyes shall see the king in his beauty**: they shall behold the land that is very far off" (v. 17, bold emphasis added).

The righteous see the same God; they stand in full revelation of His character; but they have sent their sins ahead to judgment and receive the righteousness of Christ. They are at home in the everlasting burnings. It is not to them a fire unquenchable but the desire of their hearts.

The sinner could not be happy in God's presence:

> The sinner could not be happy in God's presence; he would shrink from the companionship of holy beings. Could he be permitted to enter heaven, it would have no joy for him. The spirit of unselfish love that reigns there—every heart responding to the heart of Infinite Love—would touch no answering chord in his soul. His thoughts, his interests, his motives, would be alien to those that actuate the sinless dwellers there. He would be a discordant note in the melody of heaven. *Heaven would be to him a place of torture*; he would *long to be hidden from Him* who is its light, and the center of its joy. *It is no arbitrary decree on the part of God that excludes the wicked from heaven; they are shut out by their own unfitness for its companionship. The glory of God would be to them a consuming fire. They would welcome destruction, that they might be hidden from the face of Him who died to redeem them.* (White, *Steps to Christ*, pp. 17, 18, emphasis added)

The "torture" of heaven to the wicked is what they endure at the final arraignment before the bar of God. They will ultimately "welcome destruction." Their intent, at last, is to die.

The Investigative Judgment Burns Up the Wicked Ahead of Time

> "For we will surely die and *become* like water spilled on the ground, which cannot be gathered up again. Yet God does not take away a life; but He devises means, so that His banished ones are not expelled from Him." (2 Samuel 14:14, NKJV)

We want to be burned up now, i.e., have our sins taken away now, so that we might love His appearing.

> And it shall come to pass, *that he that is* left in Zion, and *he that* remaineth in Jerusalem, shall be called holy, *even* every one that is written among the living in Jerusalem: When the Lord shall have washed away the filth of the daughters of Zion, and **shall have purged the blood of Jerusalem from the midst thereof by the spirit of judgment, and by the spirit of burning**. (Isaiah 4:3, 4, bold emphasis added)

> Behold, I will send my messenger, and he shall prepare the way before me: and the Lord, whom ye seek, shall suddenly come to his temple, even the messenger of the covenant, whom ye delight in: behold, he shall come, saith the LORD of hosts. But who may abide the day of his coming? and who shall stand when he appeareth? for he *is* like **a refiner's fire**, and like fullers' soap: And he shall sit *as* a refiner and purifier of silver: and **he shall purify the sons of Levi, and purge them as gold and silver**, that they may offer unto the LORD an offering in righteousness. (Malachi 3:1–3, bold emphasis added)

One author discusses this point as follows:

> When Paul say[s] that, "Some men's sins are open beforehand, going before to judgment; and some men they follow after"

(*1 Timothy* 5:24), he means that believers, through the experiential process of the investigative judgment, have their sins opened to their awareness before God prior to the final day of reckoning, whereas the lost choose to not allow their sins to come to light in the preliminary judgment and must face them later on, once they are irrevocably settled into them. Those who submit to the investigative judgment prior to the close of probation effectively offload their guilt from the conscience so that it is not there to rise up and crush them in the final judgment. The wicked, on the other hand, retain their guilt by means of impenitence, … [self-justification] and blame-casting, so that when they finally stand before God they must bear the whole psychological weight of their shame. (Ty Gibson, private communication, February 8, 2018)

The Agony of the Cross and the Burden of Sin

The agony is a realization, both in the sense of *distinct understanding* and *actualization*, of the "burden of sin." The bearing of sin is more than revelation; it is the stress of anguish and coming to terms with eternal death. It is the fire that cannot be quenched because it will "burn" to final cessation of existence—the second death.

> *His heart was broken by His mental agony.* And the hearts of all who seek the Lord and find Him will be broken as they see the result of sin. ("Christ and the Law," *The Signs of the Times*, April 14, 1898, emphasis added)
>
> *Christ felt the woe that sinners will feel when they awake to realize the burden of their guilt*, to know that they have forever separated themselves from the joy and peace of Heaven.
>
> Angels beheld with amazement the agony of despair borne by the Son of God. His anguish of mind was so intense that the pain of the cross was hardly felt. (White, *The Story of Jesus*, p. 145, emphasis added)

Those who reject the mercy so freely proffered, will yet be *made to know* the worth of that which they have despised. *They will feel the agony which Christ endured upon the cross* to purchase redemption for all who would receive it. And they *will then realize* what they have lost—eternal life and the immortal inheritance....

When sinners are *compelled to look* upon Him who clothed His divinity with humanity, and who still wears this garb, their confusion is indescribable. The *scales fall from their eyes*, and *they see* that which before they would not see. *They realize* what they might have been had they received Christ, and improved the opportunities granted them. *They see* the law which they have spurned, exalted even as God's throne is exalted. *They see* God Himself giving reverence to His law.

What a scene that will be! No pen can describe it! The accumulated *guilt of the world will be laid bare*, and the voice of the Judge will be heard saying to the wicked, "Depart from me, ye that work iniquity."

Then those who pierced Christ *will remember* how they slighted His love and abused His compassion; how they chose in His stead Barabbas, a robber and murderer; how they crowned the Saviour with thorns, and caused Him to be scourged and crucified; how, in the agony of His death on the cross, they taunted Him ... They will seem to hear again His voice of entreaty. Every tone of solicitude *will vibrate as distinctly in their ears* as when the Saviour spoke to them. *Every act* of insult and mockery done to Christ will be as *fresh in their memory* as when the satanic deeds were done.

They will call on the rocks and mountains to fall on them and hide them from the face of Him that sitteth on the throne and from the wrath of the Lamb. "The wrath of the Lamb"— One who ever showed Himself full of tenderness, patience, and long-suffering, who, having given Himself up as the sacrificial offering, was led as a lamb to the slaughter, to save sinners from *the doom now falling upon them because they would not allow Him to take away their guilt.* (White, *The SDA Bible Commentary*, Vol. 6, pp. 1069, emphasis added)

No human being can bear the guilt of his own sin.... If it were so indeed, his life would be crushed out. (White, *Manuscript Releases*, p. 8)

Notice the similar descriptions of the agony of Christ at the cross and of the wicked impenitent at the day of the Lord:

My God, my God, why hast thou forsaken me? *why art thou so* far from helping me, *and from* the words of **my roaring**? ... I am poured out like water, and all my bones are out of joint: **my heart is like wax; it is melted in the midst** of my bowels. (Psalm 22:1, 14, bold emphasis added)

Howl ye; for the day of the LORD *is* **at hand; it shall come as a destruction from the Almighty.** Therefore shall all hands be faint, and **every man's heart shall melt**: And they shall be afraid: pangs and sorrows shall take hold of them; they shall be in pain as a woman that travaileth: they shall be amazed one at another; their faces *shall be as* flames. Behold, the day of the LORD cometh, cruel both with wrath and fierce anger, to lay the land desolate: and he shall destroy the sinners thereof out of it. (Isaiah 13:6–9, bold emphasis added)

The burden of *sin removed* is *rest*; having the burden of sin upon the soul is *wrath*.

Christ longs to give those who do not understand him, *correct views of his character*, to set them right, to *take away their burden of sin and resistance*, and *give them rest*.... The sinner *sees not* Jesus, but fastens his gaze upon the cloud of darkness, and

> *desires not the Lord of life and glory*. He does not realize that Jesus alone can give him peace and rest, and *quiet the tempest that Satan has created in the human soul*, and so he does not come unto him. *Under the dark cloud of impenitence, sinners are in a state of insanity*. ("Variance Between Believers and Unbelievers," *The Signs of the Times*, November 26, 1894, emphasis added)

Again, a key text that we would do well to memorize: *"He [the sinner] will realize* that because of transgression, *his soul is cut off from God*, and that *God's wrath abides on him. This is a fire unquenchable, and by it every unrepentant sinner will be destroyed"* ("Christ and the Law," *The Signs of the Times*, April 14, 1898, emphasis added).

> And the smoke of their torment ascendeth up for ever and ever: and they have **no rest day nor night**. (Revelation 14:11, bold emphasis added)

> The sinner's own thoughts are his accusers; and there can be no torture keener than the stings of a guilty conscience, which give him no rest day nor night. (White, *The Desire of Ages*, p. 223)

> For we are consumed by thine anger, and by thy wrath are we troubled. Thou hast set our iniquities before thee, our secret *sins* in the light of thy countenance. (Psalm 90:7, 8)

> In the day of final judgment, *every lost soul will understand the nature of his own rejection of truth*. The *cross will be presented*, and *its real bearing will be seen* by every mind that has been blinded by transgression. Before *the vision* of Calvary with its mysterious Victim, sinners will stand condemned. *Every lying excuse will be swept away. Human apostasy will appear* in its heinous character. *Men will see what their choice has been. Every question* of truth and error in the long-standing controversy *will then have*

> been made plain. *In the judgment of the universe, God will stand clear of blame for the existence or continuance of evil*. It will be demonstrated that the divine decrees are not accessory to sin. *There was no defect in God's government, no cause for disaffection*. When the thoughts of all hearts shall be revealed, both the loyal and the rebellious will unite in declaring, "Just and true are Thy ways, Thou King of saints. Who shall not fear Thee, O Lord, and glorify Thy name? … for Thy judgments are made manifest." (White, *The Desire of Ages*, p. 58, emphasis added)

I must interrupt the flow at this point to share an observation. The previous statement has an extremely significant point that may be easily overlooked. We tend to think of the GWT judgment primarily as a judgment of the wicked, but what is really going on here in this "day of final judgment"? Who and what is actually being judged? Notice the *universe* is doing the judging. *God* is the One who is cleared of blame, and *His government* stands unblemished! The wicked are part of the universe; they too are standing in judgment of God and declaring His name as "just and true." Praise the Lord!

> Christ felt the woe that sinners will feel when they *awake to realize the burden of their guilt, to know* that they have forever separated themselves from the joy and peace of Heaven. (White, *The Story of Jesus*, p. 145, emphasis added)

> Calvary alone can reveal the terrible enormity of sin. If we had to bear our own guilt, it would crush us. (White, *Thoughts from the Mount of Blessing*, p. 116)

> The *heaviest burden* that we bear is *the burden of sin*. If we were left to bear this burden, it *would crush us*. But the Sinless One has taken our place. "The Lord hath laid on Him the iniquity of us all." Isaiah 53:6. He has borne *the burden of our guilt*. (White, *The Desire of Ages*, p. 328, emphasis added)

> Christ [on the cross] felt much as sinners will feel when the vials of God's wrath shall be poured out upon them. Black despair, like the pall of death, will gather about their guilty souls, and then they will realize to the fullest extent the sinfulness of sin. (White, *Testimonies for the Church*, p. 210)

This all serves to show there are most significant aspects of Christ's second-death experience that correlate to the guilty sinner's second-death experience. In many cases, the language is that of "realization"—of "seeing"—the full revelation of the results of sin. Jesus, on the cross, suffered this full realization *actually*, not *vicariously*, for in His sinful human flesh, He died eternally, in the way the lost sinner will die.

However, at the same time, we must remember that on His divine side, He did not die. (There is mystery in this, of course, and we can only go so far until we get into speculation.) For instance, the phenomenal burst of light that came from the cross at His expiration, shining "with a glory like the sun" (White, *The Desire of Ages*, p. 756), would have been His divinity that was also present there. This is the life He took back up when He arose in His glorified body.

The struggle of the finally impenitent has to do with this full realization that God is the source of life, and to be in Him is the only way one can live. For this to have been a reality, it would have meant a dying to self and submission to God, looking upon Him and receiving His character for the transformation of their character. To use the common tech-talk vernacular, only the transformed are "plug and play" ready for eternal life in a clean, righteous universe. This, the wicked realize, is something they *did* not want, *do* not want, and never *will* want. Their minds are irrevocably seared with sin. They see it. They see it all: that only in God is there life. They do not want His life. They therefore understand they want death and that it is by choice, for they cannot have life and sin simultaneously. They cannot have self to rule self and yet live. They cannot take the place of God.

They must come to full admission of the enormity of sin; that life cannot continue in it; that they are bringing grace, mercy, and patience to an end because in this realization, there is no more place found for them. This is the process that eradicates sin and sinners. In this, we find it is true that God is wiping away all tears. He is leaving all that has been tainted with sin to go to nothingness by drawing out from them the "fire in the midst," the realization of the fire of His character of love and sustaining power.

From now on, everything is returning to the dominion of righteousness, and God will be everywhere manifest. The wicked know they cannot dwell—neither desire to dwell—in that presence, for this is the everlasting burnings of the inhabitation of the righteous, which to those bearing sin is the fire unquenchable that brings about searing torture of soul.

The impenitent have come to the final moment where they must say, "God, you are right, just, and true in all your ways, but I don't want it. Let me go." This is the final vindication of God, which comes from the lips of the wicked. Every being is given to be a witness for Him, or a judge of Him, whether in life or death. As the lost process this burden of sin upon their souls, from the weakest to the strongest in wickedness, they die.

The burden of sin is not only its guilt and shame, but the crushing loss of all hope in the full realization of the goodness of God and the reality of eternal existence only being possible in righteousness, as we have seen depicted in the GWT judgment. "The wicked shall see it and be grieved."

Another author wrote the following, coming to the same conclusion that I have found:

> In the awful glory, in the awful goodness of God's presence they acknowledge they rejected not an evil God, but a good God. They realize they are guilty of "crucifying" God in their minds. They have themselves destroyed their ability to love and honor God. They stand condemned. They understand they are guilty of rejecting a good God and must suffer the "wrath and indignation" of this God. He must give them over to what they

> have become. They have become beings, who in God's presence experience tremendous guilt and condemnation. This is a burden that the wicked cannot bear. God gives them over to this result. This is God's wrath. They have sown the seed and God allows the fruit. (Rogers, *Wrath of God*, p. 35)

Sinners at the end of the age will be brought to the realization of their own guilt and consequent, eternal separation from life. They do not love God, but they love existence. The selfish sinners, above all things, want to live, but they will be cut off from God, who is the Source of life. They realize they cannot live when God "comes" to them in His glory. What agony! They want to live yet not with God. He is still their enemy. If they could only get rid of Him.

In both cases, the realization of guilt and eternal death is that which destroys. Jesus came to this agony in the sense of the Father leaving Him. Sinners come to this same agony in the experience of God "coming" to them. It takes the presence of God for sinners to finally acknowledge their guilt for rejecting Him. They then understand their fate. This agony—this mental anguish—consumes the wicked. It is an unquenchable "fire" that destroys (see *Ibid.*, p. 27).

Emotional/Psychological Stress Can Cause Death

Emotional pain and grief can cause great suffering and even death. The following report from Religion News Today is evidence of this fact:

> During the January 17, 1994, Northridge/Los Angeles earthquake, over one hundred Californians literally died of fright. This was the conclusion of Robert Kloner, cardiologist at Good Samaritan hospital in Los Angeles. Apparently a terrorized brain can trigger the release of a mix of chemicals so potent it can cause the heart to contract—and never relax again.

(*Journal of the American College of Cardiology*, November 1, 1997, pp. 1174–1180)

Medical scientists have discovered that extreme stress can cause the body to secrete excessive amounts of adrenalin, which can cause the heart to stop beating, resulting in death. This condition is known as *acute stress cardiomyopathy* or "broken heart syndrome."

We would be safe to assume that no human being has ever undergone the stress that Jesus endured. "*Is it* nothing to you, all ye that pass by? behold, and see if there be any sorrow like unto my sorrow, which is done unto me, wherewith the LORD hath afflicted *me* in the day of his fierce anger. From above hath he sent fire into my bones" (Lam. 1:12, 13).

Sweating blood under extreme duress is a human biological phenomenon. A news item by Sharon Kirkey in the October 24, 2017 issue of the weekly Canadian newspaper *The National Post* (p. A8) reports that the Canadian Medical Association Journal, in that same week, discusses the phenomenon of "hematohidrosis," a condition that manifests a "spontaneous discharge of 'blood sweat'" coming from normal skin, exhibiting no relevant, underlying causes. It is hypothesized, as reported in the "Indian Journal of Dermatology," that "under conditions of extreme physical or emotional stress," the capillary blood vessels supplying the sweat glands rupture and this is how the blood gets into the perspiration. "Acute fear and intense mental contemplation are the most frequent causes," says the authors of that report, citing six cases of prisoners facing execution and another case during the 1941 London Blitz. Medical historian Dr. Jacalyn Duffin, of Canada's Queen's University, found, in her research of medical literature from 1880–2017, forty-two published articles on the phenomenon. Twenty-eight new cases were reported in peer-reviewed journals between 2004 and 2017.

We must derive all our understandings from the cross. Note the following sequence: "*He bore the guilt and shame of sin*, and the *hiding of his Father's face*, till the *woes of a lost world broke His heart*, and *crushed out His life* on Calvary's cross" (White, *The Great Controversy*, p. 651, emphasis added).

Now, it has been a point often made that it was not the physical rigors of the cruel lashings and the cross that caused the death of Christ, and that is true. Yet what has been claimed is that He died of a ruptured heart, this physical condition brought about by the mental stress He suffered in taking the burden of sin upon Himself. I believe it goes beyond this simple formula, and there is more to it than this.

Sin being imputed to Him, Jesus died the second death in some respects, much like the sinner will die it, under the formula "wages of sin = death." We must not miss the fact that Jesus' death is a type of the final death of the wicked. We know the wicked must face the living presence of God, revealed in all the glory of the truth of His righteous character and government, while enduring a full knowledge of their status as hardened rebels. They will surely endure tremendous mental stress, even unto death, just like Jesus did. However, we cannot focus on the mental stress causing physical trauma, which then caused death, such as would be found by postmortem examination.

> The *mystery of the cross explains all other mysteries*. In the light that streams from Calvary, the *attributes of God* which had filled us with fear and awe appear beautiful and attractive. Mercy, tenderness, and parental love are seen to blend with holiness,

justice, and power. While we behold the majesty of his throne, high and lifted up, *we see His character* in its gracious manifestations, and *comprehend, as never before*, the significance of that endearing title, "Our Father." (White, *The Great Controversy*, p. 652, emphasis added)

Jesus was to go through a complete process of giving Himself up to the fate of the wicked, as "numbered with the transgressors" (Isa. 53:12). His death was not brought about by physical trauma, even as surely His physical vitality was being worn away unto inevitable death. In reading John 10:15–18, we see that Jesus said He "lays down" His life—that He had the power in Him to lay down and take up His life again. Mark, Luke, and John tell us He "gave up the ghost."

Jesus Himself, the author of the Jewish system of sacrifices and rites, knew the exact moment when He would die: right at the stroke of the evening Passover sacrifice (see Mark 15:33–37); and as He did, He cried with a loud voice, signifying He still had vitality and vigor in His body. Normally, a physically dying individual's voice will fade out; there is no strength for crying out. When He cried forth this way, His words reveal the truth of His claim that He would be laying down His life voluntarily, in that He said, "Father, into thy hands I commend my spirit."

Truly, Jesus would have experienced terrible mental stress from the burden of sin and separation from His Father, beginning in the garden of Gethsemane with the bloody sweat, but the cessation of His life was after His realization of separation from the Father—after three hours of heavy darkness—as He shouted, "My God, my God, why hast thou forsaken me?" (v. 34). At this point, His physical organism would have simultaneously gone through a physical stress that produced the water that came from His side.

The point is that He surrendered His life in the blackness of bearing sin; so too will all the wicked surrender their lives in this "outer darkness" of agony of soul, where there is "weeping and gnashing of teeth," a condition of utter hopelessness. They will have to come to the point of giving themselves over to the second death, desiring it, admitting the justice of their end. Unlike Christ, however, they will at the same time scream at God with curses as they implore Him to let them go to their chosen end.

> All they that hate me love death. (Proverbs 8:36)

> For as ye have drunk upon my holy mountain, *so* shall all the heathen drink continually, yea, they shall drink, and they shall swallow down, and they shall be as though they had not been. (Obadiah 16)

> And death shall be chosen rather than life by all the residue of them that remain of this evil family, which remain in all the places whither I have driven them, saith the LORD of hosts. (Jeremiah 8:3)

While the mental anguish is definitely a lead up to death, the actual time when this stress is allowed to have its physical effect is the moment of surrender to the blackness of sin's consequences. The proof of this is in a careful observation of Jesus giving Himself over to His own death. This is how the eternally lost will feel when they are forsaken by God forever. They too will give themselves over, at which point there will be a physical causation. The physical causation may or may not be observable from the outside, but the process of giving themselves up will be visibly observed by all.

Judas is also a type of the guilt-bearing in the forever death of the finally impenitent. His desire for self-exaltation was manifest in his attempt to force Christ to take His position on the throne, where he assumed that he, Judas, would sit among the ruling generals in the Lord's army, directing the violent suppression of the Roman forces and all the world beyond. In fact, he thought he would be the second in command. He, being a type of those who reject Christ, suffered a bitter remorse and guilt-forced confession without repentance. He hung himself in despair, self-condemnation, and apprehension of coming judgment (read *The Desire of Ages*, chapter 76, entitled "Judas"). Judas and that factotum of Satan, the papacy, are both referred to as the "son of perdition." "While I was with them in the world, I kept them in thy name: those that thou gavest me I have kept, and none of them is lost, but the son perdition; that the scripture might be fulfilled" (John 17:2). Also, "Let no man deceive you by any means: for [that day shall not come], except there come a falling away first, and that man of sin be revealed, the son of perdition" (2 Thess. 2:3). These are of the stock of those whose governing principle is opposition to God and self-exaltation, showing their own selves to be God.

Satan "burns" the longest and is the last one to give over to his fate. It will be a horrible struggle for him as he has been so entirely committed to the war against God, right up to the point where he bows and confesses before Him, yet arises from his knees and rushes into the midst of the wicked to stir them to war against the city. He will determine he is not yet finished with the controversy. He has more ground to cover in his own "swallowing down" in his descent into oblivion, his personal hell.

We find that the devil has followers no more. They won't go with him into battle, having withdrawn all support from him. These ones all go through their own process of letting go of life until only Satan stands. In the final throes of his own agony, caged in on every side by the reality of his own choices, he at last realizes his full end—that he must let it go. He stands as a solitary figure in the universe, whose cause is neutralized forever. He has not a particle of hope left of building or retaining any kingdom. All the rest of the sentient beings in the universe are now *in* God and *of* God. Utterly alone, has no place to go. He is finished. At last, he will relent and also ask God to release him to eternal night.

Let us note that the inner fires of the earth have been releasing also, and this would be forming a scene of rivers of fire, explosions, and flames raining down molten sulfur and magma, transforming the landscape into a scene that would resemble a vast, seething lake of fire. Bodies will likely be involved in a process of physical burning in these geophysical fires, as in the garbage dump outside Jerusalem of old, *Gehenna*, from where the New Testament word "hell" is derived. Like *Gehenna* and *Tophet* in the Old Testament (see Isa. 30:33), these are not the fires that kill them; they only reduce the elements of physical bodies into their constituents.

They have already died. These are not the fires of final dissolution, either. The matter that comprised fleshly bodies is still in existence. We will unpack this further as we go along.

Satan's expiration is the climax of the great controversy. What follows will be spectacular and dramatic. The palette is cleared for the new creation, *ex nihilo*, as Christ declares, "Behold, I make all things new" (Rev. 21:5). The earth and its environs will disintegrate, and the New Jerusalem will ride on this sea of fire, as did Noah's ark on the waters. In the final consummation, it can now be said, "Upon *all things*, from the least to the greatest, the Creator's name is written, and *in all* are the riches of his power displayed" (White, *The Great Controversy*, p. 678, emphasis added).

There is *no place* found for the wicked. The character of God is upon all things. The riches of His power are displayed in the symbol of His wounded side. The "bright beams" that come "out of His side" ("Manasseh and Josiah," *The Review and Herald*, July 15, 1915) signify the plan of redemption, which is entailed in the elevation of humanity to His throne. This is a marriage of humanity with divinity. This happens in every individual who accepts Christ, and all the individuals together, as the body of redeemed, form the bride of Christ. This marriage union, or abode in God, is impossible for the wicked, and the realization of the truth consumes them unto death. Habakkuk 3:4 reveals the wounds of Christ as tokens of His humiliation that symbolize His power to save, and the rejection of which is His strength to execute justice or allow the finally impenitent to reap death from their severance from the Source of life.

Fire of Dissolution

Introduction to the Metaphor of the Fire in the Midst

> For our God *is* a consuming fire. (Hebrews 12:29)

> And the angel of the LORD appeared unto him in a flame of **fire out of the midst** of a bush: and he looked, and, behold, the

bush burned with fire, and the bush *was* not consumed. (Exodus 3:2, bold emphasis added)

And the LORD spake unto you **out of the midst of the fire:** ye heard the voice of the words, but saw no similitude; only *ye heard* a voice. (Deuteronomy 4:12, bold emphasis added)

And ye said, Behold, the LORD our God hath shewed us his glory and his greatness, and we have heard his voice **out of the midst of the fire:** we have seen this day that God doth talk with man, and he liveth. Now therefore why should we die? for **this great fire will consume us:** if we hear the voice of the LORD our God any more, then we shall die. For who *is there of* all flesh, that hath heard the voice of the living God speaking **out of the midst of the fire**, as we *have*, and lived? (Deuteronomy 5:24–26, bold emphasis added)

And I looked, and, behold, a whirlwind came out of the north, a great cloud, and **a fire** infolding itself, and a brightness *was* about it, and **out of the midst** thereof as the colour of amber, **out of the midst of the fire.** (Ezekiel 1:4, bold emphasis added)

Yea, I will gather you, and blow upon you in **the fire of my wrath**, and ye shall be **melted in the midst thereof.** (Ezekiel 22:21, bold emphasis added)

Thou *art* the anointed cherub that covereth; and I have set thee *so*: thou wast upon the holy mountain of God; thou hast walked up and down **in the midst of the stones of fire**.... I will destroy thee, O covering cherub, from the **midst of the stones of fire**.... therefore will I bring forth a **fire from the midst of thee**, it shall devour thee, and I will bring thee to ashes upon the earth in the sight of all them that behold thee. (Ezekiel 28:14, 16, 18, bold emphasis added)

> For I, saith the LORD, will be unto her **a wall of fire** round about, and will be **the glory in the midst** of her. (Zechariah 2:5, bold emphasis added)

Looking at the above texts, we can readily perceive that this fire has to do with the presence of God. As such, the presence or absence of God has a bearing upon our examination of the other fires: 1) the psycho-emotional experience, which is the unquenchable fire of judgment; 2) the incendiary fires arising from the release of both nature and the passion of the wicked; and 3) the final fire that dissolves all matter. It is not a distinct fire of its own. It is a metaphor also, which has to do with the action of the other fires. This section undertakes the task of defining some of the nuances of the "fire in/from the midst."

Atomic/Cosmic Fire that Sustains

The fire from the midst is, in one sense, the sustaining fire of God's presence in the form of His power, *not* His personality, lest we find ourselves off the path and into the weeds of pantheism or panentheism. It is the cognizant and active will of God that functions to hold creation together. This sustaining power is the word of God in the functional role of holding matter together in organized form. That is, we know all things that exist *materially*, animate and inanimate, are sustained by the word of God (see Col. 1:16, 17; Heb. 1:2, 3; John 1:1–3).

We are not here focusing on the aspect of the word of God, which is the life of God in the *animating* sense, that, by grace—by the virtue of the merits of Christ—allows all people to have conscious existence (see Acts 17:28), or in the *restorative* sense, by which we are created anew in His own image (see Eph. 2:10). We are speaking simply of the energy or binding force that holds elemental materials in place, from the grand level of the cosmos—the stars, planets, and systems of the macrouniverse, down to the rudimentary level of the physical universe—that of "inner space"—the molecule, atom, and sub-atom.

Stephen Haskell writes about the throne of God: "By *the power* which centers there, worlds are held in space, and suns complete their circuits. The power which holds the universe in space, and *binds atoms together*, emanates from this throne of life" (Haskell, *The Story of the Seer of Patmos*, pp. 96, 97, emphasis added).

> Many teach that matter possesses vital power,—that certain properties are imparted to matter, and it is then left to act through its own inherent energy; and that the operations of nature are conducted in harmony with fixed laws, with which God himself cannot interfere. This is false science, and is not sustained by the word of God. Nature is the servant of her Creator. God does not annul his laws, or work contrary to them; but he is continually using them as his instruments. *Nature testifies of an intelligence, a presence, an active energy, that works in and through her laws.* There is in nature the continual working of the Father and the Son. Christ says, "My Father worketh hitherto, and I work." (White, *Christian Education*, pp. 194, 195, emphasis added)
>
> God is perpetually at work in nature. She is His servant, directed as He pleases. Nature in her work testifies of *the intelligent presence and active agency of a being who moves in all His works according to His will.* It is not by an original power inherent in nature that year by year the earth yields its bounties and continues its march around the sun. The hand of infinite power is perpetually at work guiding this planet. It is *God's power momentarily exercised* that keeps it in position in its rotation.
>
> The mechanism of the human body cannot be fully understood; it presents mysteries that baffle the most intelligent. It is not as the result of a mechanism, which, once set in motion, continues its work, that the pulse beats and breath follows breath. In God we live and move and have our being. Every breath, every throb of the heart, is a continual evidence of *the power of an ever-present God*. (White, *Counsels for the Church*, pp. 324, 325, emphasis added)

As we think about how God speaks, we know that what He speaks comes into existence. "For he spake, and it was *done*; he commanded, and it stood fast" (Ps. 33:9). To understand how things go *out* of existence, we would reverse the process. All He must do is *not speak*. In this, He would effectively state, "It is undone," or perhaps more accurately, "I am not in it," and we would find that, hereby, His word is "withdrawn," with the result being that where His voice is no longer sounding, there can be nothing. If, by His word, it stands fast, then, by corollary, it is found that by the absence of His word, it no longer stands.

This is His strange act, for He never intends that when His word is sent forth, it should be withdrawn. His strange act, when carried to the fullest, results in a returning to the formless void of that which is "given up." It is not an arbitrary decree that makes this so. It is based upon the reality of immutable laws that govern the very existence of matter.

It is the strangest thing for God to "withdraw" His word, as it is against who He is. Anything that comes from God is perfect; therefore, it is intended to endure forever. Yet there is a high and lofty governing principle—even a superseding principle at work—and that principle is *freedom of choice* to all. We therefore use the word "withdrawn" also in the modality of the language of wrath, in that it is not that He turns and angrily stomps out of the room, but rather that He is shown the door in no uncertain terms. His withdrawal brings certain punishment, yet is an acquiescence to the choice of the free moral agent, rather than an imposition upon him or her.

> In simplicity and truth we would speak to the impenitent in regard to the way in which men destroy their own souls.... No soul is ever finally deserted of God, given up to his own ways, so long as there is any hope of his salvation. ("The Measure of Light Given Measures Our Responsibilities," *The Review and Herald*, October 24, 1912)
>
> Man turns from God, not God from him. (White, *Thoughts from the Mount of Blessing*, p. 93)

God grants sinners the choice to move away from Him, and though He implores them to come to Him, He does not prevent them from rejecting and ejecting Him. Therefore, if created beings no longer desire His Word in them, He honors them in their choice and allows them to leave—to stand in the place of Himself, as though they would think to be their own god to sustain their own lives. Of course, it cannot be, for outside God, there is nothing. There would be "no place found for them," to use the biblical phrase. They will reveal their choice to not have God in their experience or abide by the righteous principles of life, and they will give themselves over to death, for that is the only option. They will ultimately perish, and then the material body will also go out of existence.

> For **by him were all things created**, that are in heaven, and that are in earth, visible and invisible, whether *they be* thrones, or dominions, or principalities, or powers: all things were created by him, and for him: And he is before all things, and **by him all things consist.** (Colossians 1:16, 17, bold emphasis added)
>
> In the beginning was the Word, and the Word was with God, and **the Word was God.** The same was in the beginning with God. **All things were made by him**; and without him was not any thing made that was made. (John 1:1–3, bold emphasis added)

> **By the word of the LORD were the heavens made**; and all the host of them **by the breath of his mouth**.... For **he spake**, and it was *done*; he commanded, **and it stood fast**. (Psalm 33:6, 9, bold emphasis added)

> Hast thou marked the old way which wicked men have trodden? Which were cut down out of time, whose foundation was overflown with a flood: Which said unto God, *Depart from us: and what can the Almighty do for them*? (Job 22:15–17, emphasis added)

By the Word, a thing or person stands; by the choice of the person to eject the Word, he or she ceases to exist. As discussed earlier, we know there is a definite connection between the departure from God of sentient beings possessing moral capabilities and the natural environment that supports them. This starts right at home, in the degradation of their physical bodies. When God is ejected from the mind, the physical surroundings are also subject to the introduction of entropic action. This increases in effect with the level of iniquity in the moral creature. It is a direct correlation.

The Fire of Dissolution, Described as Nuclear Fire

The sense in which we are looking at the fire of God here is that of *nuclear* fire. When it is withdrawn, in a flash of dissipating energy, the basic particles of matter cease to exist. It is the matter-to-energy conversion with which humanity has become horrifically acquainted through tampering with the elements in the development of nuclear fissile materials. What we have not pondered is that all the elements are "fissile," for when God withdraws from a thing, it is no more.

The metaphors of devouring fire, smoke, and ashes are used to depict this fire. The figure of smoke represents the ultimate cessation of matter, resulting in the loss of energy into space, not physical particles and gases, as we normally observe in the physical process of oxidative combustion. In other words, though physical fires will be the penultimate means of reducing the bodies of the wicked, the material vapors and smoke will be ultimately obliterated in a different kind of fire.

> But the wicked shall perish, and the enemies of the LORD *shall be* as the fat of lambs: they shall consume; **into smoke shall they consume away**. (Psalm 37:20, bold emphasis added)

> And **the smoke of their torment ascendeth up for ever** and ever: and they have no rest day nor night, who worship the beast and his image, and whosoever receiveth the mark of his name. (Revelation 14:11, bold emphasis added)

> For, behold, **the day cometh, that shall burn** as an oven; and all the proud, yea, and all that do wickedly, shall be stubble: and the day that cometh shall burn them up, saith the LORD of hosts, that **it shall leave them neither root nor branch**. (Malachi 4:1, bold emphasis added)

> Yea, I will gather you, and blow upon you in **the fire of my wrath**, and ye shall be **melted in the midst** thereof.... Therefore have I poured out mine indignation upon them; I have **consumed them with the fire of my wrath: their own way have I recompensed upon their heads**, saith the Lord GOD. (Ezekiel 22:21, 31, bold emphasis added)

These verses in Ezekiel 21 are key in tying together the concepts of the fire of divine wrath as the "melting in the midst"—the consequence of their own choices and actions.

> Thou hast defiled thy sanctuaries by the multitude of thine iniquities, by the iniquity of thy traffick; therefore will **I bring forth a fire from the midst of thee, it shall devour thee, and I will bring thee to ashes upon the earth in the sight of all them that behold thee**. (Ezekiel 28:18, bold emphasis added)

> And ye shall tread down the wicked; for **they shall be ashes** under the soles of your feet in the day that I shall do *this*, saith the LORD of hosts. (Malachi 4:3, bold emphasis added)

What about these ashes under the feet of the wicked? What is that? As we spoke of a metaphoric smoke, these ashes are also metaphoric, not a literal substance, for after the "lake of fire," "melting of the elements with fervent heat" event, there will be no physical ashes. If it were molten earth material being depicted in this event, physical flesh would be so incinerated that there would be no ashes. This kind of heat would vaporize bodies completely into smoke. Therefore, no matter how one would look at this fire, ashes *must* be a figurative depiction of total annihilation—soul *and* body.

Lake of Fire

The term itself is used five times, only in Revelation. As with the "fire from the midst," this fire, the "lake of fire," can also be viewed from different angles, depending on the context. It is, in one sense, the same as the "unquenchable fire," which is drawn forth from the minds of the wicked when the books are opened in the execution of the great-white-throne judgment, brought to view in Revelation 20:11–12 (see also Isa. 13:8; "The Temptation of Christ," *The Review and Herald*, April 1, 1875). This would fit well with the symbol of waters as people (see Rev. 17:15) who, en masse, are depicted as a lake; whose constituents are in the throes of the mental agony of the fire of revelation, which elicits self-judgment.

Second, it can be seen as the vast surface of the earth is a molten mass, under the release of the physical forces to chaotic action. Finally, the term can also refer to the final eradication of the elements when all things blow up.

The lake of fire, being associated with "brimstone," invites us to have a more discerning look at the word employed. Perhaps we can gain some insight as to the nature of what, on the surface, appears to be literal molten sulfur. Several researchers into this subject have pointed out that there is more than meets the eye here.

> STRONGS NT 2303: θεῖον
>
> The Greek *theion* (THAYon):
>
> θεῖον, θείου, τό (apparently the neuter of the adjective θεῖος equivalent to divine incense, because burning brimstone was regarded as having power to purify, and to ward off contagion.

Strong's G2303 may refer to the literal element sulfur, yet it is a valid interpretation to look at it as the presence of God, as it is described in *Thayer's Greek-English Lexicon* in terms of "divine incense, because burning brimstone was regarded as having power to purify, and to ward off disease" (https://1ref.us/1gs, [accessed 12/03/2020]). It is the neuter of G2304: *theios* (in its original sense of "flashing"), which itself is from G2346: *theos*, the word for God. Putting this all together, it certainly appears as though the word, in this context, would be a perfect fit with the inspired data, depicting an unveiling of the face of God, which is intolerable with sin on the conscience.

Tophet

Tophet is a wonderful clue for a correct understanding, in that as a word of Syriac-Persic origin, it refers to a place of cremation, of "burning and burying of dead bodies," according to *Gesenius' Hebrew-Chaldee Lexicon*. This likens to the New Testament *Gehenna*, the garbage dump outside of ancient Jerusalem.

"For Tophet *is* ordained of old; yea, **for the king it is prepared**; he hath made *it* deep *and* large: the pile thereof *is* fire and much wood; the breath of the LORD, like a stream of brimstone, doth kindle it" (Isa. 30:33, bold emphasis added). The final clause is set in motion by the word of the Lord when He rises above the city to reveal Himself to the wicked and the wicked to themselves.

An interesting point to note here, which connects this passage to Satan, is in the phrase "for the king it is prepared." Of what does this remind us? "Then shall he say also unto them on the left hand, Depart from me, ye cursed, into **everlasting fire, prepared for the devil and his angels**" (Matt. 25:41, bold emphasis added).

Speaking of the enemies of God in the day of the Lord, we read of the fall of Babylon in its historical type, which applies, in a broader sense, to the millennial destructions, in obviously figurative language, focusing on the emotional torture of soul, employing simile and metaphor: "And they shall be afraid: pangs and sorrows shall take hold of them; they shall be in pain as a woman that travaileth: they shall be amazed one at another; their **faces *shall be as* flames**" (Isa. 13:8, bold emphasis added). Collectively, they are as a "lake of fire."

Here are the five texts of Revelation that refer to the "lake of fire":

- "And the beast was taken, and with him the false prophet that wrought miracles before him, with which he deceived them that had received the mark of the beast, and them that worshipped his image. These both were cast alive into a **lake of fire** burning with brimstone" (19:20, bold emphasis added).
- "And the devil that deceived them was cast into the **lake of fire** and brimstone, where the beast and the false prophet *are*, and shall be tormented day and night for ever and ever" (20:10, bold emphasis added).
- "And death and hell were cast into the **lake of fire**. This is the second death" (v. 14, bold emphasis added).
- "And whosoever was not found written in the book of life was cast into the **lake of fire**" (v. 15, bold emphasis added).
- "But the fearful, and unbelieving, and the abominable, and murderers, and whoremongers, and sorcerers, and idolaters, and all liars, shall have their part in the **lake which burneth with fire** and brimstone: which is the second death" (21:8, bold emphasis added).

Here is Isaiah's description of the same event, which is probably the literary source for John's description:

> For *it is* the day of the LORD's vengeance, *and* the year of recompenses for the controversy of Zion. And the **streams thereof shall be turned into pitch**, and the dust thereof into brimstone, and **the land thereof shall become burning pitch**. It shall not be quenched night nor day; **the smoke thereof shall go up for ever:** from generation to generation it shall lie waste; none shall pass through it for ever and ever. (Isaiah 34:8–10, bold emphasis added)

Again, we are looking at highly poetic and figurative language. We see dust being "turned into" molten sulfur. This is not alchemy. It is language—a representation of what was seen in vision as a complete annihilation of all things, using words and concepts available to the writer at the time. Notice the things that are being cast into the lake of fire are states, concepts, and systems. Death, hell (the grave), the beast, and the false prophet all cease to exist in this final judgment. These things are not cognizant entities, but consequences, conditions, and political-religious ideologies brought into existence by living beings seeking to escape God.

It is often claimed that Revelation 20:14 proves that the lake of fire is the second death, per se, but this is a hasty conclusion. It can and does refer, in one sense, to the second-death *process* or *experience*, but not a torment of living beings by literally imposed fire created by the power of God. The subject of this particular sentence is "death and hell." As already discussed, the lake of fire should be viewed as both its process (outer darkness, suffering of mental anguish) and end (the grand climax of the annihilation of matter).

The beast and false prophet are "cast alive" into the lake of fire (see 19:20). How is this so, seeing as these are religious-political-philosophical *systems*? It is found in the fact that the individual members of the wicked realm of impenitent humans and fallen angels have been expiring from the unquenchable-fire experience over a time period, and as they go down at various points on a timeline, the beast and false prophet are represented as being cast alive into the lake of fire.

It is highly likely that there will be an overlap of geophysical fires (to be discussed later as the "fire reservoir") encroaching upon the local scenes of human sufferings, with eruptions from the earth coming in, forming streams and lakes of lava, and the bodies of the wicked may end up being mingled in with these fires. Yet it is important that their expiry not be viewed as primarily caused by physical fires, or we come right back to the idea that God is using power to burn them. Their death would be by the experience of the mental fire that comes from the books being opened, wherein they ultimately surrender to their hopeless condition. This has been depicted in inspiration as that experience by which "every word they have spoken against the world's Redeemer will be reflected back upon them, and will one day burn into their guilty souls like molten lead" ("The Working of Satan," *The Signs of the Times*, April 12, 1883).

At this point of their observable surrender and declaration of the justice of God, it is not for us to say it would be impossible for anyone to get caught in physical fires and immediately perish, as is common to burning—by smoke inhalation and/or the destruction of the lungs with searing hot gases. Perhaps this will be the fate of some or even many. The main issue is that however it might unfold in its details, it must be apparent that it is in distinct contrast to the view that God simultaneously exerts His power in both positive and negative directions, i.e., using regenerating/creating power in keeping the function of nerve and brain intact while directly imposing a physical torture that would instantly kill were it not for His sustaining power. To dwell upon such a thought is hideous in its implications. God, being infinite in power, could bear down in this fashion to degrees unimaginable. This is monstrous, and we shall not try to imagine it, as many hell-fire advocates, past and present, have conjured up in the place of our "loving and kind" God. Never forget Luke 9:54–56 and the Lord's rebuke to those who would call down fiery torture on the heads of the wicked.

In yet another sense, the beast and false prophet are ultimately embodied in one individual: Satan. He will be the last one to succumb to his fate, so he can be represented truly as being "cast alive" into that lake. It is at that point that the ultimate lake of fire ignites. Satan's unquenchable-fire experience ends at the exact point where the lake-of-fire dissolution begins. The careful reader will understand by now that it is *all* "lake of fire."

In Revelation 20:10, the beast and false prophet are said to be present in the lake of fire. Again, these are ideological entities/philosophical systems built on principles of force and deception. The wicked are going extinct, and it is true that in the individuals are embodied the beast and false prophet systems. The fuel, which is separation from God through sin, for the final ignition of the lake of fire is being built up in a great heap upon the earth, as in the "much wood" of Tophet (see Isa. 30:33).

It appears as if they are alive and being tormented in it, but this is a representation of the Hebrew mind. Things aren't necessarily sequential, oftentimes written in a recapitulatory fashion. Their torment came in the form of the realization of the burden of sin, as we have discussed, but in this verse, the subject is not the torment of the wicked followers, but of the devil. "And the devil that deceived them was cast into the lake of fire and brimstone ... and shall be tormented day and night for ever and ever." The torment of Satan is the same as that of all the rest, only of longer duration and intensity.

Lake of Fire/Fire from the Midst as a Dual Metaphor

To recap with a brief comment, understand that the focus taken here may seem fuzzy, and that is because we are dealing with dual application.

On one hand, it is a depiction of the lake of fire/fire from the midst as having to do with its *endpoint* or that final blast that takes all matter out of existence. Do angels have matter? We don't know. If they do, this would be when it gets disposed. It may be that they just flash out of existence as energetic or spirit beings. It is "immaterial" in any case.

Yet, on the other hand, we rewind to emphasize an important point: the "lake of fire" and "fire from the midst" can also conceivably refer to that which transpires before—that process of the bearing of the burden of sin, which is a searing conscious suffering experience of the mind, in the unquenchable fire. There is room to make overlapping applications to various terms, while being careful to rule out that God uses His power to torture souls for even one second. As soon as we go there, we have a despot Deity.

The Fire of Fervent Heat that Dissolves Elements

There is another figure of speech used by Peter: the fire of "fervent heat," which melts the elements and burns them up. This represents the same as the "fire from the midst" and the "lake of fire" in its *final* phase, which is the cessation of matter in nuclear dissolution.

> But the day of the Lord will come as a thief in the night; in the which the **heavens shall pass away with a great noise**, and **the elements shall melt with fervent heat**, the earth also and the works that are therein shall be burned up.... Looking for and hasting unto the coming of the day of God, wherein **the heavens being on fire shall be dissolved, and the elements shall melt with fervent heat**? (2 Peter 3:10, 12, bold emphasis added)
>
> *While the earth was wrapped in the fire of destruction, the righteous abode safely in the Holy City.* Upon those that had part in the first resurrection, the second death has no power. *While God is to the wicked a consuming fire, He is to His people both a sun and a shield....*

> "I saw a new heaven and a new earth: for the first heaven and the first earth were passed away." Revelation 21:1. *The fire that consumes the wicked purifies the earth. Every trace of the curse is swept away*. No eternally burning hell will keep before the ransomed the fearful consequences of sin. (White, *The Great Controversy*, pp. 673, 674, emphasis added)

Just to make one observation of the above statement, "The fire that consumes the wicked purifies the earth," we would have to ask, Which fire is that? as we have several fires under consideration in this study. It is not unreasonable to understand this as pertaining to the *entire gamut* of fires.

1. The *unquenchable fire* consumes the wicked, and the earth is purified of wickedness.
2. The *literal fires of nature* will consume the dead bodies and, in some cases, likely instantly kill living persons—but this fire is not the one that is "prepared for the devil and his angels," for literal fires do not burn spiritual beings. That fire is the unquenchable fire. Though the literal fires will have their part in purifying the earth as well, they are not the entire picture.
3. The *final fire of fervent heat* (dissolution of matter) consumes the wicked dead and purifies the earth.

> When the flood of waters was at its height upon the earth, it had the appearance of a boundless lake of water. *When God finally purifies the earth, it will appear like a boundless lake of fire*. As God preserved the ark amid the commotions of the flood, because it contained eight righteous persons, he will preserve the New Jerusalem, containing the faithful of all ages, from righteous Abel down to the last saint which lived. Although the whole earth, with the exception of that portion where the city rests, will be wrapped in a sea of liquid fire, yet *the city is preserved as*

was the ark, by a miracle of Almighty power. It *stands unharmed amid the devouring elements*. "But the day of the Lord will come as a thief in the night; in the which the heavens shall pass away with a great noise, and the elements shall melt with fervent heat, the earth also, and the works that are therein shall be burned up." (White, *Spiritual Gifts*, pp. 87, 88, emphasis added)

The temperatures that are required to melt certain elements cannot be achieved by ordinary fires—not even the temperatures found inside the earth. We find in 2 Peter (above) that even the innards of the earth will be "burned up," so the heat at which we are here looking is hotter than this. The rocks themselves will burn up. Have we seen this before?

The Fire of Elijah's Altar as a Type of the Fire of Fervent Heat

This "fire of the LORD" is a type of the final consummation. "Then **the fire of the LORD** fell, and **consumed the burnt sacrifice**, and **the wood**, and **the stones**, and **the dust**, and licked up **the water** that *was* in the trench" (1 Kings 18:38, bold emphasis added).

The altar of sacrifice was situated in the outer court of the ancient sanctuary, which is a type of the earth, where Jesus came in His "outer court ministry." In the showdown at Elijah's altar between *YHWH* and Ba'al, we can see the lake of fire in type, in which ultimately the elements are themselves dissolved. They "melt with fervent heat." On top, we have the slain sacrifice, the symbol of sin and sinners. In the sense of metaphoric representation of the elemental dissolution, we can view the bullock as animal life. The wood is plant life. The stones and dust are the mineral base of the earth, as found in rocks and soil. The water represents all the bodies thereof. Atmosphere is not mentioned here, but it is mentioned elsewhere as the heavens that detonate loudly (see 2 Peter 3:10). We could very well assume that this fire also consumes the air surrounding the altar.

The Supper of the Great God

Birds are a symbol of dissolution/decomposition after death. "Yet within three days shall Pharaoh *lift up thy head from off thee*, and shall hang thee on a tree; and *the birds shall eat thy flesh* from off thee" (Gen. 40:19, emphasis added). There are no physical birds at end of millennium.

> I beheld the earth, and, lo, *it was* without form, and void; and the heavens, and they *had* no light. I beheld the mountains, and, lo, they trembled, and all the hills moved lightly. I beheld, and, lo, *there was* no man, and **all the birds of the heavens were fled**. I beheld, and, lo, the fruitful place *was* a wilderness, and all the cities thereof were broken down at the presence of the LORD, *and* by his fierce anger. For thus hath the LORD said, **The whole land shall be desolate; yet will I not make a full end**. (Jeremiah 4:23–27, bold emphasis added)

Christ is the ravenous bird from the east:

> Remember this, and shew yourselves men: bring *it* again to mind, O ye transgressors. Remember the former things of old: for I *am* God, and *there is* none else; *I am* God, and *there is* none like me, Declaring the end from the beginning, and from ancient times *the things* that are not *yet* done, saying, My counsel shall stand, and I will do all my pleasure: **Calling a ravenous bird from the east, the man that executeth my counsel from a far country**: yea, I have spoken *it*, I will also bring it to pass; I have purposed *it*, I will also do it. Hearken unto me, ye stouthearted, that *are* far from righteousness: **I bring near my righteousness**: it shall not be far off, and my salvation shall not tarry: and I will place salvation in Zion for Israel my glory....

> For thou hast trusted in thy wickedness: thou hast said, None seeth me. Thy wisdom and thy knowledge, it hath perverted thee; and thou hast said in thine heart, I *am*, and none else beside me. Therefore shall evil come upon thee; thou shalt not know from whence it riseth: and mischief shall fall upon thee; thou shalt not be able to put it off: and desolation shall come upon thee suddenly, *which* thou shalt not know.... Behold, they shall be as stubble; the fire shall burn them; they shall not deliver themselves from the power of the flame: **there shall not be a coal to warm at, nor fire to sit before it.** (Isaiah 46:8–13; 47:10, 11, 14, bold emphasis added)

See how, in this rich passage, God reveals His righteousness and establishes Himself as sovereign through the execution of His counsel via Christ, the "ravenous bird from the east," to those who would declare self as supreme, the result of which is desolation (or God abandonment) and death by fire unquenchable. It's all there.

The lake of fire, in its aspect of cleanup after the death of the wicked, is also represented by the figure of scavenging birds:

> And **out of his mouth goeth a sharp sword, that with it he should smite the nations:** and he shall rule them with a rod of iron: and he treadeth the winepress of the fierceness and wrath of Almighty God. And he hath on *his* vesture and on his thigh a name written, KING OF KINGS, AND LORD OF LORDS. And I saw an angel standing in the sun; and he cried with a loud voice, **saying to all the fowls that fly in the midst of heaven, Come and gather yourselves together unto the supper of the great God; That ye may eat the flesh of kings, and the flesh of captains, and the flesh of mighty men, and the flesh of horses, and of them that sit on them, and the flesh of all *men*, *both* free and bond, both small and great.** And I saw the beast, and the kings of the earth, and their armies,

gathered together to make war against him that sat on the horse, and against his army. And the beast was taken, and with him the false prophet that wrought miracles before him, with which he deceived them that had received the mark of the beast, and them that worshipped his image. These both were **cast alive into a lake of fire** burning with brimstone. And the remnant were **slain with the sword of him that sat upon the horse, which *sword* proceeded out of his mouth: and all the fowls were filled with their flesh**. (Revelation 19:15–21, bold emphasis added)

Note in verse 21 that the "remnant" were slain with the sword. This sword smites all the wicked (see vs. 15, 18). The remnant is not a group left over after all the others are slain. It is a representation of all those who were not caught up with Christ at the second coming.

This thought poses an interesting question in that, contextually, we are looking at the second coming. This means that there would likely be some birds, and we could take that literally. However, this would also mean the lake of fire has a pre-millennial counterpart. This makes sense, as we understand the lake of fire is primarily associated with the unquenchable-fire torment of the wicked coming face to face with God. (See them flee His presence and call for destruction on their heads in Revelation 6:16.) Therefore, that lake begins to seethe and boil at that time, yet it does not encompass all the wicked who ever lived or burn to its conclusion. It is only a representation of what is yet to come. There must be a final reckoning of all the wicked of history, together in the formal setting of the great-white-throne judgment scene.

The idea of two lakes of fire is not original to this study. This phrase, "lake of fire," immediately turns the reader's mind to an identical phrase in Revelation 20:10, which in turn seems to call for the conclusion that these phrases refer to the same fiery event, namely, the destruction of the wicked at the end of the thousand years. However, to do so presents a problem. Chapter 19 is most evidently discussing events in connection with the second coming of Christ. It is, therefore, a reasonable premise that there is a fiery judgment from God, both at the beginning and end of the millennium. There is certainly no inconsistency or contradiction in speaking of a lake of fire at both ends.

James White wrote thus on this point: "So, if you please, there are two lakes of fire, one at each end of the one thousand years" (RH Jan. 21, 1862) (*Seventh-day Adventist Bible Commentary*, Vol. 7, pp. 875, 876). This presents an interesting thought as we look at Peter's writing, which seems to be saying the day of the Lord has to do with the millennium (see 2 Peter 3:4–10). As the saints review the records of the wicked during the millennium, they are engaged in confirming the righteousness of God. In this sense, it is the day of the Lord—the millennial sabbath rest from His suffering of the creation in rebellion. It is the day that the work of His full vindication is carried forward: "Let God be true, but every man a liar; as it is written, That thou mightest be justified in thy sayings, and mightest overcome when thou art judged" (Rom. 3:4).

The Lake of Fire as a Cleanup Operation

One author provides further evidence to show that the lake of fire is a final cleanup and not an actual scene of mass torture, set up by God to punish sinners:

> First, the following text from Isaiah describes that same scene—*"And they shall go forth, and look upon the carcasses of the men that have transgressed against me: for their worm shall not die, neither shall their fire be quenched; and they shall be an abhorring unto all flesh."* (Isaiah 66:24)....
>
> Next, Jesus spoke of this also—*"And if thy hand offend thee, cut it off: it is better for thee to enter into life maimed, than having two hands to go into hell, into the fire that never shall be quenched."* (Mark 9:43) The word "hell" is translated from the Greek word

"Gehenna" which refers to the valley of Gehinnon, a place south of Jerusalem that had become a trash dump. That was where the trash and the dead animals and the bodies of dead criminals who had no relatives to bury them were thrown out to be burned. They did not throw people alive into that fire; it was only dead bodies that were thrown into the fire. (Bill Chambers, *The Healing Model: A Better Way to Understand Salvation*, pp. 152)

Yet more evidence is found in the Old Testament sacrificial system. David said in Psalm 73:3-5 *"For I was envious at the foolish, when I saw the prosperity of the wicked. For there are no bands in their death: but their strength is firm. They are not in trouble as other men; neither are they plagued like other men"* Then verse 17 says: *"Until I went into the sanctuary of God; then understood I their end."* David said he didn't understand the fate of the wicked until he went to the sanctuary. The sacrifices made at the sanctuary pre-figured the death of the sinner as well as Christ's death since He died the death of the sinner. When the lamb was placed on the altar to be burned was it alive or dead? It was dead of course. And by the way, who killed the lamb? Not God, but the sinner. Who killed Christ, the Lamb of God? Sinners!

Note another sacrificial ceremony in Solomon's day referred to in II Chronicles 7:1 *"Now when Solomon had made an end of praying, the fire came down from heaven, and consumed the burnt offering and the sacrifices."* In this passage, fire comes down from God out of heaven and devours the dead bodies of those animals on the altar, just as it will come down and consume the dead bodies of the wicked at the Great White Throne Judgment. I believe this is evidence enough to conclude that the wicked will be dead when *"fire comes down from God out of heaven and devours them."* (Bill Chambers, *The Healing Model: A Better Way to Understand Salvation*, pp. 153, 154)

The Fire of Dissolution at the Cross

We must find every doctrine centering in Christ and His cross, especially in relation to the events of His death and resurrection. The results of sin, we see there; the final death of the wicked, we must find there; even the final dissolution of the matter of the sinful body, we must observe there. To show that Jesus' body goes to the lake of fire/fire of fervent heat/fire from the midst, we must understand that these fleshly bodies do not go into eternal existence. The new body is a spiritual body. The matter that makes up the old body is taken out of existence—left behind.

> We must find every doctrine centering in Christ and His cross, especially in relation to the events of His death and resurrection.

Here are some points to keep in mind as we consider that the old body goes to hell, which is the grave, and this hell/grave goes to the "lake of fire" or non-existence:

- At the end of the millennium, the grave, called *hades* or "hell," is cast into the lake of fire, which is a fire of dissolution. Everything that goes there goes out of existence.
- *Christ* left His old body of sinful flesh, subject to death, in hell (or the grave); He arose glorified.
- *Those who have died in Christ* likewise leave the old body in the grave and come forth "with Him," glorified and incorruptible (see 1 Cor. 15:50–53; Rom. 6:5, 8:17; Col. 3:4).
- *The wicked dead* have come back into existence in these material, corruptible bodies, which "bear the traces of disease and death" (White, *The Great Controversy*, p. 662), and these bodies will again fall on the earth and be subject to the fire of fervent heat that converts them to energy.
- *The righteous living* are instantly changed at His coming, and their old bodies are gone out of existence.

There are undoubtedly some studies in quantum mechanics to be applied here, into which our physicists will delight to delve in the eternal future, but we don't have enough light or science to intelligently discuss the underlying cessation of the corruptible bodies of the righteous at the resurrection and translation in particular. I am not engaging in pure speculation here, but extrapolating from what has been revealed about the resurrection of the dead at the second coming:

> Our personal identity is preserved in the resurrection, *though not the same particles of matter or material substance as went into the grave*. The wondrous works of God are a mystery to man. The spirit, the character of man, is returned to God, there to be preserved.... *There is no law of God in nature which shows that God gives back the same identical particles of matter* which composed the body before death. God shall give the righteous dead a body that will please Him. (White, *The SDA Bible Commentary*, Vol. 6, p. 1093, emphasis added)

As all sin-tainted matter goes out of existence in the fire of fervent heat, so too would the matter of the old bodies. God does not use that matter to recreate new, glorified, spiritual bodies. The new creation is of entirely new material, brought into existence by the word of God—from nothing. He formed the first man, Adam, from the earth and breathed into him the breath of life, and he is described as "earthy" in 1 Corinthians 15:47–49. The second Adam, Jesus, is heavenly, and we will bear His image, both in thought, mind, and character *and* our tangible existence as dimensional beings wherein that mind resides.

Notice what we discover regarding the resurrection body:

> The Sadducees reasoned that *if* [in the resurrection] *the body is to be composed of the same particles of matter in its immortal as in its mortal state, then when raised from the dead it must have flesh*

> *and blood*, and must resume in the eternal world the life interrupted on earth....
>
> In answer to their questions, *Jesus lifted the veil from the future life....* He showed that the Sadducees were wrong in their belief. *Their premises were false.* "Ye do err," He added, "not knowing the Scriptures, nor the power of God." He did not charge them, as He had charged the Pharisees, with hypocrisy, but with *error of belief*. (White, *The Desire of Ages*, p. 605, emphasis added)

In this discussion, it is paramount that we study 1 Corinthians 15:35–37 and 42–53. We find there a very clear teaching that the old, flesh-and-blood bodies, the corrupt, sinful bodies in which we now live, are going to be no more. Where do they go? Not out like a light, but out of existence altogether. No empty shell is left behind.

Will there be a flash of light and heat in an energy release, or will it be a clean conversion, with that energy being used to bring the glorified spiritual body into existence in the very same moment as the "twinkling of an eye" about which Paul speaks? We do not know and can only wait and see, but these are interesting things to ponder as we look forward to beholding and understanding.

Christ did not leave behind a body, and neither will the resurrected and translated saints. The wicked are in a radically different situation, in that they are raised corruptible:

> At the close of the thousand years, Christ again returns to the earth.... As He descends in terrific majesty He bids the wicked dead arise to receive their doom. They come forth, a mighty host, numberless as the sands of the sea. *What a contrast to those who were raised at the first resurrection! The righteous were clothed with immortal youth and beauty. The wicked bear the traces of disease and death.* (White, *The Great Controversy*, p. 662, emphasis added)

These corruptible bodies will expire through the process of the great-white-throne judgment and revelation and lie on the earth, to be devoured by the elements and at last puff out of material existence entirely in the fire of fervent heat. Let's read the Bible:

> But **some** *man* **will say, How are the dead raised up? And with what body do they come?** *Thou* **fool, that which thou sowest is not quickened, except it die: And that which thou sowest, thou sowest not that body that shall be, but bare grain**, it may chance of wheat, or of some other *grain*… **So also** *is* **the resurrection of the dead. It is sown in corruption; it is raised in incorruption**: It is sown in dishonor; it is raised in glory: it is sown in weakness; it is raised in power: **It is sown a natural body; it is raised a spiritual body**. There is a natural body, and there is a spiritual body. And so it is written, The first man Adam was made a living soul; **the last Adam** *was made* **a quickening spirit**. Howbeit that *was* not first which is spiritual, but that which is natural; and afterward that which is spiritual. **The first man** *is* **of the earth, earthy: the second man** *is* **the Lord from heaven**. As *is* the earthy, such *are* they also that are earthy: and as *is* the heavenly, such *are* they also that are heavenly. And as we have borne the image of the earthy, we shall also bear the image of the heavenly. Now this I say, brethren, that **flesh and blood cannot inherit the kingdom of God; neither doth corruption inherit incorruption**. Behold, I shew you a mystery; We shall not all sleep, but **we shall all be changed**, In a moment, in the twinkling of an eye, at the last trump: for the trumpet shall sound, and **the dead shall be raised incorruptible**, and we shall be changed. For **this corruptible must put on incorruption**, and this mortal *must* put on immortality. (1 Corinthians 15:35–37, 42–53, bold emphasis added)

And Jesus answered them, saying, **The hour is come, that the Son of man should be glorified**. Verily, verily, I say unto you,

> **Except a corn of wheat fall into the ground and die**, it abideth alone: but **if it die, it bringeth forth much fruit**. (John 12:23, 24, bold emphasis added)

Jeremiah depicts fire at the cross:

> *Is it* nothing to you, all ye that pass by? behold, and **see if there be any sorrow like unto my sorrow**, which is done unto me, **wherewith the LORD hath afflicted** *me* **in the day of his fierce anger**. From above hath **he sent fire into my bones**, and it prevaileth against them: he hath spread a net for my feet, he hath turned me back: he hath **made me desolate** *and* faint all the day. (Lamentations 1:12, 13, bold emphasis added)

Primarily, this lament is for Jerusalem. However, Ellen White connects it to the experience of Christ:

> During His thirty years of life on earth His heart was wrung with inconceivable anguish. The path from the manger to Calvary was shadowed by grief and sorrow. He was a man of sorrows, and acquainted with grief, enduring such heartache as no human language can portray. He could have said in truth, *"Behold, and see if there be any sorrow like unto my sorrow."* (White, *God's Amazing Grace*, p. 172, emphasis added)

The Fire Reservoir

Under the hand of God, nature ministers against the transgressors of God's laws. She holds her destructive elements in her bosom till the time when they shall break forth to destroy man and purify the earth. (White, *Manuscript Releases*, Vol. 3, p. 344)

How shall I give thee up, Ephraim? *how* shall I deliver thee, Israel? how shall I make thee as Admah? *how* shall I set thee as Zeboim? (Hosea 11:8)

Frequently we hear of earthquakes, of tempests and tornadoes, accompanied with thunder and lightning. Apparently these are capricious outbreaks of seemingly disorganized, unregulated forces. But God has a purpose in *permitting these calamities to occur*....

Local *disturbances in nature are permitted to take place* as symbols of that which may be expected all over the world when the angels loose the four winds of the earth. The forces of nature are under the direction of an Eternal Agency. Science, in her pride, may seek to explain strange happenings on land and on sea; but science fails of tracing in these things the workings of Providence. (White, *Manuscript Releases*, Vol. 19, pp, 279, 280, emphasis added)

The Relationship Between Nature and Sin

We have covered this ground under the previous section and now come back to it to discuss the mechanics of how nature goes to chaos and its relationship to increased levels of wickedness. The powers of nature are not fueled by non-renewable resources. What is the "glue" that we call weak and strong nuclear forces, magnetism, and gravity? These are all to be considered as maintained by the unseen hand of God, with a power that emanates directly from His being (see Acts 17:28; Col. 1:17).

God has finished his creative work, but *his energy is still exerted in upholding the objects of his creation*. It is not because the mechanism that has once been set in motion continues its work by its own inherent energy that the pulse beats and breath follows breath; but every breath, every pulsation of the heart, is an evidence of the all-pervading care of Him in whom we live and have our being.

> It is not because of inherent power that year by year the earth produces her bounties and continues her motion around the sun. *The hand of God guides the planets*, and keeps them in position in their orderly march through the heavens. *It is through his power that vegetation flourishes*, that the leaves appear and the flowers bloom. *His word controls the elements*, and by him the valleys are made fruitful. He covers the heavens with clouds, and prepares rain for the earth; he "maketh grass to grow upon the mountains." "He giveth snow like wool; he scattereth the hoar frost like ashes." "When he uttereth his voice, there is a multitude of waters in the heavens, and he causeth the vapors to ascend from the ends of the earth; he maketh lightnings with rain, and bringeth forth the wind out of his treasures." ("Science and the Bible in Education," *The Signs of the Times*, March 20, 1884, emphasis added)

There is a link between the dominion that humanity was given over the earth and the state of nature. The smooth operation of all nature, as a totally beneficent circuit of provision for the perfect function of all things animate and inanimate, would proceed continually as His created beings continued under His loving care. Conversely, we must expect nature to be fatally damaged through impaired function if humanity were to turn from God. The same power that guides and sustains humanity would be withdrawn from nature as it also withdraws from humanity through its apostasy. There is a direct relationship.

> And unto Adam he said, Because thou hast hearkened unto the voice of thy wife, and hast eaten of the tree, of which I commanded thee, saying, Thou shalt not eat of it: cursed *is* the ground for thy sake; in sorrow shalt thou eat *of* it all the days of thy life; Thorns also and thistles shall it bring forth to thee; and thou shalt eat the herb of the field. (Genesis 3:17, 18)

> *Christ never planted the seeds of death in the system.* Satan planted these seeds when he tempted Adam to eat of the tree of

knowledge, which meant disobedience to God. Not one noxious plant was placed in the Lord's great garden, but after Adam and Eve sinned, poisonous herbs sprang up. In the parable of the sower the question was asked the master, "Didst not thou sow good seed in thy field? From whence then hath it tares?" The master answered, "An enemy hath done this." [Matthew 13:27, 28.] *All tares are sown by the evil one.* Every noxious herb is of his sowing, and by his ingenious methods of amalgamation he has corrupted the earth with tares. (White, *Manuscript Releases*, Vol. 16, p. 247, emphasis added)

But not only had man come under the power of the deceiver, *but the earth itself, the dominion of man, was usurped by the enemy.* ("The Plan of Salvation," *The Signs of the Times*, February 13, 1893, emphasis added)

The first curse was pronounced upon the posterity of Adam and upon the earth, because of disobedience. The second curse came upon the ground after Cain slew his brother Abel. The third most dreadful curse from God, came upon the earth at the flood. (White, *Spiritual Gifts*, Vol. 4a, p. 121)

The evil consequent upon the indulgence of depraved appetite is widespread, and *the earth is corrupted under the inhabitants thereof.* The earth withereth under the curse of its sin, and the very cattle are diseased. What is the trouble? *Why is this? It is because the people have forsaken the law of God, and the earth is cursed under its transgression.* Notwithstanding the warnings of God's word, *transgression has increased since the days of Adam, and more and more heavily has the curse pressed upon the human family, on the beasts of the earth, and on the earth itself.* Continual transgression of the law of God has brought its sure results. ("The Liquor Traffic Working Counter to Christ," *The Review and Herald*, May 8, 1894, emphasis added)

> **There is a link between the dominion that humanity was given over the earth and the state of nature. The smooth operation of all nature, as a totally beneficent circuit of provision for the perfect function of all things animate and inanimate, would proceed continually as His created beings continued under His loving care. Conversely, we must expect nature to be fatally damaged through impaired function if humanity were to turn from God.**

Thus, we can see that as mankind departs further and further from God and His righteousness, nature also becomes more and more chaotic. The great flood is "exhibit A" in this testimony against humanity. "Hast thou marked the old way which wicked men have trodden? Which were cut down out of time, whose foundation was overflown with a flood: Which said unto God, Depart from us: and what can the Almighty do for them?" (Job 22:15–17)

Nature cannot function aright without God in it. As He is the power that upholds nature, it would not make sense for Him to be told to leave and expect He should stay to uphold it so that it might continue to function as always through His momentary provision for the upkeep of beings that have sent Him away. It may be that the rebel does not in words say, "Go away, God," but a disregard for His law communicates that very thing. Actions are louder than words are. The words may be, "We love you God, bless us we pray," while the soul is in flagrant disobedience of His Word. This is insincere and destructive. It grants even more power to the enemy to work:

> There are many who profess the name of Christ whose hearts are not engaged in his service. They have simply arrayed

themselves in a profession of godliness, and by this very act they have made greater their condemnation, and have become more deceptive and more successful agents of Satan in the ruin of souls. ("Nothing is Hidden," *The Review and Herald*, March 27, 1888)

In the Scriptures, there is the portrayal, in figurative language, of the earth as having a mouth. The earth receives sin:

And the LORD said unto Cain, Where *is* Abel thy brother? And he said, I know not: *Am* I my brother's keeper? And he said, What hast thou done? the **voice of thy brother's blood crieth unto me from the ground**. And now *art* thou **cursed from the earth, which hath opened her mouth to receive thy brother's blood** from thy hand. (Genesis 4:9–11, bold emphasis added)

This ingestion of sin makes the earth sick:

And the land is defiled: therefore I do visit the iniquity thereof upon it, and the land itself vomiteth out her inhabitants.... (For all these abominations have the men of the land done, which *were* before you, and the land is defiled;) That the land spue not you out also, when ye defile it, as it spued out the nations that *were* before you. (Leviticus 18:25, 27, 28)

Seeing that increased wickedness is the cause of increased entropy in nature, it only makes sense that at the height of total wickedness, all nature will come apart.

Behold, **the LORD maketh the earth empty, and maketh it waste**, and turneth it upside down, and scattereth abroad the inhabitants thereof.... The land shall be utterly emptied, and utterly spoiled: for the LORD hath spoken this word. The **earth**

mourneth *and* **fadeth away**, the world languisheth *and* fadeth away, the haughty people of the earth do languish. The **earth also is defiled under the inhabitants thereof**; because they have transgressed the laws, changed the ordinance, broken the everlasting covenant. Therefore hath the curse devoured the earth, and they that dwell therein are desolate: **therefore the inhabitants of the earth are burned**, and few men left. (Isaiah 24:1, 3–6, bold emphasis added)

Just prior to the revealing of Christ at the second coming, the entire mass of humanity will close in, with murderous intent, upon a relatively small group of those who remain faithful. At this point, the earth convulses in a total upheaval of nature in one "great conflagration," yet it does not finish before all the wicked expire. There are all the wicked *fallen angel* inhabitants left alive to bicker and growl among themselves, along with the unfinished business with the millions of sleeping souls who do not come up until the end of the millennium, when nature again spends herself in chaos.

At the end, all the wicked beings of all time, both angels and humans, are together united against the God of heaven and Lord of all creation. Their attack on the Holy City is their final declaration of separation from God, and it will bring about a complete collapse of nature that will cause not only the wicked beings but the elements themselves to go to a full cessation of existence. "Behold, the righteous shall be recompensed in the earth: much more the wicked and the sinner" (Prov. 11:31).

At the Second Coming, There Is Geophysical Fire Under the Seventh Plague

This is not to say that it is the *only* fire at that time, for there is also a taste of the unquenchable fire, which will burn to its conclusion at the end of the millennium as the wicked are terrified at being visibly, physically confronted with divinity. Our focus in this section is upon the physical fires with which we are more familiar—the stuff of disasters.

> And saying, Where is the promise of his coming? for since the fathers fell asleep, all things continue as *they were* from the beginning of the creation. For this they willingly are ignorant of, that by **the word of God the heavens were of old**, and the earth standing out of the water and in the water: Whereby the world that then was, being overflowed with water, perished: But **the heavens and the earth, which are now, by the same word are kept in store**, **reserved unto fire** against the day of judgment and perdition of ungodly men. (2 Peter 3:4–7, bold emphasis added)

In this text, you have a depiction of the old world being upheld by the word of God. In that world, you had an entirely different ecology. There was a water reservoir in the mantle above the earth and great reservoirs beneath. The flood occurred as these were both released. The changes wrought in this cataclysmic event have now predisposed the world for another destruction, only not by water this time. The water event cannot happen again. It has broken forth already. Now there is a geophysical destabilization in the earth's crust and massive amounts of vegetative matter buried under the earth. Both of these together are a reservoir of fire and will be "called forth," to use the biblical parlance, when again the Lord should withdraw His protective and sustaining powers.

> In the day of the Lord, *just before the coming of Christ*, God will send *lightnings from Heaven in His wrath, which will unite with fire in the earth*. The *mountains will burn* like a furnace, and will *pour forth terrible streams of lava*, destroying gardens and fields, villages and cities; and as they *pour their melted ore, rocks and heated mud* into the rivers, will cause them to boil like a pot, and send forth massive rocks and scatter their broken fragments upon the land with indescribable violence. Whole rivers will be dried up. The earth will be convulsed, and there will be dreadful eruptions and earthquakes everywhere. God will

plague the wicked inhabitants of the earth until they are destroyed from off it.

The *earth shall reel to and fro like a drunkard*, and be removed as a cottage. The *elements shall be in flames*, and the *heavens shall be rolled together as a scroll.*

The *earth's crust will be rent by the outbursts of the elements concealed in the bowels of the earth.* These elements, once broken loose, will sweep away the treasures of those who for years have been adding to their wealth by securing large possessions at starvation prices from those in their employ.

The great general conflagration is but just ahead, when all this wasted labor of life will be swept away in a night and day.

There will be … great destruction of human life. But as in the days of the great deluge Noah was preserved in the ark that God had prepared for him, so in these days of destruction and calamity, God will be the refuge of His believing ones. Through the psalmist He declares, "Because thou has made the Lord, which is my refuge, even the most High, thy habitation; there shall no evil befall thee, neither shall any plague come nigh thy dwelling." "For in the time of trouble he shall hide me in his pavilion…." Then shall we not make the Lord our surety and our defense? (White, *Maranatha*, p. 283, emphasis added)

In the day of His [Christ's] coming, the last great trumpet is heard, and there is a terrible shaking of earth and heaven. The whole earth, from the loftiest mountains to the deepest mines, will hear. Everything will be penetrated by fire. The tainted atmosphere will be cleansed by fire.

The fire having fulfilled its mission, the dead that have been laid away in the grave will come forth—some to the resurrection of life, to be caught up to meet their Lord in the air, and *some to behold the coming of Him whom they have despised*, and whom they now recognize as the judge of all the earth. (White, *Manuscript Releases*, Vol. 8, p. 347, emphasis added)

> *All the righteous are untouched by the flames. They can walk through the fire*, as Shadrach, Meshach, and Abednego walked in the midst of the furnace heated seven times hotter than it was wont to be heated. The Hebrew worthies could not be consumed, because the form of the fourth, the Son of God, was with them. So in the day of the coming of the Lord, smoke and flame will be powerless to harm the righteous. Those who are united with the Lord will escape unscathed. Earthquakes, hurricanes, flame, and flood cannot injure those who are prepared to meet their Saviour in peace. (White, *The Upward Look*, p. 261, emphasis added)

The Fire Reservoir Plays a Part After the Millennium

In the previous text, we have given clear references to the geophysical fires coming forth at the second coming. In the following text, we have these fires also being applied at the final destruction after the thousand years:

> Those majestic trees which God had caused to grow upon the earth, for the benefit of the inhabitants of the old world, and which they had used to form into idols, and to corrupt themselves with, *God has reserved in the earth, in the shape of coal and oil to use as agencies in their final destruction*. As he called forth the waters in the earth at the time of the flood, as weapons from his arsenal to accomplish the destruction of the antediluvian race, *so at the end of the one thousand years he will call forth the fires in the earth as his weapons* which he has reserved for the final destruction, not only of successive generations since the flood, *but the antediluvian race who perished by the flood*.
>
> When the flood of waters was at its height upon the earth, it had the appearance of a boundless lake of water. *When God finally purifies the earth, it will appear like a boundless lake of fire. As God preserved the ark amid the commotions of the flood,*

because it contained eight righteous persons, *he will preserve the New Jerusalem, containing the faithful of all ages*, from righteous Abel down to the last saint which lived. Although *the whole earth, with the exception of that portion where the city rests, will be wrapped in a sea of liquid fire, yet the city is preserved as was the ark, by a miracle of Almighty power. It stands unharmed amid the devouring elements.* "But the day of the Lord will come as a thief in the night; *in the which the heavens shall pass away with a great noise, and the elements shall melt with fervent heat*, the earth also, and the works that are therein shall be burned up." (White, *Spiritual Gifts*, Vol. 3, pp. 87, 88, emphasis added)

Note that the "day of the Lord" is a phrase applied to events both before and after the millennium. Both ends of this period have to do with all the fires under discussion, except for the final dispersion of matter into energy, which is at the very end of the post-millennial GWT scene. To unpack this further, in the previous quote, we have a depiction of the fires in the earth: the geophysical fire, *morphing* into the fire of fervent heat, which is the atomic fire, in the completion of the lake-of-fire sequence. She has seen the geophysical fire play a part in the ruination of the earth at the second coming, and it could not have, at that time, spent itself entirely if it is again called forth at the end of the millennium.

Even as it comes forth in this final scenario, it cannot be the same as the fire of fervent heat, which, at the end of the "lake of fire," takes all things out of existence. In that fire, the elemental earth, with all its inner workings, burns up, and the heavens pass away with a great noise (see 2 Peter 3:10). Not all elements melt, burn up, or "consume away" at ordinary fire temperatures or even augmented temperatures achievable by human technology. The elements may change states yet remain in existence no matter how much heat we apply to them. The only exception to this is certain fissile materials that exist as isotopes of certain elements. Unfortunately, we have learned how to take some forms of matter out of existence altogether.

At the beginning of the thousand-year period, there is a great fire, but matter is left behind. The earth is still here, a broken-down pile of rubble; a dark hunk of material put on ice for a thousand years, with no light, for the sun will be extinguished (see Isa. 13:9, 10; 24:21–23; Ezek. 32:7; Joel 2:10; etc.). It will be a most dismal prison house for the devils.

The post-millennial replay of geophysical fire would also present to the prophetic, visionary eye as a great "boundless lake of fire," but it is not the same type of fire as is the dissolving fire of fervent heat. As Satan expires, his unquenchable-fire experience, along with the physical fires from the earth environment, give way to the fire that melts the elements, which is the nuclear fire of the power of God that operates as the binding forces that hold together the material universe. These two fires end with the dissolving of matter.

There arises a question regarding how unprotected human beings, in the GWT environment, can survive the outbreaks of geophysical-atmospheric fires. We cannot say with certainty, but we can think of some plausible explanations:

- Perhaps, in the sequence of events, this postmillennial round of geophysical fire would come in just as the entirety of the wicked *human* population will have expired. God will surely release nature according to righteousness, seeing the need for timing, so that the wicked be preserved long enough to fully process their individual hell. This is how, in the biblical language, God "torments them day and night forever and ever"; or
- perhaps these fires break out at geographic locations *away* from the environs of the Holy City, where all the wicked are congregated to execute war but find instead they have finally come up before the judgment bar of God; or
- it may be that humans are in these fires, not being tortured in them, but miraculously preserved from being subject to them until it is appropriate to let them go. In this scenario, as the various individual rebels come to the end of their process, they would be given up to whatever

death awaits, whether by stress-induced heart attack (cardiomyopathy), violence among themselves, suicide, lightning, meteoric explosions, or volcanic eruption.

Why this is a point of discussion is because we must have an observable phenomenon where it is seen that the second death of the wicked occurs from a cognitive process ending in an acknowledgment of their choice and its consequence of eternal death. This would be understood by all as a request for God to let them go. The observing universe would understand completely that their expiry is not the result of the proactive use of divine power to execute the wicked. All the wicked must clearly demonstrate they are going into oblivion by choice. The Scriptures declare that every knee will bow and every tongue confess the righteousness of God. When the finally impenitent, wicked soul shall make such a declaration with full cognition of the consequences, it is a request for it to be over—for God to let them expire forever.

A point to note is that demons can be alive and untouched by the geophysical fires, so while the earth is again breaking apart, they are still suffering the unquenchable fire as they process seven millennia of pure, dedicated evil, which saturated every thought and intent of their hearts and minds.

To close this section, I would again refer to Bill Chambers' *The Healing Model* for further thought on why we have all this final revelation in the climax of the great controversy:

> Now that they acknowledge and bow before Him, would the Lord have mercy on them if they would now surrender their heart to Him? Before you answer, remember God said *"I change not"*—He is the same *"Yesterday, today, and forever."*
>
> The Bible says *"His mercy is from everlasting to everlasting"* (Psalm 103:17) That means it never ends! So, instead of, 'Will God give them another chance?' shouldn't the question be, since the wicked now see the truth about God so clearly, "Will they now surrender their hearts to Him?" Sadly, the answer is that even if God gave them another chance, they would not take advantage of it. They will not repent no matter what. At the Great White Throne Judgment, it will be clear that if even as the wicked witness everything God has done with their own eyes, they still *will not* repent!
>
> In this way the entire universe will witness the result of sin on the human heart. Sin changes people—not in a superficial or legal way, but sin, if not reversed or healed, changes and hardens the heart against God and His law of unselfish love to the point that there is no hope of recovery! They will never change! They can't, they are incurable! And being incurable, they will die.
>
> God could prevent their death, but He has said He *'will by no means clear the guilty"*—He will give them up to *"reap that which they have sown."* (Bill Chambers, *The Healing Model: Understanding How God Saves,* pp. 103, 104)

Like the waters of the Flood the fires of the great day declare God's verdict that the wicked are incurable. They have no disposition to submit to divine authority. Their will has been exercised in revolt; and when life is ended, it is too late to turn the current of their thoughts in the opposite direction, too late to turn from transgression to obedience, from hatred to love. (White, *The Great Controversy*, p. 543)

Summing Up the Three Fires

[Note: See also Appendix B: A Synopsis of the Fires]

Unquenchable Fire—Synonymous metaphors include "the worm that does not die," "chains of everlasting darkness," and "outer darkness." It is at the full revelation of Deity in His character-glory that the books of the mind are opened, bringing terrible realization. This is the personal bearing of sin, causing anguish and psycho-emotional hell, with weeping, despair, and "gnashing of teeth." The sweet release of physical death comes at the right time as they make either tacit or open requests for God to give them up.

Geophysical/Meteorological/Cosmic Fires (forces of nature)—These kill nobody before the unquenchable fire does its work. These are fires of natural forces gone to chaos—fires from in the earth, from storms, lightning, incoming space objects, etc. This fire also produces what could be called a "lake of fire" in a more literal and visible sense, but we must be careful never to put living sufferers in this fire as though sustained by God *in it*, to be kept there roasting alive for a duration of torture. Once a physical body is embroiled in flame, if it is not already a dead body, it is one that will expire in seconds.

Fire of Fervent Heat—This is the final and ultimate withdrawal of God's power—His "strange act"—from all matter that has been tainted with sin and its effects. The terms "fire from the midst" and the "lake of fire" also embrace this fire, when viewed in reference to their endpoint.

We have looked at three kinds of fires having to do with the demise of sinners and final eradication of all that has been touched by sin, without implicating God as the executioner of the sentence against transgression. In biblical language, the entire discussion, with its classification and qualifications of the fires, comes under the heading "Fire from God out of

Heaven." Additionally, it is all the "lake of fire" and "fire from the midst" in their various nuances or phases of operation.

We have covered how sinners are first consumed by the experience called the "unquenchable fire," which is the realization of the truth about God and their own role in the great controversy, as well as a coming to terms with their present status and choice. We examined how they will, at last, one by one, give up their struggle and accept the death they understand they have *chosen*. This all takes place in the context of the great-white-throne judgment and its aftermath. This unquenchable fire is also represented as the worm that does not die, the place of outer darkness, weeping, and gnashing of teeth, and like depictions. It is hell. This suffering is also depicted by the metaphor of the lake of fire in its *process phase*.

The wicked fall at different points of time, some taking much longer than do others as their burden of sin is much greater, and each one must process through the guilt, shame, and bearing in themselves, without blaming God or others, all their sin and wickedness, as we read that every act will come before them in review.

As all this is happening, there is a point where God's sustaining power is withdrawn further from natural forces, resulting in geological upheavals. There are firestorms and molten elements, but these are not the thing that destroys the wicked in the primary sense. That process that ends the life is a cognitive one, which gives way at last to the physical.

The wicked must clearly demonstrate their choice is to reject God, and it cannot be seen that He is in any way creating an arbitrary execution of the death sentence that is upon them due to sin itself. Their death is not by His decree but entirely of their own determination. This entire demonstration is not only for their own mental closure but also the mental closure of all the redeemed and the onlooking universe. It is the only way the final security of the entire inhabited universe can be achieved. There can never be any more question about the character of God or the nature of sin.

Satan takes the longest to process his own sin. As he goes down, the time will have arrived when God releases the entirety of sin-tainted creation. All of its physical elements come apart in that which is called the "lake of fire" in its *culmination phase,* a term synonymous with "fire of fervent heat" or "the fire from/in the midst," as described with metaphors like "smoke ascending forever," "smoke consuming away," "fire from the Lord," or even scavenging birds. These are all depictions of matter going out of existence.

Note that ordinary fires of oxidative combustion cannot cleanse the earth and solar system of all traces of sin. There are radioactive poisons that will not be destroyed in this way and which are even now spreading all over the earth, as well as many other detrimental compounds. Heat will not neutralize or cleanse some of these. Some of them have "half-lives" of thousands of years. God is letting all these elements dissolve at the atomic level. He is letting them go to the "mother of all chain reactions," where every atom and molecule coverts to pure energy. This will be a tremendous nuclear explosion, while the righteous ride through it in the ark of the Holy City. After this, God will recreate all things from nothing, as He did in the beginning. "Behold, I make all things new," says our God (Rev. 21:5).

Let us hasten the day as we prepare our hearts to stand in His sight, dwelling in the everlasting burnings with eternal joy, gladness, praise, and thanksgiving.

Appendix A: *The Great Controversy*, Chapter 42

A Study of the Sequence of Events in "The Controversy Ended"

Note: The reader is encouraged to work through this content not only to gain insights into the language used in the Spirit of Prophecy and the flow/timeline of its narrative, but also for some of the additional discussion points or nuances that may not have been brought forward in the main body of this study.

Guide to Reading

- The following numbered list is given as an advance summation of the narrative of chapter 42 of *The Great Controversy* (1888 version, rather than 1911). The points are in their order, following the original writing from beginning to end.
- **Then in the analysis section, each point functions as a section heading, in bold, followed by full citation of the corresponding segment from chapter 42 of *The Great Controversy*, in black.**
- **Finally, interspersed within the text of chapter 42 is the author's discussion and analysis.**

1. Christ and the redeemed return to earth at the end of the thousand years, and He raises the wicked dead. The unwilling lips of the wicked say, "Blessed is He that cometh in the name of the Lord."
2. Satan determines not to yield the controversy.
3. Satan moves among the people, declaring it was his power that raised them up. He works miracles to strengthen them and continues to teach them that he is the rightful ruler of the earth and God has stolen the kingdom from him. He declares that God would be a most cruel tyrant over them, should He win this war. The mighty people of earth solidify plans and organize their forces to produce again the implements of war. They marshal themselves into armies in preparation for an attack upon the city of God and its inhabitants. *This* is an army such as never was ever before on the earth.
4. They march against the city.
5. They are stopped in their tracks as Christ appears above the city and His brightness floods the land.
6. The King of kings is duly coronated in the presence of the angels and all who have ever lived on the earth.
7. The great-white-throne judgment begins. Consciousness of sin begins to bear down upon them.
8. God produces a panoramic view above the throne, wherein there is a great visual/psychological replay of the plan of salvation, and each one sees the part he or she played in rejecting God. All this includes Satan and his angels. Every eye is riveted to the scene.
9. There is an unfolding of realization—of *seeing*—of awakening—with the clarity of a total recall of not only the choices and actions, but also of motives—the thoughts and intents of the heart. They are awash in revelation, made fully aware of absolute and ultimate reality. Lost souls see they have no excuse for themselves. They are unable to avoid coming to the full psychological and

spiritual appropriation of what they have forfeited—eternal life. They desire to hide from the face of Christ.

10. Satan himself goes through the same process. As he beholds the majesty of Christ, he sees the mighty angel that now has the place that he forsook. He remembers his former station in heaven, where he dwelt in complete peace and contentment. The whole story of his own rebellion is brought back to his view, and he is reminded how he made no effort to turn from the path of folly when he had the chance to do so. He knows his position is false, as he has already been subjected to numerous defeats in the great controversy. Satan sees that he has unfitted himself for heaven and its environment would be torture. His accusations are silenced. He bows and confesses the justice of his sentence. Satan's confession reveals that he knows God is right, and he has gone beyond the point of no return and therefore must go out of existence.

11. Even though Satan has openly confessed God's justice before Him and all the inhabitants of the universe—both the righteous and the wicked—and knows very well that it is finished for him, he is not yet ready to let go. In an enraged and fevered state of mind, he attempts to whip up his host into immediate warfare.

12. There are none who will go Satan's way anymore. They are done with him. Yet, like their ruler whom they chose, they are not changed in heart in any way. They still have no desire for God. They are filled only with despair and rage as they see their hopeless condition. They are infuriated against Satan and his agents of deception.

13. The wicked "turn upon" Satan and his agents. They "draw their swords against the beauty of Satan's wisdom and they defile his brightness, bringing him down to the pit." He is "cast to the ground." "The terrible of nations," "kings of the earth," behold him. In their sight he is "brought to ashes." He is destroyed.

An Analysis and Commentary of "The Controversy Ended"

1. **Christ and the redeemed return to earth at the end of the thousand years, and He raises the wicked dead. The unwilling lips of the wicked say, "Blessed is He that cometh in the name of the Lord."**

    "*At the close of the thousand years, Christ again returns to the earth.* He is accompanied by the host of the redeemed, and attended by a retinue of angels. As he descends in terrific majesty, *he bids the wicked dead arise to receive their doom.* They come forth, a mighty host, numberless as the sands of the sea. What a contrast to those who were raised at the first resurrection! The righteous were clothed with immortal youth and beauty. The wicked bear the traces of disease and death.

    "Every eye in that vast multitude is turned to behold the glory of the Son of God. *With one voice the wicked hosts exclaim, 'Blessed is He that cometh in the name of the Lord!' It is not love to Jesus that inspires this utterance. The force of truth urges the words from unwilling lips.* As the wicked went into their graves, so they come forth, with the same enmity to Christ, and the same spirit of rebellion. *They are to have no new probation, in which to remedy the defects of their past lives. Nothing would be gained by this. A life-time of transgression has not softened their hearts. A second probation, were it given them, would be occupied as was the first, in evading the requirements of God and exciting rebellion against him*" (p. 662, emphasis added).

    This will be proven as they work right along with Satan and his agenda to overcome the city.

    "Christ descends upon the Mount of Olives, whence, after his resurrection, he ascended, and where angels repeated the promise of his return. Says the prophet, 'The Lord my God shall come, and all the saints with thee.' 'And his feet shall stand in that day upon the Mount of Olives, which is before Jerusalem on the east, and the Mount of Olives shall cleave in the midst thereof, ... and there shall be a very great valley.' 'And the Lord shall be King over all the earth. In that day shall there be one Lord, and his name one.' [Zechariah 14:5, 4, 9.] As the New Jerusalem, in its dazzling splendor, comes down out of Heaven, it rests upon the place purified and made ready to receive it, and Christ with his people and the angels, enters the holy city'" (p. 662).

2. **Satan determines not to yield the controversy.**

"Now Satan prepares for a last mighty struggle for the supremacy. While deprived of his power, and cut off from his work of deception, the prince of evil was miserable and dejected; but as the wicked dead are raised, and he sees the vast multitudes upon his side, his hopes revive, and he determines not to yield the great controversy" (p. 663, emphasis added).

3. **Satan moves among the people, declaring it was his power that raised them up. He works miracles to strengthen them and continues to teach them that he is the rightful ruler of the earth and God has stolen the kingdom from him. He declares that God would be a most cruel tyrant over them, should He win this war. The mighty people of earth solidify plans and organize their forces to produce again the implements of war. They marshal themselves into armies in preparation for an attack upon the city of God and its inhabitants.** *This* **is an army such as never was ever before on the earth.**

"He will marshal all the armies of the lost under his banner, and through them endeavor to execute his plans. The wicked are Satan's captives. In rejecting Christ they have accepted the rule of the rebel leader. They are ready to receive his suggestions and to do his bidding. *Yet, true to his early cunning, he does not acknowledge himself to be Satan. He claims to be the Prince who is the rightful owner of the world, and whose inheritance has been unlawfully wrested from him. He represents himself to his deluded subjects as a redeemer, assuring them that his power has brought them forth*

from their graves, and that he is about to rescue them from the most cruel tyranny. The presence of Christ having been removed, Satan works wonders to support his claims. He makes the weak strong, and inspires all with his own spirit and energy. He proposes to lead them against the camp of the saints, and to take possession of the city of God. With fiendish exultation he points to the unnumbered millions who have been raised from the dead, and declares that as their leader he is well able to overthrow the city, and regain his throne and his kingdom" (p. 663, emphasis added).

Modern spiritualism, as it functions in the occult and through secret societies such as Freemasonry, Skull and Bones, Illuminati, etc., teaches through its high priests and their writings that Lucifer is still the light bearer and the savior of the race from the tyranny of God.

The New Age religions and their channelers also transmit the big lies, "You shall not surely die" and "You shall be as gods." The masses believe the lies, following the popular teachings rampant in society. They are now seen here, at the end of the millennium, as fully captive to the very same deceptions that had taken in almost all the world before Christ came the second time. They will demonstrate their continued belief in the lies by their willingness to war upon the city, the redeemed, and even God Himself.

"In that vast throng are multitudes of the long-lived race that existed before the flood; *men of lofty stature and giant intellect*, who, yielding to the control of fallen angels, devoted all their skill and knowledge to the exaltation of themselves; *men whose wonderful works of art led the world to idolize their genius*, but whose cruelty and *evil inventions*, defiling the earth and defacing the image of God, caused him to blot them from the face of his creation. *There are kings and generals who conquered nations, valiant men who never lost a battle, proud, ambitious warriors whose approach made kingdoms tremble.* In death these experienced no change. As they come up from the grave, they resume the current of their thoughts just where it ceased. They are *actuated by the same desire to conquer that ruled them when they fell.*

"Satan consults with his angels, and then with these kings and conquerors and mighty men. They look upon the strength and numbers on their side, and declare that the army within the city is small in comparison with theirs, and that it can be overcome. *They lay their plans to take possession of the riches and glory of the New Jerusalem. All immediately begin to prepare for battle. Skillful artisans construct implements of war. Military leaders, famed for their success, marshal the throngs of warlike men into companies and divisions*" (pp. 663, 664, emphasis added).

4. **They march against the city.**

"At last the order to advance is given, and the countless host moves on,—an army such as was never summoned by earthly conquerors, such as the combined forces of all ages since war began on earth could never equal. Satan, the mightiest of warriors, leads the van, and his angels unite their forces for this final struggle. Kings and warriors are in his train, and the multitudes follow in vast companies, each under its appointed leader. *With military precision, the serried ranks advance over the earth's broken and uneven surface to the city of God.* By command of Jesus, the gates of the New Jerusalem are closed, and the armies of Satan surround the city, and make ready for the onset" (p. 664, emphasis added).

5. **They are stopped in their tracks as Christ appears above the city and His brightness floods the land.**

"*Now Christ again appears to the view of his enemies*. Far above the city, upon a foundation of burnished gold, is a throne, high and lifted up. Upon this throne sits the Son of God, and around him are the subjects of his kingdom. The power and majesty of Christ no language can describe, no pen portray. The glory of the Eternal Father is enshrouding his Son. *The brightness of his presence fills the city of God, and flows out beyond the gates, flooding the whole earth with its radiance*" (pp. 664, 665, emphasis added).

SIDEBAR STUDY on the brightness of His coming: This physical brightness does not at this time destroy the wicked. Neither did the physical brightness of His coming the second time destroy them. Yet it is the "brightness of His coming" that surely destroys them, as we read:

"Then shall they that obey not the gospel be consumed with the spirit of His mouth and be destroyed with the brightness of His coming. 2 Thessalonians 2:8. *Like Israel of old the wicked destroy themselves*; they fall by their iniquity. By a life of sin, they have placed themselves so out of harmony with God, their natures have become so debased with evil, that *the manifestation of His glory is to them a consuming fire*" (p. 37, emphasis added).

Herein, "it is affirmed that the wicked destroy themselves. It is not the work of God but their own. They have sown the seed and they must reap the harvest.

"Most significant, is the parallel drawn between the way in which Israel perished and the destruction in the last days. As the one perished, so will the other. This is to indicate that the Israelites were likewise destroyed with the brightness of His coming" (Wright, *Behold Your God*, p. 499).

The *"brightness of His coming"* is an equivalent expression to the *"manifestation of His glory,"* which is *the revelation of His Character*. We are told in many instances what is the glory of Christ or of God: "The glory of Christ is his character" (White, *God's Amazing Grace*, p. 322; *Reflecting Christ*, p. 214; *That I May Know Him*, p. 131).

This means that when they had the opportunity, during the loud cry, they spurned Jesus, as revealed by the 144,000, and sought to exterminate God's people. *This rejection placed them outside His protection during the seven last plagues, and they fell under these devastating events, which also include His coming in the seventh plague.* While the brightness of the event will surely be blinding to the natural eyes, it is primarily a psycho-spiritual phenomenon as a result of being unsheltered in the presence of God with an unregenerate mind. It is therefore not "directed-energy weapons" (i.e., sheets of physical energy emanating from Jesus) that lethally damage the physical organism; they die, rather, in the general upheaval of nature, called "the great final conflagration," which is an expression of the wrath of God being displaced from His normal role as Protector and Sustainer. Yet this is not the end; it is not their final destruction. It is only the sleep-death from which they will be resurrected at the end of the millennium.

This same "brightness of His coming," revealed first when Jesus came to earth and died on the cross, then through the final-generation loud cry and ensuing battle of Armageddon, is finally and fully revealed in the great-white-throne judgment at the end of the millennium—the battle of Gog and Magog (see Rev. 20:7–11). This final revelation is what kindles the ultimate, unquenchable fire that sends them to the second death—that process of taking on the agony of the guilt and burden of sin, which is defined as the *realization that* "because of transgression, his soul is cut off from God, and that God's wrath abides on him" ("Christ and the Law," *The Signs of the Times*, April 14, 1898).

A careful study of the thoughts presented in the following passage reveals how it is the brightness of *His coming*, aka the *revelation of His character*, that destroys the wicked:

"Christ presented to His countrymen and to the world *brightness*, beauty, and holiness, the divine nature, by which they might be bound close to the heart of Infinite Love; *He brought light into the world to dispel spiritual darkness, and to reveal truth. But they would not receive* the heavenly gift. The apostle inquires, 'Who hath bewitched you, that ye should not obey the truth?' It is through the deceptive working of Satan that fatal delusions have been brought even into the religious world, and *error and falsehood have been accepted instead of the light of truth. When light is rejected, darkness covers the earth, and gross darkness the people*" ("Christianity A Sword," *The Bible Echo*, March 12, 1894, emphasis added; note that elsewhere, Ellen White speaks of this gross darkness as a "misapprehension of the character of God" ["The Privilege of the Follower of Christ," The Review and Herald, July 5, 1892]).

"Men professing the name of Christ have worked against His cause, and the *blessing brought to men at infinite cost has been turned into a curse*;

for *when truth is rejected because it is out of harmony with the corruption of the natural heart, it becomes a sword to destroy. The truth, which was to restore and renew, is a destroyer of evil; and when evil is persistently cherished, it becomes a destroyer of the sinner also.*

"Strife and opposition have been the sure result of resistance on the part of men, incited by evil angels, to God's plan of mercy. *Man's perversity, his resistance of the truth, makes the mission of Christ appear to be what He announced to His disciples,—the sending of a sword upon the earth; but the strife is not the effect of Christianity, but the result of opposition in the hearts of those who will not receive its blessings*" ("Christianity A Sword," *The Bible Echo*, March 12, 1894, emphasis added).

This is the modality that we call "Bible language." The truth destroys in the same way that God destroys: by giving choice to accept or reject. The reality is that God, who is truth, is life. These three are an inseparable package. To accept one is to accept all; to reject one is to reject all. It is common today to hear of "his truth," "her truth," "your truth," or "my truth," but there is no such thing. There is only God. "God forbid: yea, let God be true, but every man a liar; as it is written, That thou mightest be justified in thy sayings, and mightest overcome when thou art judged" (Rom. 3:4).

> **It is common today to hear of "his truth," "her truth," "your truth," or "my truth," but there is no such thing. There is only God.**

"Nearest the throne are those who were once zealous in the cause of Satan, but who, plucked as brands from the burning, have followed their Saviour with deep, intense devotion. Next are those who perfected Christian characters in the midst of falsehood and infidelity, those who honored the law of God when the Christian world declared it void, and the millions, of all ages, who were martyred for their faith. And beyond is the 'great multitude, which no man could number, of all nations, and kindreds, and people, and tongues,' 'before the throne, and before the Lamb, clothed with white robes, and palms in their hands.' [Revelation 7:9.]

Their warfare is ended, their victory won. They have run the race and reached the prize. The palm branch in their hands is a symbol of their triumph, the white robe an emblem of the spotless righteousness of Christ which now is theirs.

"The redeemed raise a song of praise that echoes and re-echoes through the vaults of heaven, 'Salvation to our God which sitteth upon the throne, and unto the Lamb.' And angel and seraph unite their voices in adoration. As the redeemed have beheld the power and malignity of Satan, they have seen, as never before, that no power but that of Christ could have made them conquerors. In all that shining throng there are none to ascribe salvation to themselves, as if they had prevailed by their own power and goodness. Nothing is said of what they have done or suffered; but the burden of every song, the key-note of every anthem, is, Salvation to our God, and unto the Lamb" (p. 665).

6. **The King of kings is duly coronated in the presence of angels and all who have ever lived on the earth.**

"In the presence of the assembled inhabitants of earth and Heaven the final coronation of the Son of God takes place" (p. 665).

7. **The great-white-throne judgment begins. Consciousness of sin begins to bear down upon them.**

"And now, invested with supreme majesty and power, the King of kings pronounces sentence upon the rebels against his government, and executes justice upon those who have transgressed his law and oppressed his people. Says the prophet of God: 'I saw a great white throne, and Him that sat on it, from whose face the earth and the heaven fled away; and there was found no place for them. And I saw the dead, small and great, stand before God; and the books were opened; and another book was opened, which is the book of life; and the dead were judged out of those things which were written in the books, according to their works.' [Revelation 20:11, 12.]

"As soon as the books of record are opened, and the eye of Jesus looks upon the wicked, they are conscious of every sin which they have ever committed. *They see just where their feet diverged from the path of purity and holiness,* just how far pride and rebellion have carried them in the violation of the law of God. The seductive temptations which they encouraged by indulgence in sin, the blessings perverted, the messengers of God despised, the warnings rejected, the waves of mercy beaten back by the stubborn, unrepentant heart,—*all appear as if written in letters of fire*" (pp. 665, 666, emphasis added).

This principle of consciousness of every sin ever committed is one of the main constituents of the suffering of the wicked and explains why some suffer more than others do, because not every individual human or fallen angel is equal in depths of degradation, sin, or evil. The language of fire and burning is used to describe this experience of the realization of sin: "Every word they have spoken against the world's Redeemer ... will one day burn into their guilty souls like molten lead" (White, *Confrontation*, p. 87); the sinner "will realize that because of transgression, his soul is cut off from God, and that God's wrath abides on him. This is a fire unquenchable, and by it every unrepentant sinner will be destroyed" ("Christ and the Law," *The Signs of the Times*, April 14, 1898).

"Then I turned, and lifted up mine eyes, and looked, and behold a flying roll. And he said unto me, What seest thou? And I answered, I see a flying roll; the length thereof is twenty cubits, and the breadth thereof ten cubits. Then said he unto me, This is the curse that goeth forth over the face of the whole earth: for every one that stealeth shall be cut off as on this side according to it; and every one that sweareth shall be cut off as on that side according to it. I will bring it forth, saith the LORD of hosts, and it shall enter into the house of the thief, and into the house of him that sweareth falsely by my name: and it shall remain in the midst of his house, and shall consume it with the timber thereof and the stones thereof" (Zechariah 5:1–4).

"Against every evildoer God's law utters condemnation. He may disregard that voice, he may seek to drown its warning, but in vain.

It follows him. It makes itself heard. It destroys his peace. If unheeded, it pursues him to the grave. It bears witness against him at the judgment. *A quenchless fire, it consumes at last soul and body"* (White, *Education*, pp. 144, 145, emphasis added).

American psychiatrist and author, Tim Jennings, sums it up thus, using the very same words I could very well have written myself:

"Where does the suffering and torment take place? In the presence of the holy angels and the Lamb. And what kind of suffering is this? Mental anguish, suffering of heart, pain of mind, torment of psyche as each person comes face to face with the truth about themselves, their history, their opportunities rejected. They come face to face with the pain and suffering they have caused in contrast to the total love, grace, and goodness of God. And when each individual has reviewed the truth about their own lives, when the truth has burned through all the lies and becomes too overwhelming, when the psychological pain is too great they finally experience the full separation from God they have chosen and physically die the second, eternal death. And then, after all the wicked have died of their own unhealed condition, a literal, cleansing fire comes and melts the elements with fervent heat and the earth will be made new, the eternal home of the righteous (2 Peter 3:10-12)" ("The Question of Punishment Part III," Come and Reason Ministries, https://1ref.us/1gr, [accessed 12/03/2020]).

8. **God produces a panoramic view above the throne, wherein there is a great visual/psychological replay of the plan of salvation, and each one sees the part he or she played in rejecting God. All this includes Satan and his angels. Every eye is riveted to the scene.**

"*Above the throne is revealed the cross; and like a panoramic view appear the scenes* of Adam's temptation and fall, and the successive steps in the great plan of redemption. The Saviour's lowly birth; his early life of simplicity and obedience; his baptism in Jordan; the fast and temptation in the wilderness; his public ministry, unfolding to men Heaven's most precious blessings; the days crowded with deeds of love and mercy, the nights of prayer and watching in the solitude of the mountains; the plottings of envy, hate, and malice which repaid his benefits; the awful, *mysterious agony in Gethsemane, beneath the crushing weight of the sins of the whole world*; his betrayal into the hands of the murderous mob; the fearful events of that night of horror,—the unresisting prisoner, forsaken by his best-loved disciples, rudely hurried through the streets of Jerusalem; the Son of God exultingly displayed before Annas, arraigned in the high priest's palace, in the judgment hall of Pilate, before the cowardly and cruel Herod, mocked, insulted, tortured, and condemned to die,—all are vividly portrayed.

"*And now before the swaying multitude are revealed the final scenes,—* the patient Sufferer treading the path to Calvary; the Prince of Heaven hanging upon the cross; the haughty priests and the jeering rabble deriding his expiring agony; the supernatural darkness; the heaving earth, the rent rocks, the open graves, marking the moment when the world's Redeemer yielded up his life" (pp. 666, 667, emphasis added).

9. **There is an unfolding of realization—of *seeing*—of awakening—with the clarity of a total recall of not only the choices and actions, but also of motives—the thoughts and intents of the heart. They are awash in revelation, made fully aware of absolute and ultimate reality. Lost souls see they have no excuse for themselves. They are unable to avoid coming to the full psychological and spiritual appropriation of what they have forfeited—eternal life. They desire to hide from the face of Christ.**

"*The awful spectacle appears just as it was. Satan, his angels, and his subjects have no power to turn from the picture of their own work. Each actor recalls the part which he performed.* Herod, who slew the innocent children of Bethlehem that he might destroy the King of Israel; the base Herodias, upon whose guilty soul rests the blood of John the Baptist; the weak, time-serving Pilate; the mocking soldiers; the priests and rulers and the maddened throng who cried, 'His blood be on us, and our children!'—*all behold the enormity of their guilt. They vainly seek to hide from the divine majesty of His countenance, outshining the glory of the sun, while the redeemed cast their crowns at the Saviour's feet, exclaiming, 'He died for me!'"* (p. 667, emphasis added).

People will not be able to claim they cannot remember, as is heard so often in earthly trials in the courts of law. This recall will be comprehensive, unerring, and unavoidable, for it is "downloaded" to their minds from the exacting "register of heaven," as held in the powerful minds of the recording angels. Not only do the wicked have a thorough remembrance of all their lives, activated by the angels; they are given a view of it as it really is, the setting being the scope of eternal realities. Now it is that the fact of their criminality is pressed home with ultra-high-resolution clarity, producing a psychological force of an enormous weight of guilt upon their souls.

"Amid the ransomed throng are the apostles of Christ, the heroic Paul, the ardent Peter, the loved and loving John, and their true-hearted brethren, and with them the vast host of martyrs; while outside the walls, with every vile and abominable thing, are those by whom they were persecuted, imprisoned, and slain. There is Nero, that monster of cruelty and vice, beholding the joy and exaltation of those whom he once tortured, and in whose extremest anguish he found Satanic delight. His mother is there *to witness the result of her own work*; *to see how* the evil stamp of character transmitted to her son, the passions encouraged and developed by her influence and example, have *borne fruit in crimes* that caused the world to shudder.

"There are papist priests and prelates, who claimed to be Christ's ambassadors, yet employed the rack, the dungeon, and the stake to control the consciences of his people. There are the proud pontiffs who exalted themselves above God, and presumed to change the law of the Most High. Those pretended fathers of the church have an account to render to God from which they would fain be excused. *Too late they are made to see that the Omniscient One is jealous of his law, and that he will in nowise clear the guilty. They learn now* that Christ identifies his interest with that of his suffering people; and *they feel the force* of his own words, 'Inasmuch as ye have done it unto one of the least of these my brethren, ye have done it unto me.' [Matthew 25:40.].

"The whole wicked world stand arraigned at the bar of God, on the charge of high treason against the government of Heaven. They have none to plead their cause; *they are without excuse*; and *the sentence of eternal death is pronounced against them*.

"*It is now evident to all that the wages of sin is not noble independence and eternal life, but slavery, ruin, and death. The wicked see what they have forfeited by their life of rebellion*. The far more exceeding and eternal weight of glory was despised when offered them; but how desirable it now appears. *'All this,'* cries the lost soul, *'I might have had; but I chose to put these things far from me*. Oh, strange infatuation! I have exchanged peace, happiness, and honor, for wretchedness, infamy, and despair.' All see that their exclusion from Heaven is just. By their lives they have declared, 'We will not have this Jesus to reign over us.'

"As if entranced, *the wicked have looked* upon the coronation of the Son of God. *They see* in his hands the tables of the divine law, the statutes which they have despised and transgressed. *They witness* the outburst of wonder, rapture, and adoration from the saved; and as the wave of melody sweeps over the multitudes without the city, *all with one voice exclaim, 'Great and marvelous are thy works, Lord God Almighty; just and true are thy ways, thou King of saints;' and falling prostrate, they worship the Prince of life*" (pp. 667–669, emphasis added).

This worship by the wicked is of a completely different character as that of the righteous. It is not from a heart of gratitude and praise. They are mad with rage, anguish, and mental turmoil. The realization of truth is so overwhelming and pure that they have no other proclamation they can make. They now bow down, completely stripped of any pretense, manipulation of the facts, false coloring of motives, or excuses for the choices they have made in life, seeing they have made them only for gratification of self, without regard for others.

Those choices have just been replayed with perfect reproduction on heaven's Hi/Wi-Fi system. Each mouth is stopped, other than to say, if not in words, but in the action of bowing down itself, "God, you are right. Rebellion is not viable. We would ruin the universe if it were ours. I do not deserve life. Moreover, I understand there is no life without connection to You, the Source. I will not have You to reign over me. I reject You; therefore, I reject life."

I call heaven and earth to record this day against you, that I have set before you life and death, blessing and cursing: therefore choose life, that both thou and thy seed may live (Deut. 30:19).

And death shall be chosen rather than life by all the residue of them that remain of this evil family, which remain in all the places whither I have driven them, saith the LORD of hosts (Jer. 8:3).

10. Satan himself goes through the same process. As he beholds the majesty of Christ he sees the mighty angel that now has the place that he forsook. He remembers his former station in heaven, where he dwelt in complete peace and contentment. The whole story of his own rebellion is brought back to his view and he is reminded how he made no effort to turn from the path of folly, when he had the chance to do so. He knows his position is false, as he has already been subjected to numerous defeats in the great controversy. In fact, even while developing his rebellion in heaven, he knew he was wrong. Conviction came to him even then:

"Lucifer was convinced that he was in the wrong. He saw that "the Lord is righteous in all His ways, and holy in all His works" (Psalm 145:17); that the divine statutes are just, and that he ought to acknowledge them as such before all heaven. Had he done this, he might have saved himself and many angels. He had not at that time fully cast off his allegiance to God." (White, *Patriarchs and Prophets*, p. 39)

Satan sees that he has unfitted himself for heaven and its environment would be torture. His accusations are silenced. He bows and

confesses the justice of his sentence. Satan's confession reveals that he knows God is right, and he has gone beyond the point of no return and therefore must go out of existence.

"*Satan seems paralyzed as he beholds the glory and majesty of Christ*. He who was once a covering cherub remembers whence he has fallen. A shining seraph, 'son of the morning;' how changed, how degraded! From the council where once he was honored, he is forever excluded. *He sees another now standing near to the Father, veiling his glory. He has seen the crown placed upon the head of Christ by an angel of lofty stature and majestic presence, and he knows that the exalted position of this angel might have been his.*

"*Memory recalls* the home of his innocence and purity, the peace and content that were his until he indulged in murmuring against God, and envy of Christ. His accusations, his rebellion, his deceptions to gain the sympathy and support of the angels, *his stubborn persistence in making no effort for self-recovery when God would have granted him forgiveness,*—all come vividly before him. He reviews his work among men and its results,— the enmity of man toward his fellow-man, the terrible destruction of life, the rise and fall of kingdoms, the overturning of thrones, the long succession of tumults, conflicts, and revolutions. He recalls his constant efforts to oppose the work of Christ and to sink man lower and lower. He sees that his hellish plots have been powerless to destroy those who have put their trust in Jesus. As Satan looks upon his kingdom, the fruit of his toil, he sees only failure and ruin. *He has led the multitudes to believe that the city of God would be an easy prey; but he knows that this is false. Again and again, in the progress of the great controversy, he has been defeated, and compelled to yield. He knows too well the power and majesty of the Eternal.*

"The aim of the great rebel has ever been to justify himself, and to prove the divine government responsible for the rebellion. To this end he has bent all the power of his giant intellect. He has worked deliberately and systematically, and with marvelous success, leading vast multitudes to accept *his version of the great controversy* which has been so long in progress.

For thousands of years this *chief of conspiracy* has palmed off falsehood for truth. *But the time has now come when the rebellion is to be finally defeated, and the history and character of Satan disclosed.* In his last great effort to dethrone Christ, destroy his people, and take possession of the city of God, the arch-deceiver has been fully unmasked. Those who have united with him see the total failure of his cause. Christ's followers and the loyal angels behold the full extent of his machinations against the government of God. He is the object of universal abhorrence" (pp. 669, 670, emphasis added).

This is where the fury of the wicked turns back upon Satan, and he is brought down to the pit. This is where the brightness of his wisdom is defiled (see Ezek. 28:17). His lies are exposed. His entire premise and proposed system of government is seen not only as utterly futile, bankrupt in every way, but as nothing more than a bid to have all power and exercise it for himself only, as supreme dictator. To understand what this means, just comb through history and its line of despots, and there is the character of Satan exemplified.

Satan has worked through the elite circles of the world, mystic philosophies, false sciences, and Luciferian doctrines to promise a great new age; a new world order; a grand era of peace, prosperity, and freedom. His followers see how they have ordered their selfish lives in pursuit of lies and have worked his agenda, thinking to preserve themselves on top (see Luke 17:33). They were in full agreement with the plan to exterminate any who would disagree with them. These religious, fanatic dissidents (Sabbath keepers) were viewed as the primary threat to their totalitarian system.

The false Christian world has also now been awakened to see that their system, too, was set up to fight against the true God and that their god was actually Satan. They had believed his lies about the true God, in which he attributed to Him his own evil character traits, accusing Him as one who destroys His enemies in order to maintain His authority. Satan claimed that those who allied themselves with his own agenda would be rewarded as rulers over the world. Thinking to do God service, they

sought to kill those who were trying to save them, calling them to repentance in the gospel appeal.

"*Satan sees that his voluntary rebellion has unfitted him for Heaven.* He has trained his powers to war against God; *the purity, peace, and harmony of Heaven would be to him supreme torture.* His accusations against the mercy and justice of God are now silenced. The reproach which he has endeavored to cast upon Jehovah rests wholly upon himself. *And now Satan bows down, and confesses the justice of his sentence.*

"'Who shall not fear thee, O Lord, and glorify thy name? for thou only art holy: for all nations shall come and worship before thee; for thy judgments are made manifest.' [Revelation 15:4.] *Every question of truth and error in the long-standing controversy has now been made plain. The results of rebellion*, the fruits of setting aside the divine statutes, *have been laid open* to the view of all created intelligences. The working out of Satan's rule in contrast with the government of God, has been presented to the whole universe. *Satan's own works have condemned him. God's wisdom, his justice, and his goodness stand fully vindicated.* It is seen that all his dealings in the great controversy have been conducted with respect to the eternal good of his people, and the good of all the worlds that he has created. 'All thy works shall praise thee, O Lord; and thy saints shall bless thee.' [Psalm 145:10.] The history of sin will stand to all eternity as a witness that with the existence of God's law is bound up the happiness of all the beings he has created. *With all the facts of the great controversy in view, the whole universe, both loyal and rebellious, with one accord declare, 'Just and true are thy ways, thou King of saints.'*

"Before the universe has been clearly presented the great sacrifice made by the Father and the Son in man's behalf. The hour has come when Christ occupies his rightful position, and is glorified above principalities and powers and every name that is named. It was for the joy that was set before him,—that he might bring many sons unto glory,—that he endured the cross and despised the shame. And inconceivably great as was the sorrow and the shame, yet greater is the joy and the glory. He looks upon the redeemed, renewed in his own image, every heart bearing the perfect impress of the divine, every face reflecting the likeness of their King. He beholds in them the result of the travail of his soul, and he is satisfied. Then, in a voice that reaches the assembled multitudes of the righteous and the wicked, he declares, 'Behold the purchase of my blood! For these I suffered; for these I died; that they might dwell in my presence throughout eternal ages.' And the song of praise ascends from the white-robed ones about the throne, 'Worthy is the Lamb that was slain to receive power, and riches, and wisdom, and strength, and honor, and glory, and blessing.' [Revelation 5:12]" (pp. 670, 671, emphasis added).

11. **Even though Satan has openly confessed God's justice before Him and all of the inhabitants of the universe—both the righteous and the wicked—and he knows very well that it is finished for him, he is not yet ready to let go. In an enraged and fevered state of mind, he attempts to whip up his host into immediate warfare.**

"*Notwithstanding that Satan has been constrained to acknowledge God's justice, and to bow to the supremacy of Christ, his character remains unchanged. The spirit of rebellion, like a mighty torrent, again bursts forth. Filled with frenzy, he determines not to yield the great controversy.* The time has come for a last desperate struggle against the King of Heaven. *He rushes into the midst of his subjects, and endeavors to inspire them with his own fury, and arouse them to instant battle.*" (pp. 671, 672, emphasis added).

12. **There are none who will go Satan's way anymore. They are done with him. Yet, like their ruler whom they chose, they are not changed in heart in any way. They still have no desire for God. They are filled only with despair and rage as they see their hopeless condition. They are infuriated against Satan and his agents of deception.**

"But of all the countless millions whom he has allured into rebellion, there are none now to acknowledge his supremacy. His power is at an end.

The wicked are filled with the same hatred of God that inspires Satan; but they see that their case is hopeless, that they cannot prevail against Jehovah" (p. 672).

13. The wicked "turn upon" Satan and his agents. They "draw their swords against the beauty of Satan's wisdom and they defile his brightness, bringing him down to the pit." He is "cast to the ground." "The terrible of nations," "kings of the earth," behold him. In their sight he is "brought to ashes." He is destroyed.

"*Their rage is kindled against Satan and those who have been his agents in deception, and with the fury of demons they turn upon them.*

"Saith the Lord: 'Because thou hast set thine heart as the heart of God; behold, therefore *I will bring strangers upon thee, the terrible of the nations; and they shall draw their swords against the beauty of thy wisdom, and they shall defile thy brightness. They shall bring thee down to the pit.*' '*I will destroy thee*, O covering cherub, from the midst of the stones of fire.... *I will cast thee to the ground. I will lay thee before kings*, that *they may behold thee.*' 'I will *bring thee to ashes* upon the earth *in the sight of all them that behold thee*.... Thou shalt be a terror, and never shalt thou be any more.' [Ezekiel 28:6–8, 16–19.]" (p. 672, emphasis added).

Satan is cast to the ground *in the unmasking*. By beholding the full truth about him, his formerly deceived followers cast him to the ground by their realization, full understanding, and conviction that he is a complete liar and they have been fully (albeit willingly) deceived. This is what brings Satan's reign to an utter end. This terrible epiphany is also an intrinsic element of the process of unquenchable fire that brings all wicked beings to their end, including Satan himself (see "Christ and the Law," The Signs of the Times, April, 14, 1898).

What about the military thrust? Yes, there will be a great arms build-up, but the strangest thing is there won't be a shot fired in the intended war—at least, not upon the city and its inhabitants. Those weapons could be conceivably turned upon each other in a chaotic unleashing of blame. The wicked are going to have all the wind taken out of their sails at the judgment as they finish the panoramic view of history in the sky. They will have fury for Satan as they no longer support his cause, yet he is a spirit being, so it is impossible to harm him or any of his demon army in any physical way. Remember that *God does nothing arbitrary. Satan will not be reduced to human physicality*, as some suggest in a theory that the wicked will at last lay hands on Satan to destroy him, based upon Isaiah 14:15–16 and other passages such as we see referenced above. The language in these passages is poetic imagery to portray that Satan's support is gone and therein, his kingdom falls.

This is the ultimate "drying up of the great river Euphrates" event. At the premillennial time of the sixth plague, before the second coming of Christ, the ruling elite saw that the Luciferian and religious systems of the world were failing, crumbling, and even fighting God. Therefore, the support for these Babylonian systems was withdrawn, and tremendous violence and upheaval ensued, resulting in the immediate emancipation of God's people from the oppression of darkness, with Christ and His angels coming in to take them away from the dying planet.

In like manner does this final unmasking take the rebellion to its postmillennial conclusion, as the "man" behind it all is even more fully revealed. At the second coming, this scenario is witnessed mainly by the final generation of living souls. At the great white throne (GWT) scene, it is witnessed by all who have ever lived on earth. It is seen in great detail how he used all these earthly systems to promote his own agenda. They were deceived, but they know it came upon them willingly, through their own selfish desires and stifled consciences—the voice of the Holy Spirit of God.

Though now they have none but themselves to blame, they have no change of heart. There can no more be any development of higher thoughts and motives. Love is gone. They have only hate. They hate Satan for his work against them, and in their understanding of what has transpired, they lay down their arms and say, "No. You are finished, we are finished, it is all over. You are a thief, murderer, and liar, and we will not make war in your cause. You are wrong."

The reference to Satan as a "man" points only to the fact that he would have appeared in human form, such as angels are known on occasion to do. See Genesis 18:2 for an instance where three angels appeared to Abraham as men. One of those men was Christ, and at this time, before His incarnation, He also had an angelic form, Michael, yet He also appeared as a man. (see also 19:1, 5). In Daniel 9:21, Gabriel, the angel who occupies Satan's former position next to the throne, is called a man.

"'Every battle of the warrior is with confused noise, and garments rolled in blood; but this shall be with burning and fuel of fire.' 'The indignation of the Lord is upon all nations, and his fury upon all their armies: he hath utterly destroyed them, he hath delivered them to the slaughter.' 'Upon the wicked he shall *rain quick burning coals, fire and brimstone*, and *a horrible tempest*: this shall be the portion of their cup.' [Isaiah 9:5; 34:2; 11:6 (MARGIN).] *Fire comes down from God out of Heaven. The earth is broken up. The weapons concealed in its depths are drawn forth. Devouring flames burst from every yawning chasm. The very rocks are on fire. The day has come that shall burn as an oven. The elements melt with fervent heat, the earth also, and the works that are therein are burned up.* [Malachi 4:1; 2 Peter 3:10.] *The earth's surface seems one molten mass,—a vast, seething lake of fire.* It is the time of the judgment and perdition of ungodly men,—'the day of the Lord's vengeance, and the year of recompenses for the controversy of Zion.' [Isaiah 34:8; Proverbs 11:31.]" (pp. 672, 673, emphasis added).

Done. This is not, at least primarily, a war of weapons such as humans would wage against each other. There may be some of that included in the fire that is generated at this time, but this is mainly the earth being let go to release the rest of its fire that wasn't spent in the premillennial conflagration, at the time of the second coming. As all wicked beings process the burden of sin, receiving its wages, they fall dead in the experience of unquenchable fire of mental anguish and realization, coming to the point where they reconcile to their death and desire of God to release them from life and any connection to Him. All perish in this process.

As it comes down to the expiration of the last wicked one, Satan, the time comes when everything ever touched by sin goes out of existence, except the redeemed, whose own annihilation (death to self) transpired in Christ. Now the "fervent heat" that "melts" the very elements takes matter out of existence. This is the endpoint of the lake of fire/fire in the midst (remember these terms also apply to the process of unquenchable fire of cognitive suffering). This is the fullness of wrath. God withdraws His power, which upholds and sustains all things, and anything that loses this "fire" dissipates into the universe as energy.

Now, in the text, we cycle back for a recap. First, to tie off the preceding narrative, there is a snapshot of the final-cleanup, nuclear fire:

"The wicked receive their recompense in the earth. [Isaiah 34:8; Proverbs 11:31.] They 'shall be stubble; and the day that cometh shall burn them up, saith the Lord of hosts.' [Malachi 4:1]" (p. 673).

Then the narrative returns to a view of the process of the "fire unquenchable" process of realizing the consequence of sin and coming to the decision to take their death. Another Bible student discusses the structure of the writing:

"In the Bible we find what is called the principle of "repeat and expand". Sometimes a Bible writer will cover a time line from beginning to end and then come back and look at a portion of what he has previously written about. He would expand in more detail on this particular portion of the time line. We see this in the second chapter of Genesis. We see this principle in Daniel and Revelation and other places throughout the Bible.

"I believe this is exactly what Ellen White begins to do in the first paragraph on page 673, which begins 'The wicked receive their recompense …'"

"Beginning at page 662 and through to page 672 paragraph two, she covers the time period from the raising of the wicked to the 'works that are therein burned up'—the end of the wicked. A major portion of chapter 42 has been devoted to this time line.

"Now in the first paragraph on page 673 she 'repeats' a portion of what she has covered previously and 'expands' upon it. We read, 'Some are destroyed as in a moment, while others suffer many days. All are punished according to their deeds.' We have concluded that this suffering is caused by the physical fire that burns people while they are yet alive. We have associated the physical fire that burns up the works of the earth (p. 672 par. 2, last part) with the experience of the wicked that suffer many days. (p. 673, par. 1).

"The wicked are not destroyed by physical fire. Again, E.G. White wrote that they are destroyed by the realization of guilt and the realization that they are cut off from life. (ST April 14, 1898 par. 13) Therefore, the suffering in paragraph one page 673 must be speaking of mental anguish." (Roland Rogers, "Wrath of God," p. 55)

"Some are destroyed as in a moment, while others *suffer* many days. All are punished 'according to their deeds'" (*Ibid.*, emphasis added).

As the wicked work through the process of realizing their end, we find them dying in awful mental stress, for they must work out their own chosen end, requesting at last of God to give them over to that end as they fully acquiesce to His righteousness. There is no question left in their minds or the minds of those looking upon this process that a) the wicked have completely understood that this place to which they have come was a product of their own life choices, and b) God had done all He could have ever done to save them. The divine heart and principles are ever the same, as when He declared, "Jerusalem, Jerusalem, how often would I have gathered thy children together, and ye would not!" (Matt. 23:37). What more could He have done?

He gave His own self in full demonstration of His character and the principles of His governance. The wicked know they have realized the full burden of sin and its cost, and the redeemed recognize this too. They have chosen not to have God's way and understand this means death.

They would rather have death than have life in God's presence, for that is to them a torture, a fire unquenchable, which they are now enduring. Now is fully realized the horror of the statement, "All they that hate me love death" (Prov. 8:36).

Now is the time that the statement of God, long deferred in mercy through the interposition of His blood, comes to its ultimate fulfillment regarding eating of the fruit of the tree of knowledge of good and evil. This is an experiential knowledge that they were not to have, for it means, in its fullest sense, not the first death but the permanent cessation of existence known as second death, in that God had said, "In the day that ye eat of the fruit of this tree, ye shall surely die." This is the day when they not only eat it but swallow it down (see Obad. 16), for it is the inevitable fruit of the decision to replace God with self; the eternal with the finite; the Creator with the created.

Some would argue that this statement of God's warning refers only to the first death, but ultimately it *must* be the death from which there is no hope of resurrection. Obadiah 16 brings it home by the metaphor employed. The fact of the

> *That cup of iniquity is filled with the pure juice of that fruit, is it not? It is the full measure of denying God's word and seeking self-rule. When taken to the fullest choice to separate from God, it can only mean a realization of the ultimate consequence of that choice, which is the second death.*

matter is that while disobedience brought the first death upon all, to stay in that state ultimately brings second death. It is certain. Only within the safety of the law—of obedience to the Word of God—can life be maintained, with all its liberties to move, make choices, and have one's being. Sin brings one into ever-increasing bondage to selfish desires, with all the painful consequences, and ultimately locks the sinner down in the ultimate prison house: death.

What is particularly striking is this "swallowing down" set forth in Obadiah. That cup of iniquity is filled with the pure juice of that fruit, is it not? It is the full measure of denying God's word and seeking self-rule. When taken to the fullest choice to separate from God, it can only mean a realization of the ultimate consequence of that choice, which is the second death. Jesus didn't just "taste" the fruit; He swallowed its death on behalf of every human. He drank the cup to its dregs, enduring that separation experience for all. Yet, not all would enter into His joy and be saved, for they decided to drink their own cup. So it is that on that last *day*, when they declare the righteousness of God yet, at the same time, are determined to have none of it, they are not just tasting but "swallowing down" that fruit. They are going the full distance of *experience*, which is *knowledge* in the biblical usage. They now shall *know* intimately the full bond and oneness with self and sin, and it is ultimately the choice to *not be* anymore.

Which death was it that "passed upon all men"? Notice the following passage:

"In the midst of Eden grew the tree of life, whose fruit had the power of perpetuating life. Had Adam remained obedient to God, he would have continued to enjoy free access to this tree and would have lived forever. But when he sinned he was cut off from partaking of the tree of life, and he became subject to death. The divine sentence, 'Dust thou art, and unto dust shalt thou return,' *points to the utter extinction of life.*

"Immortality, promised to man on condition of obedience, had been forfeited by transgression. Adam could not transmit to his posterity that which he did not possess; and there could have been no hope for the fallen race had not God, by the sacrifice of His Son, brought immortality within their reach. While 'death passed upon all men, for that all have sinned,' Christ 'hath brought life and immortality to light through the gospel.' Romans 5:12; 2 Timothy 1:10. And only through Christ can immortality be obtained. Said Jesus: 'He that believeth on the Son hath everlasting life: and he that believeth not the Son shall not see life.' John 3:36. Every man may come into possession of this priceless blessing if he will comply with the conditions. All 'who by patient continuance in well-doing seek for glory and honor and immortality,' will receive 'eternal life.' Romans 2:7.

"The only one who promised Adam life in disobedience was the great deceiver. And the declaration of the serpent to Eve in Eden—"Ye shall not surely die"—was the first sermon ever preached upon the immortality of the soul. Yet this declaration, resting solely upon the authority of Satan, is echoed from the pulpits of Christendom and is received by the majority of mankind as readily as it was received by our first parents. The divine sentence, 'The soul that sinneth, it shall die' (Ezekiel 18:20), is made to mean: The soul that sinneth, it shall not die, but live eternally. We cannot but wonder at the strange infatuation which renders men so credulous concerning the words of Satan and so unbelieving in regard to the words of God" (White, *The Great Controversy*, pp. 532, 533, emphasis added).

"The warning given to our first parents—'In the day that thou eatest thereof thou shalt surely die' (Genesis 2:17)—did not imply that they were to die on the very day when they partook of the forbidden fruit. But on that day the irrevocable sentence would be pronounced. Immortality was promised them on condition of obedience; by transgression they would forfeit eternal life. That very day they would be doomed to death" (White, *Patriarchs and Prophets*, p. 60, emphasis added).

"The sins of the righteous having been transferred to Satan, he is made to suffer not only for his own rebellion, but for all the sins which he has caused God's people to commit. His punishment is to be far greater than that of those whom he has deceived. *After all have perished who fell by his deceptions, he is still to live and suffer on. In the cleansing flames the wicked are at last destroyed*, root and branch,—Satan the root, his followers the branches. The full penalty of the law has been visited; the demands of justice have been met; and Heaven and earth, beholding, declare the righteousness of Jehovah" (p. 673, emphasis added).

As the process of unquenchable fire has taken every other wicked being to the second death, Satan suffers on, having no followers left, and is the very last one to give over to his fate. He sees he has no kingdom, and all things, animate and inanimate, are to be made new and restored, that the fullness of the glory of God will forevermore be shone upon and through them. He sees there is at last no place found for him—*anywhere*. He at last gives up his futile struggle, bows down, and expires. At this point, the entire earth and its environs "melt" in the final blast of fervent heat, the endpoint of the lake of fire/fire brought from the midst.

"Satan's work of ruin is forever ended. For six thousand years he has wrought his will, filling the earth with woe, and causing grief throughout the universe. The whole creation has groaned and travailed together in pain. Now God's creatures are forever delivered from his presence and temptations. 'The whole earth is at rest, and is quiet; they [the righteous] break forth into singing.' [Isaiah 14:7.] And a shout of praise and triumph ascends from the whole loyal universe. 'The voice of a great multitude,' 'as the voice of many waters, and as the voice of mighty thunderings,' is heard, saying, 'Alleluia; for the Lord God omnipotent reigneth.'

"While the earth was wrapped in the fire of destruction, the righteous abode safely in the holy city. Upon those that had part in the first resurrection, the second death has no power. [Revelation 20:6; Psalm 84:11.] *While God is to the wicked a consuming fire, he is to his people both a sun and a shield*. [Revelation 20:6; Psalm 84:11.]

"'And I saw a new heaven and a new earth; for the first heaven and the first earth were *passed away*.' [Revelation 21:1.] *The fire that consumes the wicked purifies the earth*. Every trace of the curse is swept away. No eternally burning hell will keep before the ransomed the fearful consequences of sin" (pp. 673, 674, emphasis added).

In this one line, "The fire that consumes the wicked purifies the earth," you have a view to the total process. The unquenchable fire consumes the wicked in the process of sinking under the burden of sin and realizing its results. They die from this, seeking release at last in saying to God, "Since there is nothing for us to live for, we want death." They lose the will to live. God lets them go. How they die, at this point, is immaterial. It can be from stress, shock, murder, suicide, or catastrophism in nature.

The error that must not be made with regard to the death of the finally impenitent is to leap to the idea that God exercises power to punish. Rather, He withdraws power according to the cognizant choice of the finally impenitent, and the result is called their "punishment." This fire of withdrawal is that which has been "prepared" for the devil and his angels, in the sense of it being their rightful and natural consequence of separating from God, but held in reserve until the end of the thousand years. As Satan comes to his own end, in the same way, the process is completed for all the wicked host.

At this point, the fire of God's sustenance of matter itself is withdrawn, and the earth and all the dead inhabitants go into nonexistence, with the physical substance converting to raw light and heat energy. Spiritual beings are also subject to the same process, although in a way that we cannot now define or understand, for we do not have any knowledge of the physical principles involved in their makeup.

"One reminder alone remains: our Redeemer will ever bear the marks of his crucifixion. Upon his wounded head, upon his side, his hands and feet, are the only traces of the cruel work that sin has wrought. Says the prophet, beholding Christ in his glory, *'He had bright beams coming out of his side; and there was the hiding of his power.'* [Habakkuk 3:4 (MARGIN)] *That pierced side whence flowed the crimson stream that reconciled man to God,—there is the Saviour's glory, there 'the hiding of his power.' 'Mighty to save,' through the sacrifice of redemption, he was therefore strong to execute justice upon them that despised God's mercy.* And *the tokens of his humiliation* are his highest honor; through the eternal ages the wounds of Calvary will show forth his praise, and *declare his power*" (p. 674, emphasis added).

When the wicked fully realize who God is and what He has done to give them life, they are convinced of His justice in that they realize they have not wanted His life, then or now. They understand that by the rejection of His grace, they have rejected life. They understand that the gospel that could have saved them is now "destroying" them by their rejection of it. This is the glory and power that consumes them—the brightness of His coming; the revelation of His character, which is the foundation of His government—total freedom, total non-coercion, total selfless, all-for-others, agape love.

The wicked do not want to live by this system. They want governance of *self*, *by* self, and *for* self, at the expense of others, though they do understand it is wrong and there is no existence in that way. It cannot function; it is fatally flawed, for it requires one to be self-sustaining and aspire to the impossible—to become God. They, like their leader, have succumbed to strange delusions to the point of being irredeemable. Left to itself (assuming God would continue to sustain their lives and physical environment), that system of governance, without any restraining influence of the Holy Spirit, would rapidly result in a total breakdown of society by lawless greed and bloodshed, as the stronger would continually kill the weaker until there would be none left.

"The tokens of His humiliation ... declare His power." Wow! In our darkness, we once thought the power of God was smashing the teeth of His enemies. No! True power is revealed in these tokens: the scars borne in His body. These are telling the story of redemption unto eternal life, which, once understood by the impenitent, has the strength to bring them to their end as they understand their rejection of it means they must die, and it is their choice to die. They see that God is the rightful owner of all the universe and love will reign. They know they would abhor life in such a giving flow and purity of heart.

The love of God, shown by the sacrifice of Christ in assuming our sinful flesh, even that of a common man, and taking it to the second death in exchange for His righteous life and Spirit, is what saves all who will be saved, while that same thing, rejected, destroys the wicked as they declare they do not want it. They demonstrate an insanity whereby they have allowed themselves to be "grafted into the stock of Satan," demonstrating that they actually love the principles of death more than they love the principles of God and His love. They love self more than they love God, even though there is no life in self. In this full manifestation of His righteousness and goodness, He declares justice in His strange act of letting them go to destruction, not forcing them to live.

"'O Tower of the flock, the stronghold of the daughter of Zion, unto thee shall it come, even the first dominion.' [Micah 4:8; Ephesians 1:14.] The time has come, to which holy men have looked with longing since the flaming sword barred the first pair from Eden,—the time for 'the redemption of the purchased possession.' [Micah 4:8; Ephesians 1:14.] The earth originally given to man as his kingdom, betrayed by him into the hands of Satan, and so long held by the mighty foe, has been brought back by the great plan of redemption. All that was lost by sin has been restored. 'Thus saith the Lord … that formed the earth and made it; he hath established it, he created it not in vain, he formed it to be inhabited.' [Isaiah 45:18.] God's original purpose in the creation of the earth is fulfilled as it is made the eternal abode of the redeemed. 'The righteous shall inherit the land, and dwell therein forever.' [Psalm 37:29.]" (p. 674).

[*Note: here we are omitting a portion of the chapter that describes the hereafter.*]

"*Upon all things, from the least to the greatest, the Creator's name is written, and in all are the riches of his power displayed.*

"And the years of eternity, as they roll, will bring richer and *still more glorious revelations of God and of Christ*. As knowledge is progressive, so will love, reverence, and happiness increase. The more men learn of God, *the greater will be their admiration of his character*. As Jesus opens before them the riches of redemption, and the amazing achievements in the great controversy with Satan, the hearts of the ransomed thrill with more fervent devotion, and with more rapturous joy they sweep the harps of gold; and ten thousand times ten thousand and thousands of thousands of voices unite to swell the mighty chorus of praise.…

"The great controversy is ended. Sin and sinners are no more. The entire universe is clean. One pulse of harmony and gladness beats through the vast creation. From Him who created all, flow life and light and gladness, throughout the realms of illimitable space. *From the minutest atom to the greatest world, all things, animate and inanimate*, in their unshadowed beauty and perfect joy, *declare that God is love*" (p. 678, emphasis added).

Appendix B: A Synopsis of the Fires

FIRE FROM GOD OUT OF HEAVEN	
Great White Throne Arraignment	----> Dissolution of Matter
---->Natural Fires	----> Dissolution of Matter
Unquenchable Fire	----> Fire of Fervent Heat
Lake of Fire	----> Lake of Fire
Fire from the Midst	----> Fire from the Midst

Fire from God out of Heaven—This title refers to the entire final sequence, with all its fires. The moving picture in the sky of the drama of the ages, tailored to every personal experience, is aptly called "fire out of heaven," as it involves the terrible processing of the burden of sin and guilt. The eruption of natural fires will rain down burning elements, and there could very well be incoming hot material from space, as well as lightnings from heavy atmospheric turbulence, all of which are "fire from God," as, in biblical terms, natural disasters are said to be "from God" (e.g., Job 1:16). The final eradication of all matter will be the result of God's withdrawal, an action "from God."

The Great White Throne Arraignment—When the wicked march against the city, the gates are closed, and the coronation of Christ takes place, beginning the fires. It ends with the dissolving of the earth and heavens.

The Dissolution of Matter—When Satan, the last wicked being alive, is finished with his rebellion, he perishes. At this point, the next event in the eradication of sin is to remove all that has been tainted by sin and set up a new heaven and earth. Like the original creation, it will not be dependent on preexisting material, but will come to exist by the word of God, *ex nihilo*. When God gives up the matter, it converts to energy and dissipates into space.

Unquenchable Fire—The process of coming to accept the results of one's lost condition, realizing there is no hope of living on one's own terms apart from God—and there is no desire for repentance—death is chosen.

The Fire of Fervent Heat—This is the final fire of dissolution that takes matter out of existence, after all the wicked have perished. It is a special fire, beyond that of normal chemical processes of oxidation. It is nuclear fire—the removal of God's sustaining power at the atomic level.

Lake of Fire—The term embraces all the fires. In one sense, it is the unquenchable fire. The masses of the wicked (the lake) are in outer darkness with weeping and gnashing of teeth (the fire). This is a psycho-emotional lake of fire. The geophysical, meteorological issues, and cosmic hail will contribute to an earth that is represented in inspired pictorial as a "vast, seething lake of fire," while the final dissolution also fits the description perfectly, with the New Jerusalem as the antitypical ark of safety.

Fire from the Midst—This refers primarily to the unquenchable-fire experience, that which is represented as the destruction of Lucifer. It is the burden of guilt and the horror of realization of loss brought out from the records of memory. It burns all the wicked host as every individual, from both the spirit realm and human realm, has to meet the judgment. It ends with the fire of fervent heat and dissolution of matter.

Natural Fires—As the wicked go through the unquenchable-fire experience, the Lord will also begin to let go of inanimate creation in the earth and its solar environs. What fires were not spent at the second coming will now issue forth again to completion. The impenitent do not all expire at once. Some are finished quickly, while others take much longer, in accordance with the burden upon them and their tenacity in rebellion. It is not clear to us what happens with the wicked who carry on for longer periods—how they are preserved from the natural destruction of physical chaos. Regardless of how we might imagine or speculate on this, we must be careful not to depict God in any way as simultaneously using His physical power to produce fire of any kind at the same time He uses creative and sustaining power to keep the wicked alive for the purpose of physical torture or punishment.

> *The impenitent do not all expire at once. Some are finished quickly, while others take much longer, in accordance with the burden upon them and their tenacity in rebellion.*

God will release them when they are finished in their own minds, not when He is satisfied that they've been tortured long enough. It is quite possible that when He releases them, the natural fires will destroy them quickly, but we cannot say that it will be the same for all. Some will die of other causes such as heart failure or perhaps even suicide. It would be impossible to represent physical fires as that which were prepared for the devil and his angels, as natural fires will not affect spirit beings. We are talking about fires of nature with respect to their effects upon flesh only.

Appendix C: Why so Difficult?

By Pastor Roland Rogers
[The following material is excerpted from an unpublished and undated paper, "Wrath of God," by Pr. Roland Rogers, pp. 48, 49.]

One might ask a question. Why doesn't the Bible or E.G. White simply state, very clearly, that the wicked die from mental anguish and not from fire? Perhaps it is not simply stated because it isn't the truth. Perhaps what has been accomplished in this document is the result of leaving things out; twisting things; taking statements out of context or putting it together in such a way as to make it arrive at a predetermined conclusion. This certainly is a possibility. So the reader must be careful.

But, on the other hand, there could be a reasonable explanation that would help us understand just why the Bible and E.G. White did not record in simple declarative statements the answer to this question: "Why do the wicked suffer and what takes their life?"

Let's ask some more questions. When Jesus talked about hell, why didn't He make it crystal clear that hell is not forever? Why didn't Paul make it very clear that when you die you don't go to heaven or hell, you remain in your grave? Why didn't he specifically state that the Sabbath was still binding after the cross? Why didn't Paul make it clear when addressing the subject of perfection? Why did Paul leave us to struggle with the concepts of justification and sanctification? Why isn't the important truth of righteousness by faith so clear that no one could misunderstand it? When the Bible speaks of the death of Christ why doesn't it clearly state that Jesus died from mental anguish and not from the physical abuse He was subjected to?

What about our church's history in its struggle to find the truth? What about our doctrine of the sanctuary and the investigative judgment? What about 1844? Why didn't God make it abundantly clear to our pioneers that Jesus wasn't returning to the earth at that time? Why did the pioneers have to study, search, wrestle, stay up all night and pray before they arrived at these truths? Why didn't God just simply make it very clear in the Scripture? Why did they have to go "here and there" gathering bits of evidence as they went and then through the long search to finally arrive at the truth?

Why have men and women in every generation struggled to "unearth the gems"? Why aren't they lying on the "surface"? Maybe God wanted them to do some hard thinking. Could it be that they needed the struggle and effort? Could it be that the hard search makes the truth more important to us? Isn't it true that the more you invest in something the more important it is to you and the more you struggle to obtain it the more valuable it becomes?

And there could be another reason why God "hides" truth. The more you work at it, the longer you work with it, the easier it is to retain in your mind. It seems that the more valuable and important a truth is the harder the struggle to find it.

Why doesn't the Bible and E.G. White make it so easy that there is no room for doubt? Why isn't it crystal clear? Why is the struggle to find the truth so necessary? Perhaps it is this way because truth is so very important.

I would encourage the reader of this document to go back over this paper slowly, carefully with a heart to know the truth about God's treatment of His enemies. What does He do to His forever enemies?

It's not how God treats His friends that is so important, it's how God treats His enemies. We are the enemy. This is our clearest revelation of the love of God. This is our story in the entire Bible! This is our story of God!

This is a "hidden" truth of the Bible and E.G. White! Search for it. Struggle to find it. Pray for it! And then when you find it, share it.

Bibliography

Chambers, Bill. *The Healing Model: A Better Way to Understand Salvation.* Fort Oglethorpe, GA: TEACH Services, 2009.

Crosby, Tim. "Does God Get Angry?" Biblical Research Institute, https://1ref.us/1gp (accessed 12/03/2020).

Haskell, Stephen. *The Story of the Seer of Patmos*, https://1ref.us/1hi (accessed 12/29/2020).

Holbrook, Frank B. "Does God Destroy?" Biblical Research Institute, https://1ref.us/1go (accessed 12/03/2020).

Jennings, Tim. "The Question of Punishment Part III," Come and Reason Ministries, https://1ref.us/1gr (accessed 12/03/2020).

Moore, Marvin, *Reflections on the Wrath of God*, https://1ref.us/1hh (accessed 12/29/2020).

Rodriguez, Angel Manuel. "What is the wrath of God?" Biblical Research Institute, https://1ref.us/1gq (accessed 12/03/2020).

Rogers, Roland. "Wrath of God." Unpublished manuscript.

Straub, Kevin, *As He Is …* Fort Oglethorpe, GA: TEACH Services, 2012.

White, Ellen G. "A Living Church." *The Review and Herald*, June 3, 1880.

———. "A Message for Today." *The Review and Herald*, June 18, 1901.

———. "A Time of Trouble." *The Review and Herald*, September 17, 1901.

———. *The Acts of the Apostles.* Mountain View, CA: Pacific Press Publishing Association, 1911.

———. "Be Zealous and Repent." *The Review and Herald*, September 4, 1883.

———. "Be Zealous and Repent." *The Review and Herald*, December 23, 1890.

———. "Camp-Meeting at Ottawa, Kansas." *The Review and Herald*, July 23, 1889.

———. "Christ and the Law." *The Signs of the Times*, April 14, 1898.

———. "Christ Our Hope." *The Review and Herald*, December 20, 1892.

———. *Christ Triumphant*. Hagerstown, MD: Review and Herald Publishing Association, 1999.

———. "Christ and the Law." *The Signs of the Times*, April 14, 1898.

———. *Christ's Object Lessons*. Washington, DC: Review and Herald Publishing Association, 1900.

———. *Christian Education*. Battle Creek, MI: International Tract Society, 1894.

———. "Christianity A Sword." *The Bible Echo*, March 12, 1894.

———. *Confrontation*. Washington, DC: Review and Herald Publishing Association, 1971.

———. *Counsels for the Church*. Nampa, ID: Pacific Press Publishing Association, 1991.

———. *Daughters of God*. Washington, DC: Review and Herald Publishing Association, 1998.

———. "Dear Brethren and Sisters." *The Review and Herald*, August 1, 1849.

———. *The Desire of Ages*. Mountain View, CA: Pacific Press Publishing Association, 1898.

———. *Early Writings*. Washington, DC: Review and Herald Publishing Association, 1882.

———. *Education*. Mountain View, CA: Pacific Press Publishing Association, 1903.

———. *Fundamentals of Christian Education*. Nashville, TN: Southern Publishing Association, 1923.

———. *God's Amazing Grace*. Washington, DC: Review and Herald Publishing Association, 1973.

———. *The Great Controversy 1888*. Mountain View, CA: Pacific Press Publishing Association, 1888.

———. *The Great Controversy*. Mountain View, CA: Pacific Press Publishing Association, 1911.

———. *Gospel Workers*. Washington, DC: Review and Herald Publishing Association, 1915.

———. "Home Duties of the Father." *The Signs of the Times*, December 20, 1877.

———. *Letter 22*. February 13, 1900.

———. "Manasseh and Josiah." *The Review and Herald*, July 15, 1915.

———. *Manuscript Releases*. Vol. 3. Silver Spring, MD: Ellen G. White Estate, 1990.

———. *Manuscript Releases*. Vol. 8. Silver Spring, MD: Ellen G. White Estate, 1990.

———. *Manuscript Releases*. Vol. 11. Silver Spring, MD: Ellen G. White Estate, 1990.

———. *Manuscript Releases*. Vol. 12. Silver Spring, MD: Ellen G. White Estate, 1990.

———. *Manuscript Releases*. Vol. 14. Silver Spring, MD: Ellen G. White Estate, 1990.

———. *Manuscript Releases*. Vol. 16. Silver Spring, MD: Ellen G. White Estate, 1990.

———. *Manuscript Releases*. Vol. 18. Silver Spring, MD: Ellen G. White Estate, 1990.

———. *Manuscript Releases*. Vol. 19. Silver Spring, MD: Ellen G. White Estate, 1990.

———. *Maranatha*. Washington, DC: Review and Herald Publishing Association, 1976.

———. *Medical Ministry*. Mountain View, CA: Pacific Press Publishing Association, 1932.

———. "Nothing is Hidden." *The Review and Herald*, March 27, 1888.

———. *Patriarchs and Prophets*. Washington, DC: Review and Herald Publishing Association, 1890.

———. *Reflecting Christ*. Hagerstown, MD: Review and Herald Publishing Association, 1985.

———. "Science and the Bible in Education." *The Signs of the Times*, March 20, 1884.

———. *Selected Messages*. Book 1. Washington, DC: Review and Herald Publishing Association, 1958.

———. *Selected Messages*. Book 2. Washington, DC: Review and Herald Publishing Association, 1958.

———. *Sermons and Talks*. Vol. 2. Silver Spring, MD: Ellen G. White Estate, 1994.

———. *The SDA Bible Commentary*. Vol. 3. Washington, DC: Review and Herald Publishing Association, 1954.

———. *The SDA Bible Commentary*. Vol. 5. Washington, DC: Review and Herald Publishing Association, 1956.

———. *The SDA Bible Commentary*. Vol. 6. Washington, DC: Review and Herald Publishing Association, 1956.

———. *The SDA Bible Commentary*. Vol. 7. Washington, DC: Review and Herald Publishing Association, 1957.

———. *The Spirit of Prophecy*. Vol. 1. Battle Creek, MI: Seventh-day Adventist Publishing Association, 1870.

———. *The Spirit of Prophecy*. Vol. 4. Battle Creek, MI: Seventh-day Adventist Publishing Association, 1884.

———. *Spiritual Gifts*. Vol. 3. Battle Creek, MI: Seventh-day Adventist Publishing Association, 1864.

———. *Spiritual Gifts*. Vol. 4a. Battle Creek, MI: Seventh-day Adventist Publishing Association, 1864.

———. *The Story of Jesus*. Nashville, TN: Southern Publishing Association, 1900.

———. *The Story of Redemption*. Washington, DC: Review and Herald Publishing Association, 1947.

———. *Testimonies for the Church*. Vol. 2. Mountain View, CA: Pacific Press Publishing Association, 1871.

———. *Testimonies for the Church*. Vol. 4. Mountain View, CA: Pacific Press Publishing Association, 1881.

———. *Testimonies for the Church*. Vol. 5. Mountain View, CA: Pacific Press Publishing Association, 1889.

———. *That I May Know Him*. Washington, DC: Review and Herald Publishing Association, 1964.

———. "The Government of God." *The Review and Herald*, March 9, 1886.

———. "The Great Controversy. Between Christ And His Angels and Satan And His Angels." *The Signs of the Times*, January 16, 1879.

———. "The Liquor Traffic Working Counter to Christ." *The Review and Herald*, May 8, 1894.

———. "The Measure of Light Given Measures Our Responsibilities." *The Review and Herald*, October 24, 1912.

———. "The New Life in Christ." *The Review and Herald*, May 10, 1906.

———. "The Plan of Salvation." *The Signs of the Times*, February 13, 1893.

———. "The Privilege of the Follower of Christ." *The Review and Herald*, July 5, 1892.

———. "The Relation of Christ to the Law Is Not Understood." *The Review and Herald*, February 4, 1890.

———. "The Temptation of Christ." *The Review and Herald*, April 1, 1875.

———. "The Working of Satan." *The Signs of the Times*, April 12, 1883.

———. "The Wrath of the Lamb." *The Bible Echo*, May 30, 1898.

———. "They That Have Done Good." *The Signs of the Times*, August 29, 1892.

———. *This Day With God*. Washington, DC: Review and Herald Publishing Association, 1979.

———. *Thoughts from the Mount of Blessing*. Mountain View, CA: Pacific Press Publishing Association, 1896.

———. *The Upward Look*. Washington, DC: Review and Herald Publishing Association, 1982.

———. "Variance Between Believers and Unbelievers." *The Signs of the Times*, November 26, 1894.

———. "Words to the Young." *The Youth's Instructor*, November 30, 1893.

———. "Words to the Young." *The Youth's Instructor*, December 21, 1893.

Wright, Fred T., *Behold Your God*. 1st ed. Queensland, Australia: Destiny Press, 1979.

TEACH Services, Inc.
P U B L I S H I N G
www.TEACHServices.com • (800) 367-1844

We invite you to view the complete
selection of titles we publish at:
www.TEACHServices.com

We encourage you to write us
with your thoughts about this,
or any other book we publish at:
info@TEACHServices.com

TEACH Services' titles may be purchased in
bulk quantities for educational, fund-raising,
business, or promotional use.
bulksales@TEACHServices.com

Finally, if you are interested in seeing
your own book in print, please contact us at:
publishing@TEACHServices.com
We are happy to review your manuscript at no charge.

www.ingramcontent.com/pod-product-compliance
Lightning Source LLC
Chambersburg PA
CBHW070756230426
43665CB00017B/2387